BY JAMES P. WARBURG

BOOKS

RECENT PAMPHLETS

THE
UNITED STATES
IN THE
POSTWAR WORLD

JAMES P. WARBURG

THE
UNITED STATES
IN THE
POSTWAR WORLD

WHAT WE HAVE DONE,
WHAT WE HAVE LEFT UNDONE,
AND
WHAT WE CAN AND MUST DO

ATHENEUM *NEW YORK*

1966

E
744
.W287

THIS BOOK IS DEDICATED
IN GRATITUDE AND AFFECTION
TO JOSEPH BARNES

INTRODUCTION

"American Library Burned in Jakarta!"—*"Mobs Demonstrate Before American Embassy in Japan!"*—*"Cambodia Declines American Aid!"*—*"De Gaulle Denounces U.S. Policy in Vietnam!"*—*"Argentinians Protest U.S. Intervention in Santo Domingo!"*

These have become familiar headlines in our press—almost as familiar as the blasts directed at the United States from Moscow or Peking. Coming from supposedly friendly nations, these messages suggest a widespread disapproval of American foreign policy even where that policy has been directed toward extending protection or help.

In late 1965, an editorial in the usually pro-American *Times* of London read in part:

> Americans generally regard themselves as peaceful folks but in the first two decades of the Cold War it was the United States and not the Soviet Union which was engaged in most of the wars since the last great war to end wars. . . . Columbia is hardly the Goddess of Peace. . . . The American Declaration of Independence asserts the right of people to abolish any form of government. President Wilson spoke of the right of little countries to determine their own polity and he was eloquently echoed by President Kennedy. Both, however, intervened in the internal affairs of small nations, as did President John-

son. Quite possibly Uncle Sam knew best, but he did not bother to ask his small Latin American nephews.

Are we, as we like to think, reasonably sensible, humane, generous and peace-loving people who respect the rights and feelings of others? Or are we, as many Europeans, Asians, Africans and Latin Americans appear to think, impatient if not trigger-happy, inconsiderate, overbearing and at times even brutal? Do we still believe in the right of all peoples to overthrow unsatisfactory governments, or have we in fact become a counterrevolutionary *status-quo* power? When we proclaim ourselves champions of freedom, do we mean what the Founding Fathers meant, or are we interested in a different kind of freedom in which property rights are perhaps more important than human rights? Finally, is our purpose truly what we say it is—to abolish war and establish the rule of law throughout the world—or are we in fact unwilling to submit to world law and to relinquish the right to use our great power unilaterally?

Our actions in the two postwar decades entitle the peoples of the world to ask these questions. We owe it to ourselves no less than to them to attempt to find the answers.

It is the writer's belief, with which others may disagree, that in the whole postwar period—from 1945 through 1965 —United States foreign policy was distorted by an obsessive fear of communism which prevented a clear perspective, caused at least two serious mistakes (Germany and China) and obscured what should have been the chief aims of our nation's policy—namely, to aid and guide a worldwide revolution into the paths of peaceful change.

In part, this failure may have derived from ignorance of

other cultures, languages, religions and value standards, which led to the somewhat naïve conviction that what is good for the United States and its people is good for the nations and peoples of the world. This conviction, in turn, was based upon a number of debatable propositions: (1) that a high living standard constituted the *summum bonum* of a "good society"; (2) that "free enterprise" capitalism was the only way to achieve affluence and a "good society"; (3) that freedom of speech, worship and the right of assembly—in other words, "human rights"—could be attained only in a society where property rights (i.e., "free enterprise") were safeguarded; and (4) that "democracy" (i.e., representative government) was the only form of government which could promote and defend "free enterprise" and, hence, the pursuit of "life, liberty and happiness."

Fear of communism combined with the foregoing debatable propositions to cause an antipathy to any form of "socialism," or state capitalism, as a step toward the abolition of all human and property rights under a communist dictatorship. The antipathy engendered by this belief alienated the United States from that two-thirds of the world in which, because there was little or no private capital, progress could be achieved only by government direction of the economy, and in which, because there had never been any freedom in the Western sense, democracy could be expected to evolve only after the most basic human needs had been satisfied.

A further point: the postwar policy of the United States (and the postwar policy of most other Western nations) has been conditioned by two major factors only one of which is fully realized and neither of which is as yet fully understood. Everyone knows that the advent of the atomic age marked a turning-point in the world's history although the full implications of that turning-point are as yet unclear. Not everyone realizes, however, that the postwar period has been dominated by the necessity for sweeping up what Walter Lippmann has aptly called "the debris of European imperialism."

The collapse of the European balance of power began in 1938 with the betrayal of Czechoslovakia. After World War I, France, in order to protect herself against another German attack, had created a system of alliances known as the "Little Entente," embracing Poland, the successor states of the Austro-Hungarian empire and most of the Balkan countries. This East European *cordon sanitaire* between Germany and Russia developed into something very like a colonial empire, with Paris as the financial center, French industry supplying the largely agricultural hinterland with manufactured goods and the East European countries providing France with raw materials. In the mid-1930's, Nazi economic penetration, guided by the notorious Dr. Hjalmar Schacht, began to undermine this system. It was then utterly destroyed by the "Peace" of Munich, which cut Eastern Europe loose from its Western moorings and left it, first, a prey to Hitler and, after Hitler's defeat, a prey to "liberation" by the Red Army.

Japan's defeat of Britain, France and Holland in the Far East early in World War II triggered the collapse of the European colonial empires. The retreat began with Britain's liberation of India, Pakistan, Burma and Ceylon; and from Asia the anti-colonial revolt spread to Africa and the Middle East. In a little over ten years, little was left of the European colonial empires except a few islands and the stubbornly-held Portuguese possessions in Africa and Asia.

All this we know. But what most of the world and we ourselves are inclined to overlook is that it fell to the United States to act as a sort of unpaid caretaker of imperial estates in liquidation—estates in which the United States had never owned an interest. It is true that the United States did not *have* to move into the vacuum left by the dissolution of the European colonial empires; but it is also true that the vacuum had somehow to be filled. Fear of communism and, in this writer's judgment, a gross overestimation of Soviet Russia's immediate postwar ambitions and capabilities led the United States to appoint itself as a global custodian, attempting to fill the vacuum in parts of the world where the United States itself had no vital national interests.

To say this is not to justify American policy but to offer a partial explanation for what appears as and to a certain extent has actually become an American neo-colonialism. That this neo-colonialism has been motivated by fear, rather than by acquisitiveness, makes very little difference to those who do not share the fear. European colonial imperialism was heartily disliked and resented by the dependent peoples, but at least it was understood. Neither the obsessive fear of communism nor the semi-altruistic paternalism that motivated American neo-colonialism was understood, and, hence, other motives were suspected. The anti-communist obsession obscured and indeed stultified the humanitarian instinct of the American people, making aid extended at least in part for altruistic motives seem wholly self-interested, and—worse—making such aid appear to have been extended for a self-interest which seemed incomprehensible and, therefore, doubly suspect.

This impression has been heightened by the fact that American altruism all too often takes the form of a naïve paternalism which proselytizes "the American way of life" as the only road to happiness, whereas it is actually wholly un-suited to the majority of the world's peoples. Even if this were not the case—even if the American way were indeed the right way for all—the American attitude of "father knows best" would be resented because it offends the dignity and self-re-spect of those to whom the advice is given. To make matters worse, American paternalism has all too often been like that of a father who scarcely knows the names of his many chil-dren, let alone their individual characteristics. The long years of living in happy isolation from the rest of the world left the people of the United States woefully ignorant with respect to the non-English-speaking world. Apart from the localized knowledge of foreign countries retained by still unassimilated immigrant groups, what little knowledge of history and geog-raphy most Americans possessed had been recently acquired through the experience of two great wars.

This was not true of two categories of Americans: mission-aries and businessmen. Both had acquired a considerable knowledge of other parts of the world and both were well known to many of the world's peoples. Both, however, clearly had had axes to grind; both were salesmen. The missionaries had come to sell Christianity; the businessmen to sell their wares, their know-how and their desire to exploit natural re-sources. Both frequently performed useful services—the mis-sionaries in the field of education, and the businessmen in promoting economic development. But the teaching of Chris-tianity implied a disrespect for other religions and was im-paired by the often un-Christian behavior of the Western countries whence the missionaries came. (In particular, Amer-ican missionaries were handicapped by the un-Christian treat-ment accorded to the Negro citizens of the United States.)

And the economic development brought by Western business-men was offset by an exploitation of human and natural resources which frequently yielded little if any benefit to the native populations.

World War II brought a new kind of American into foreign lands. Millions of young American servicemen, most of whom had never been outside of their own country, appeared in remote corners of the earth. On the whole, these young Americans were good ambassadors, not only because they fought bravely and well but also because they brought with them a friendly attitude, a lighthearted humor and a fondness for little children. Through no fault of their own, they also brought a picture of a pampered American people—a people so affluent that its soldiers had more food and candy than they could eat, more money than they could spend and more vehicles to carry them around than had ever before been seen. But —again through no fault of their own, for this was due to their upbringing—these young Americans conveyed a sense of their own superiority, not realizing that when they referred to natives as "gooks" or "wogs" they were being insulting and reflecting not only their own ignorance but also the racial prejudice in their country.

And then, when the war was over, another unfamiliar type of American appeared on the world scene—a bureaucrat sent out to administer aid, to gather intelligence and to teach anti-communism and "the American way of life." Few of these people knew the language or the history of the countries to which they were sent. For "intelligence," they were forced to rely upon English-speaking (and usually relatively rich) natives or paid interpreters. Most of these bureaucrats lived in gradually growing American enclaves, sent their children to

American schools, bought their food at American commissaries and enjoyed a living standard above that to which they had been accustomed at home. Their contacts with the people whom they had been sent out to study and help were limited. There were, of course, notable exceptions, like Chester Bowles, the United States Ambassador to India, who sent his children to Indian schools, and like some of the lower-level "ugly Americans" who learned to live with and love the people whom they were sent to help. But, on the whole, it is probably fair to say that most of the United States missions, composed as they have been of bureaucrats, military advisers and operatives of the Central Intelligence Agency, have conveyed the impression that they were there primarily to implement an American policy the main thrust of which was an anti-communist crusade comprehensible only to the privileged few who were concerned chiefly with maintaining their own local political and economic positions of power.

These are some of the factors we must bear in mind in seeking to answer the questions raised at the outset. It is not only what we have done in the postwar period that shapes world opinion of the United States but also how we have done it and, even more, what we have left undone.

The first ten chapters of this study attempt to present a rapid outline of what the United States has done in the postwar period.

Chapters 11, 12 and 13 are concerned with what the United States has left undone.

Chapter 14 endeavors to analyze how and by whom United States postwar foreign policy has been shaped.

Chapter 15 presents the writer's answer to the question raised at the outset: "To what extent are we misjudged by the world, and why?"

Finally, Chapter 16 takes a qualifiedly optimistic look into the future.

The view of postwar history expressed in these pages does not, in many respects, conform to majority opinion, although it diverges less from majority opinion today than did many of the writer's dissenting views when they were first publicly expressed in the course of the last twenty years.

An outspoken critic of much of our nation's foreign policy throughout the postwar period cannot review that period without some reference to the dissenting positions he has taken as a public servant or as an outside observer privileged to communicate his views to the makers of foreign policy. No apology is made for such references; they enable the reader to distinguish between foresight and hindsight and to evaluate present recommendations in the light of his own judgment as to the wisdom or unwisdom of recommendations made in the past.

CONTENTS

xvii

PART ONE

WHAT WE HAVE DONE

1

Roosevelt's Policy of Conciliation

President Roosevelt was a keen student of World War I history. He greatly admired Woodrow Wilson's idealism, but his own pragmatic common sense made him sharply aware of Wilson's mistakes. Tactically, as Roosevelt saw it, Wilson committed three errors when it came to making the peace: he failed to consult the Senate in advance of his attempt to organize the League of Nations; he failed to prevent adherence to the League from becoming a partisan political issue; and he was over-optimistic in assuming that American enthusiasm for participation in world affairs would continue after the war. In seeking to avoid a repetition of these mistakes, Roosevelt consulted the Senate leadership at every stage of his planning of a new world organization, making a successful effort to enlist the support of Republicans as well as members of his own party. And, in his determination to avoid a relapse into isolationism such as had occurred with a return to "normalcy" under President Harding, Roosevelt weakened the Charter of

3

the United Nations in such a way as to retain for the United States the maximum freedom of action. It was for this reason that he conceived of the new world organization not as a league of sovereign peoples with at least some attributes of a world government but as another league of sovereign nations, guided and directed by the unanimous decisions of the five great powers—the United States, Britain, France, China and the Soviet Union. In order to assure American participation, Roosevelt was satisfied to create a world organization dependent for its success in preserving the peace upon the continued cooperation of the chief members of the victorious anti-Axis coalition.

Historians differ as to whether this was a good or a bad gamble. Actually, Roosevelt had little choice. The only sort of world organization which the Soviet Union could be expected to join was one by which it could not be coerced. Stalin was every bit as touchy on this subject as the United States Senate. Moreover, there was a strong streak of nationalism in Roosevelt himself, and it seems clear that he had a rather limited idea of American postwar participation in world affairs outside of the Western Hemisphere. On a number of occasions, he warned Churchill not to count upon the continued presence of American troops in Europe. In his postwar planning, Roosevelt was again influenced by Wilson's failure to reach agreement with his wartime allies. He once remarked to the writer that, while he deplored the selfish nationalistic attitude of Lloyd George at Versailles, he thought it had been a great mistake not to give France the guarantee of her future security which she desired and to which he thought she had been entitled. With this in mind, he was determined not to let Stalin acquire a similar grievance.

4

Roosevelt realized more fully than Churchill or most of his own advisers that Stalin's suspicious and secretive nature, which had made wartime cooperation difficult, had its roots in history. He knew that the Soviet Union had at its birth incurred Western hostility by withdrawing from the war against the Central Powers, thus making Allied victory more costly and more difficult. Although Tsarist Russia had been a backward and none too popular member of the Western family of nations, it had nevertheless been a member. The Kerensky revolution of March 1917 might have increased Russian popularity, but Kerensky's overthrow in October by the Bolsheviks aroused widespread anxiety and resentment. The Bolshevik revolution appeared not only as a threat to victory and the establishment of law and order but also as a challenge to the whole ethical and religious structure of Western society as well as to the economic foundations upon which that society rested. Its doctrine of world revolution threatened the Western world's basic structure of belief and behavior. It was for this reason that the Allies and Japan had attempted to overthrow the Bolshevik regime by armed invasion, and that, when this failed, diplomatic recognition of the Soviet government had been long withheld and then only grudgingly extended.

Roosevelt was also aware that Russia, as a nation, had suffered the loss of important territory—in Asia as the result of its defeat by Japan in 1905, and in Europe at the end of World War I when the Soviet Union was forced to relinquish Finland, the three Baltic states, Poland and parts of Rumania. Thus the new Soviet state fell heir to a nationalist revisionism quite similar to the revisionist sentiment in France after the loss of Alsace-Lorraine.

Finally, Roosevelt knew that, while East-West tensions had

5

relaxed considerably during the first fifteen years of the Soviet Union's existence, a new deterioration of relations had set in when Western diplomacy had stultified itself by appeasement of Hitler and Mussolini while the Soviet Union repeatedly called for action to halt fascist aggression. He knew also that an essential aim of the appeasement policy had been to turn that aggression eastward.

This intimate knowledge of the past accounted for Roosevelt's willingness to allow Soviet annexation of the Baltic states and parts of Poland, Rumania and East Prussia in violation of the pledge against such annexations which he and Churchill had signed in the Atlantic Charter. It probably also accounted for his disagreement with Churchill over the possibility of "doing business" with the Soviet leader.

Similarly, one may suspect that Roosevelt's unwillingness to discuss the political future of Europe until military victory had been achieved derived partly from a desire not to repeat the mistakes made at Versailles and partly from what he conceived to be military expediency in seeking quick victory.[1]

To offer this explanation of Roosevelt's wartime foreign policy is not unreservedly to endorse its wisdom. Indeed, the writer opposed the territorial annexations sanctioned at Yalta; deplored the absence of a political policy with respect to the future of Europe and especially with respect to the future of Germany; and questioned the effectiveness of a United Nations that would be unable to deal with disputes among the veto-wielding great powers.[2]

[1] The State Department did not always see eye to eye with Roosevelt during the war. In general, it supported the subordination of political aims to military expediency in such matters as the Vichy policy and the deals with Darlan and Badoglio, but it was more concerned than Roosevelt with limiting the postwar influence of the Soviet Union.

[2] See Warburg, *Foreign Policy Begins at Home.*

There were other important respects in which Roosevelt's determination not to let history repeat itself bore more fruitful results. The creation of the United Nations Relief and Rehabilitation Administration (UNRRA), of the International Bank for Reconstruction and Rehabilitation (the "World Bank"), and of an International Monetary Fund (IMF) grew directly out of the experience of hunger and chaos which had followed World War I. The Lend-Lease Act was a brilliantly conceived device to enable the United States to extend aid to friendly nations without later becoming involved in a war-debt-repayment-reparations tangle such as had caused bad feeling after World War I.

All in all, one might say that where history provided a guide Roosevelt profited from past experience, but where history offered no signposts he was less sure-footed. Thus he failed lamentably to recognize the threat posed by Italian, Spanish and German fascism until it was almost too late. In this he was not alone, but his connivance at Anglo-French appeasement, culminating in the disgraceful "Peace" of Munich, constituted an error so colossal and far-reaching that, in their anxiety not to make a similar mistake, Roosevelt's successors were for years to equate any attempt at conciliation through negotiations with dishonorable "appeasement." Interestingly enough, Roosevelt himself did not draw the false conclusion that was later widely accepted by the American people and their leaders; his recognition that appeasement of Hitler and Mussolini had been both unwise and dishonorable did not lead him to reject all attempts at the peaceful settlement of disputes. This was clearly evidenced by his conciliatory attitude toward Stalin.

At Yalta, he conceded Stalin's pre-eminent interest in hav-

7

ing governments in adjacent countries friendly to the Soviet Union and somewhat reluctantly accepted the previously secret Churchill-Stalin agreement allotting varying degrees of influence to Russia and Great Britain in the Balkans. In general, he accepted the fact that the Soviet Union would have predominant power in Eastern Europe, stipulating only that the East European states should have freely elected representative governments. (This vaguely expressed stipulation was subject to conflicting interpretations and seemed to the writer wholly unrealistic.) As to the Far East, on the assumption that Stalin would enter the war against Japan as he had promised, Roosevelt conceded nothing that Stalin would not have the power to seize in any case—namely, repossession of the Kurile Islands and the northern half of Sakhalin, a warm-water port at Dairen and an equal voice with China in the control of the Manchurian railways. In return, Stalin agreed to support the government of Chiang Kai-shek as against the Chinese Communists and to allow Chinese administrators to accompany the Red Army when it marched into Manchuria. These arrangements were later embodied in a Russo-Chinese peace treaty and loyally carried out.

Shortly before Roosevelt's death, tension between Russia and the West arose over Stalin's high-handed action in imposing a communist-dominated government upon Poland—an action which Churchill regarded as a betrayal of the ambiguous Yalta agreements and which Roosevelt himself found shocking. Nevertheless, until the day of his death on April 12, 1945, Roosevelt clung firmly to the conviction which he expressed in his last message to Churchill, that this matter as well as all differences between the Soviet Union and the West could and must be peacefully ironed out.

8

Undoubtedly, Roosevelt had in mind that Stalin's position of predominant power in Eastern Europe was offset by acute economic weakness resulting from the war and the consequent need for economic aid which only the United States was in a position to extend.

When Harry Truman entered the White House, he fell heir to accomplished victory in Europe, to an almost certain triumph over Japan and to a design for peace through cooperation with the Soviet Union. In addition, although he did not know it at the time, Truman inherited an almost perfected secret weapon destined to revolutionize the world—a weapon which would present the temptation to pursue a course toward peace quite different from that steered by his predecessor.

2

Truman and Byrnes— Atomic Diplomacy and Delayed Confrontation

.

Harry Truman was a man far more characteristic of the American people as a whole than the paternalistic Hudson Valley patrician whom he succeeded in the White House. Truman's people were small farmers in the Middle West. His four grandparents had been born in Kentucky and had moved to Missouri in 1840. One was German, the three others came of English–North Irish stock.

Born at Independence in 1884, Truman attended public school, went to work at seventeen, first for the *Kansas City Star* and then as a timekeeper and helper in Kansas City banks. In 1905, aged twenty-one, he joined the Missouri National Guard and tried to enter West Point but was rejected because of defective eyesight. From 1906 until the United States entered the war, he ran his family's farm. In 1917, he entered the Field Artillery School at Fort Sill, Oklahoma, was commissioned a lieutenant and then captain in the 129th Field Artillery, was sent overseas and served in the Argonne and

St. Mihiel actions with the American Expeditionary Corps. He was discharged as a major in 1919.

Then, for about three years, he ran a not very successful haberdashery and became interested in courthouse politics, obtaining an appointment as judge of the Jackson County Court in 1922. After attending the Kansas City School of Law for two years, he ran, first unsuccessfully and then successfully, for the office of presiding judge. In 1934, at the age of fifty, he became a United States Senator and, in 1944, was chosen by Roosevelt to become Vice President, succeeding to the Presidency at Roosevelt's death in April 1945. He was then sixty-one but possessed the energy and spirit of a much younger man.

This was the man who, within two weeks of his succession to the Presidency, decided to have a showdown with Josef Stalin. And this was the man who, after waging a Cold War for almost three years, was endorsed and re-elected by the American people.

What elements in the American society, what characteristics of the American people did he reflect?

1. Like many young Americans who came from a Middle West farming background and could see no particularly bright future for themselves in agriculture or business, Truman tried for an appointment to West Point at the age of twenty-one. Had he not been rejected because of weak eyesight, one can easily imagine him as having become a professional soldier rather than a politician. His wartime experience as a field officer in the artillery was one which he enjoyed and looked back upon with pride. From it, he acquired a respect for discipline, an admiration for successful generals and admirals, and something of the spirit which pervades such veterans' organ-

izations as the American Legion.

2. Brought up in the Baptist religion, Truman acquired, like many young Americans, a fundamentalist faith in the Bible and an unhesitating conviction of revealed truth as to "right" and "wrong." On the other hand, experience with Missouri courthouse politics in the days of the notorious Pendergast machine taught him the practical value of choosing a "side" and, by loyal service to that side, achieving advancement. The two influences combined, as they do with many Americans, to make him a strong and loyal partisan with an unshakable belief in the "rightness" of the faction, political party or nation to which he belonged.

Strong partisanship, whether for nation or political party, tends to create a black-and-white view in which it becomes difficult to attribute any virtue to the other side and easy to ascribe virtue to one's own.

3. Coming from a border state in which there had been strong sympathy for the South (his mother's family had been sympathetic to the Confederacy), Truman drifted toward friendship with Southern Senators, most of them ardent believers in "white supremacy." These Southerners controlled important committee chairmanships. On the other hand, his religious convictions made Truman keenly conscious of the injustice being done to Negroes and left him with an ambivalent feeling toward the issue of race relations. It was significant that he chose as his first Secretary of State James F. Byrnes, a South Carolinian white-supremacist and apostate Roman Catholic, whom Roosevelt had rejected as a running-mate in 1944 largely because of his religion and his racial prejudice.

If one adds up these characteristics, plus an almost total un-

12

familiarity with the world outside of the United States, one obtains some insight into the factors which made Harry Truman adopt a simplistic and, as the writer sees it, a distorted view of the foreign-policy problems that he faced when he became President.

Shortly before his death, Roosevelt had asked Stalin to send his foreign minister to Washington in order to discuss the formation of the new Polish government and other matters pertaining to the Soviet position in Eastern Europe. Stalin had refused on the grounds that a Polish government had been formed but had received no invitation to attend the San Francisco Conference at which the United Nations was to be organized. (It was true that Stalin had finally invited Stanislaw Mikolajczyk, head of the Polish Government-in-Exile at London, to come to Warsaw and that the latter had agreed, but Stalin had so far refused to hold free elections and had continued to insist upon communist domination of the Warsaw government.)

After Roosevelt's death, Stalin agreed to send Molotov to see the new American President. His arrival was scheduled for April 23. Thus, within twelve days of his taking office, Truman had not only to prepare for the United Nations meeting— a task which he left largely to the hold-over Secretary of State Stettinius—but also to formulate a policy with respect to Eastern Europe.

Although many eminent historians have expressed the belief that when Truman took office he had every intention of continuing Roosevelt's conciliatory policy, there is reason to doubt this hypothesis. The records show that practically all of Truman's advisers urged him to modify Roosevelt's conciliatory policy, differing only as to the timing of a showdown with

13

Stalin. W. Averell Harriman, then United States Ambassador to Moscow, was the most articulate advocate of a confrontation, maintaining that failure to face the issues in Eastern Europe would be interpreted by Stalin as weakness and invite further aggressive expansionism, whereas a display of firmness would lead to a less aggressive Soviet policy. Harriman pointed out that the Soviet Union faced a stupendous task of reconstruction and hoped to receive something like $6 billion in American aid. Acting Secretary of State Joseph Grew (Stettinius was in San Francisco) and Navy Secretary James V. Forrestal strongly supported Harriman. Henry L. Stimson, Secretary of War, and Chief of Staff General George C. Marshall were more cautious as to the timing of a showdown—Marshall because he wished to avoid a rupture of relations which might keep the Soviet Union from declaring war on Japan, and Stimson because he thought a showdown should be postponed until Truman held in his hand the trump card of possessing a proven atomic bomb.

Perhaps because Truman as yet knew very little about what was going on at Los Alamos, perhaps because of his native belligerence, the new President decided in favor of an immediate showdown. When Molotov called at the White House on April 23, he received a dressing down in language which, according to Admiral Leahy, had no precedent in diplomatic intercourse. Molotov was shocked and dismayed. Churchill, hearing of the interview, was delighted. However, neither Truman's tough talk nor his subsequent show of force over the Trieste dispute nor his halting of Lend-Lease shipments to Russia caused Stalin to back down. The showdown having failed, Truman sent the ailing Harry Hopkins to Moscow to persuade Stalin to let Molotov attend the San Francisco Conference.

14

It is at this point that the interpretations of historians vary. The prevalent belief among such well-informed writers as Robert E. Sherwood and the historian Herbert Feis was that the Hopkins mission signified Truman's intention to resume Roosevelt's policy of endeavoring to avoid a break in Soviet-American relations. A more recent school of historians,[1] after careful study of documents not available at the time, comes to the conclusion that Stimson had persuaded Truman during the latter part of April or early May that a showdown should not be avoided but that it should be postponed until the atomic bomb had been revealed. It is on this hypothesis that the more recent studies explain Truman's unwillingness during May and June to "gang up" with Churchill against Stalin and his refusal, infuriating to Churchill, to press for an early Big Three meeting or to order the American troops to remain in that part of the Soviet zone of occupation which they had unexpectedly overrun, saying that he wanted to meet Stalin "with clean hands." These actions, according to more recent studies, were not, as commonly thought, an indication of Truman's return to a Rooseveltian policy of conciliation but merely a strategy of delayed confrontation. The interesting fact brought out and now quite fully documented is that there never was any doubt in Stimson's or Truman's mind that the bomb, if perfected, should be used. Stimson's idea was that the confrontation with Stalin should not take place until "the bomb had been laid on Japan." With this Truman apparently agreed and, for this reason, three times postponed the Potsdam meeting when progress at Los Alamos was slower than expected. It was not Stimson's idea to brandish the atomic bomb as an instrument of coercive pressure but, rather, to offer Stalin some

[1] See Denna F. Fleming, *The Cold War and Its Origins*, and Gar Alperovitz, *Atomic Diplomacy*.

15

sort of partnership in developing and controlling the use of atomic energy in exchange for certain *quid pro quos* in Eastern Europe. (This idea, however, seems never to have appealed very much to Truman and was eventually emphatically vetoed by James F. Byrnes, whom he chose to be his Secretary of State.)

The irony of this strategy of delayed confrontation was that Truman eventually committed himself to a date in July for the Potsdam Conference and that the bomb had still not been tested when he sailed for Europe, setting forth for the encounter with openly expressed reluctance.

Along with other contemporary historians writing at the time, this observer missed the main point of the July-August Potsdam meeting. The question of reaching agreement on the four-power government of Germany seemed so important that it was natural to assume that honest efforts were being made to solve it, *whereas the fact was that Truman did not wish at this time to reach an agreement on Germany or on any other issue*. Not as yet having his trump card, Truman was content to state the uncompromising American interpretations of the ambiguous Yalta Agreement, making no attempt to reconcile them with the Russian interpretations, and to postpone the settlement of all issues until the meeting at London in September of the newly appointed Council of Foreign Ministers. However, postponement of the major issues did not prevent the making of three major blunders at the Potsdam Conference.

The first was to leave the question of Germany's western frontier unsettled after deciding, to all intents and purposes, what was to be done in the East. (While determination of the Polish-German frontier was in theory left to final settlement at a German peace conference, the Polish annexations were as a

16

practical matter settled business.)

The second and almost incredible blunder was to give France a zone of occupation and an equal voice on the Allied Control Council, amounting to a veto, without obtaining French signature to the four-power contract under which the four-power government was supposed to operate.

These two blunders were closely related. The de Gaulle government wished to annex the German Saar and part of the Rhineland. Once the Atlantic Charter pledges against any annexations had gone overboard, this was not an unreasonable demand, especially if considered in the light of past French experience with Germany. On the other hand, Germany, deprived of the Silesian coal mines and industry and of its eastern breadbasket, could not live, much less become reasonably prosperous, if it were also to be deprived of its major industries and coal mines in the Ruhr. Not only Britain and the United States but also Russia recognized this and therefore refused to accede to the French demand. Not being bound by the Potsdam agreement and yet able to veto its operation, France proceeded to block every step by which the Control Council sought to carry out its mandate for governing Germany as a political and economic entity. This French obstructionism brought about the wholly unplanned division of Germany into four separate, hermetically sealed compartments among which all trade, travel and political intercourse were inhibited. It was not Russian violation of the Potsdam agreement but French intransigence that first broke down the four-power plan. Soviet exploitation of the breakdown was to come later.

The third and perhaps the most fundamental error committed at the Potsdam Conference was to make the assumption that four victorious nations could impose what amounted to a complete political and economic revolution upon a defeated Germany without having first reached agreement among themselves as to what kind of Germany they desired to create.

In addition to these three cardinal blunders, the Potsdam Conference failed to resolve the conflicting interpretations of the Yalta agreements as to reparations, laid the foundations for a disastrous farce of "denazification," and adopted from a confused American directive issued to General Eisenhower a compromise between the Morgenthau Plan for the "de-industrialization" of Germany and the War and State Departments' desire that Germany be made self-supporting as soon as possible.

Thus, while Truman wanted to postpone the settlement of all issues at Potsdam, he in fact "settled" enough questions to doom the plan for four-power government to failure.

During the conference, Stimson received word that the test of the bomb had been successful—that, in fact, it had exceeded all expectations. This delighted Truman as well as Churchill and served to make the Anglo-American leaders less than ever willing to compromise. On his way home, Truman learned that the first atomic bomb had been dropped with devastating effect upon Hiroshima. The stage was now set for a complete reversal of American policy toward the Soviet Union. At Potsdam, Truman had merely mentioned to Stalin that the United States now possessed a bomb of infinitely greater destructive power than any hitherto known—a statement which did not seem greatly to impress the Soviet leader. Both Churchill and Stimson had urged Truman not to divulge any further details until the first bomb should have been dropped upon Japan. Unless one assumes that Stalin knew about the bomb through espionage, one can imagine what must have been his feelings when he realized, after Hiroshima, that the United States now possessed what at the time seemed "the ultimate weapon."

The American public was told and believed that the two bombs had been dropped upon Hiroshima and Nagasaki to hasten Japanese surrender and to save the 500,000 casualties which would have resulted from an invasion of the Japanese home islands. This belief was fortified by the fact that the Japanese did in fact surrender within a few days after the bombs fell. As a matter of fact, the British scientist P. M. S. Blackett was right in stating as early as 1947 that there had been no military necessity for using these inhuman weapons— that the reason for using them had been strictly political and had constituted the opening gun in a political offensive against the Soviet Union. Commenting at the time on Blackett's article in the *New Statesman*, the writer expressed the opinion that Blackett was probably right.

It is now known that the Japanese government was desperately trying at the time of the Potsdam Conference to get the Soviet Union to mediate a surrender which would permit Emperor Hirohito to remain in power. Stalin was not interested because he wished to have time to enter the war and thus to gain a voice in the peace settlement. Truman was not interested because he wished, by using the bomb, to bring about surrender *before* Russia could march into Manchuria. Not a single one of Truman's military advisers, even including the cautious General Marshall, thought by this time that it was necessary to use the bomb to bring about surrender, nor did any of the military men think that an invasion of the home islands would any longer be necessary. And yet the bombs were used and used as quickly as possible after they became available. Why? It seems fairly obvious that they were used in the hope of obtaining Japanese surrender before Russia could enter the war and send her troops marching into Manchuria. Very likely sensing this purpose, Stalin declared war on Japan and launched his invasion of Manchuria three days after the first bomb fell on Hiroshima. This destroyed Japan's last hope.

Apart from the political purpose of dropping the bombs upon Japan, there were also two kinds of domestic pressure at work. Actually, there were two different bombs. The first, dropped upon Hiroshima, was a uranium bomb which seemed relatively certain to work, but it took just about all the uranium available in the United States to make it. The second bomb, dropped upon Nagasaki, was a plutonium bomb which the people at Los Alamos were particularly eager to test because, if it worked, a large supply could be manufactured. In order to prove this, about 100,000 Japanese were killed at Nagasaki. In addition, there was fear that, unless the bombs were proven, Congress might eventually attack the entire Manhattan Project as a gigantic boondoggle.

On August 11, Byrnes drafted a demand for immediate unconditional surrender, which was cabled to Harriman for Stalin's concurrence. The message provided for the surrender to be accepted by General MacArthur and for what amounted to sole American control of the occupation of Japan. When Molotov asked for time to consider the draft, he was told that this was impossible, and Stalin agreed, expressing several face-saving wishes which were largely ignored. Thus, the first objective of preventing Stalin from having any influence over Japan's future was accomplished, in spite of the fact that the surrender had not been achieved prior to the Soviet declaration of war. On August 14, the Japanese government surrendered.

On the same day, the long-delayed Soviet-Chinese treaty was signed at Moscow, with Stalin conceding almost all the points (i.e., with regard to the administration of Dairen and the Manchurian railways) that had been raised in the long negotiations with Foreign Minister T. V. Soong. Chiang Kai-shek's administrators were thus permitted to take over civilian control of Manchuria, and the United States was permitted to airlift Nationalist troops to take over control. (The Red Army subsequently withdrew in April 1946, though not without first removing a number of Manchurian industries as war booty.[2])

With the war ended, Japan under American control and Chiang Kai-shek assured of Soviet support, the primary American objectives in the Far East appeared to have been attained. In addition, the United States succeeded on August 27 in getting Stalin to agree to a public declaration affirming Soviet support for the traditional American "Open Door" policy as to China.

However, in the days immediately following upon the Japanese surrender, the American State Department was concerned not so much with the Far East as with preparation for the postponed showdown with Stalin over Eastern Europe. These preparations were so intense that Byrnes requested a postponement of the London meeting of the Foreign Ministers from September 1 to September 10.

What became of the Stimson proposal to use the atomic trump card both as a carrot and a stick—that is, to offer

[2] The fact that Stalin entered the war, and probably could not have been kept from so doing in pursuit of Soviet interests, does not alter the fact that, earlier in the year, his promise had relieved the United States of considerable anxiety. From the point of view of the Japanese, occupation by a single conqueror, contrasted to the four-power occupation of Germany, proved a distinct blessing. See Edwin O. Reischauer, *Japan, Past and Present*.

the Russians some sort of partnership in the future control and development of atomic energy in exchange for a more liberal attitude toward the East European countries over which the Soviet Union had gained physical control?

While Truman had accepted Stimson's advice to postpone a showdown until the trump card could be played, he apparently had never been favorably inclined toward the second part of Stimson's proposal. Moreover, Byrnes was strongly opposed to it, and Stimson himself had developed certain doubts. These arose from the realization that any form of international control would require safeguards involving inspection, and that a secrecy-obsessed police-state dictatorship like the Soviet Union would be unlikely to agree to open its doors to such a procedure. Among the *quid pro quos* to be expected from an offer of partnership, one could scarcely expect an agreement on the part of the Soviet Union to change fundamentally the nature of its own government, even though such a development might be hoped for in time. Stimson was soon to have further thoughts on this matter, but when Byrnes went to London for the showdown meeting, he had no idea of making any conciliatory move of this sort.

Byrnes believed that the United States could maintain a nuclear monopoly for at least seven years, during which time his tough diplomacy would be able to bring about a stabilized and tranquil Europe and to enforce an American plan for peace which would make wars and armaments unnecessary forever. These ideas had been the burden of Truman's optimistic report to the nation on August 9. Byrnes left for London with the firm intention of using the atomic weapon as an "implied threat" (the words are those used in Stimson's diary) enabling him to dictate the terms of a lasting peace.

22

As a matter of fact, as Byrnes departed from Washington, things in Europe looked rather encouraging. The Polish government had agreed to free elections and to the presence of Western newspapermen. In Germany, General Eisenhower and Marshal Zhukov were getting along well in the initial stages of planning the four-power government of Germany as a single political and economic entity, even though the reparations issue—vitally important to the Soviet Union—remained unsettled, and in spite of the fact that France was already demanding annexations of West German territory. In Hungary, the Russians had agreed to admit the Western Allies to equality on the Control Commission, to postpone the scheduled elections and to permit better facilities for free campaigning. (These later resulted, on October 7 and November 4, in a complete defeat of the Communist Party.) However, in Bulgaria and Rumania, where Churchill had agreed to recognize predominant Soviet influence, Stalin had remained adamant, demanding that the United States and Britain recognize the existing Soviet-dominated governments. Contrary to the existing agreement, the United States had, through its diplomatic representatives, encouraged the opposition parties to demand free elections and refused to recognize the existing governments.

When Byrnes put forward the flat demand that the governments of Bulgaria and Rumania be changed, Molotov refused, obviously shocked by the changed American attitude. The much-heralded Foreign Ministers' Meeting broke down without even being able to agree upon a communiqué explaining its failure. In the Secretary's words, "We had come to the crossroads." He had deliberately forced an open break in order to raise the question of the political and economic domination of Eastern Europe by the Soviet Union. "Only by refusing to bow to Soviet domination could we," he wrote, "establish sound relations for the future."

Where Roosevelt and Churchill had conceded that, short of waging war against the Soviet Union, it would not be possible to do more than seek to persuade Stalin to loosen his hold upon the Balkans, Truman and Byrnes, armed with their atomic monopoly, now sought to coerce. Stalin, no matter how militarily and economically weak might be his relative position, was a poor subject upon whom to try such tactics. The London Meeting in September 1945 marked the beginning of the Cold War.

A search of the records of this earliest period in United States postwar policy reveals a number of somewhat astonishing facts:

There seems to have been no one of importance among Truman's closest advisers who dissented from the decision to seek a showdown with Stalin over the political and economic future of Europe.

Among those in Washington who knew about the work going on at Los Alamos, there seems to have been no one who did not take for granted that the bomb, if developed, would be used; and no one who seriously considered a prior warning to the people of Japan. This may have been partly because of fear that the bomb might not work. Among some of the scientists working at Chicago and Los Alamos, a different view was held. A report drafted by Dr. James Franck in June 1945 recommended against a surprise attack upon Japan; it suggested a technical demonstration and efforts to develop means of international control in order to prevent a desperate arms race. Therefore the report warned against a first use of the

24

weapon which would prejudice the achievement of international cooperation, warning that a surprise attack involved the likelihood that "Russia and even allied countries which bear less mistrust of our ways and intentions . . . may be deeply shocked by this step." The advice of this minority was disregarded.

Before the atomic bombs were dropped, each of the Joint Chiefs of Staff advised Truman that it was highly probable that Japan could be forced to surrender without use of the bomb and without an invasion of the home islands. Generals Marshall, Arnold and LeMay and Admirals Leahy and King all held this view. The fact that General MacArthur, the Supreme Commander in the Pacific, was not even asked for an opinion shows that military considerations were not decisive. MacArthur subsequently stated that, from a military point of view, he considered the use of the atomic bombs completely unnecessary. Churchill's chief military adviser, General Hastings Ismay, shared this view and, like Eisenhower and Leahy, expressed his "revulsion" over the use of the weapons. Apparently, Dwight D. Eisenhower was the only one among the top military men who actually advised against using the bombs, arguing at Potsdam, where he heard the news from Alamogordo, that "the United States should avoid shocking world opinion." His advice was angrily rejected by Stimson.[3]

After the bomb had been dropped neither Truman nor any of his advisers expressed the slightest *moral* scruples. Truman, aboard the *Augusta* when the news came, was exultant. Only Eisenhower later expressed the revulsion he felt at the time, saying in 1963: "It wasn't necessary to hit them with that awful thing."[4]

[3] Dwight D. Eisenhower, *Mandate for Change*, pages 312–313.
[4] *Newsweek*, November 11, 1963, page 107.

Among the atomic scientists, on the other hand, the contemporary literature shows a strong sense of guilt and apprehension as to the future. And among the American people there were many, including the writer, who were deeply shocked by what seemed an act of extreme barbarity even if it had been true, as Truman claimed, that the use of the bomb had "saved millions of lives."

Stimson, however, had second thoughts—not about the dropping of the bombs on Japan, but about dealing with the Soviet Union. In a letter and memorandum to the President dated September 11, 1945, he urged an immediate approach to Moscow with regard to the future development and control of atomic energy.[5]

The two major points made by Stimson to the President were:

1. That the relations between Russia and the United States might be irretrievably embittered "if we fail to approach them now and merely continue to negotiate with them, having this weapon rather ostentatiously on our hip." To do that, Stimson said, would increase Soviet suspicions and distrust and inspire the Russians to greater efforts in "an all-out effort to solve the problem."

"The chief lesson I have learned in a long life," Stimson wrote, "is that the only way you can make a man trustworthy is to trust him; and the surest way to make him untrustworthy is to distrust him and show your distrust."

2. Stimson proposed that, after discussion with the British, the United States should offer Russia an arrangement which

---

[5] The full text of the letter and the memorandum may be found in Stimson's memoir, *On Active Service in Peace and War*, written with McGeorge Bundy.

would control and limit the use of nuclear weapons and "encourage the development of atomic power for peaceful and humanitarian purposes."

After outlining the sort of arrangement he had in mind, Stimson wrote:

> I emphasize perhaps beyond all other considerations the importance of taking this action with Russia as a proposal of the United States—backed by Great Britain, but peculiarly the proposal of the United States. Action of any international group of nations, including many small nations who have not demonstrated their potential power or responsibility in this war would not, in my opinion, be taken seriously by the Soviets. The loose debates which would surround such a proposal, if put before a conference of nations, would provoke but scant favor from the Soviet. As I say, I think this is the most important point in the program.
>
> After the nations which have won this war have agreed to it, there will be ample time to introduce France and China into the covenants and finally to incorporate the agreement into the scheme of the United Nations.

Had Stimson's advice been followed, history might have taken a very different course. The Acheson-Lilienthal (or Baruch) proposal put forward by the United States in 1946 was too late and was launched in the United Nations in precisely the manner against which Stimson had warned. It conformed in almost all respects to Stimson's specifications for a proposal which the Russians would be sure to reject.

The plan was presented not to the Soviet Union, as Stimson had recommended, but to the entire world. It provided for the creation of an International Atomic Development Authority to which would be entrusted all phases of the development and use of atomic energy, including managerial control or ownership of all atomic-energy activities potentially dangerous to world security, and the power to control, inspect and license all other atomic activities. According to this proposal, the Authority would conduct continuous inspection of all phases of production of fissionable materials, have the sole right to carry on atomic-weapons tests and to promote the peacetime benefits of atomic energy.

Thus, the American plan quite logically required all countries, including the secrecy-conscious Soviet Union, to subject their entire territory to inspection and to accept national subordination to what amounted to a supranational authority in the field of atomic-energy development.

The Soviet Union, as might have been expected, objected to the provision for inspection and for international ownership of mines and factories. It also demanded the right to veto the adoption of any "decisions relating to the control of atomic energy." Moscow countered with a proposal to ban the use, production and storing of atomic weapons and the immediate destruction of all bomb stocks. This the United States rejected on the grounds that the West, deprived of the atom bomb, would be defenseless in the face of the Soviet Union's superior strength in conventional ground forces.

28

3

Postwar Myopia

During the war, the United States earned the respect and admiration of most of the world by its great contribution to victory. No sooner had that victory been won than the behavior of the American people and their government dissipated a large part of the goodwill which they had earned. This was due in part to the Truman administration's failure to understand the nature of the postwar world, and in greater measure to the lack of consideration for the plight of others and the orgy of self-indulgence displayed by the American people and their government immediately after V-J Day.

World War II had been a struggle for survival against threatened physical conquest; but it had also been in part a revolutionary civil conflict which crossed and recrossed national frontiers. The war of survival had created strange bedfellows, throwing democracies into alliance with dictatorships. The revolutionary conflict, which did not end with the defeat of the Axis Powers, contained at least as many seeds of future

29

trouble as the wartime decisions and actions of the victorious coalition.

Both the distribution and the nature of national power had radically changed, making it no longer possible to maintain a traditional balance of power among the leading nations.

The change in the *distribution of power* was primarily due to a shift in the center of gravity of the Western world from Europe to the United States—a shift which had been going on imperceptibly throughout the first part of the century until it was accelerated by the impact of two great wars. This transference of the seat of Western power across the Atlantic left the European nations with the habit of exercising a power which they no longer possessed and the United States in possession of world power without either the experience or the inclination to exercise it. The result was the creation of a power vacuum in those parts of the world that had formerly been owned, controlled or dominated by Western Europe. Neither the United States nor the Soviet Union created this vacuum. Its cause was the decline of Western Europe, brought about by the West Europeans' centuries-old inability to live at peace with one another.

The change *in the nature of power* was, quite simply, that the invention of atomic weapons of mass murder and destruction was about to make victory in any future major conflict indistinguishable from defeat. As yet, neither of the two great nations in which power had become concentrated—the United States and the Soviet Union—had fully grasped that the advent of nuclear weapons was in the process of making war an instrument of suicide rather than an instrument of self-preservation. Nor had they grasped the fact that, with power concentrated in only two superpowers, there could either be peace through agreement or else a struggle for preponderance of power in which the two superpowers would carry on economic and propaganda warfare against each other, compete for the allegiance of the lesser nations (or for their exploitation) and so drift nearer and nearer to suicidal conflict.

The worldwide political, social and economic revolution could clearly not be arrested, though, in the absence of a struggle between the two superpowers for preponderance, the revolution might be guided toward the achievement of justice and freedom by peaceful means. Here, the outstanding fact was extremely difficult for Western statesmen to understand and accept—namely, that the world had reached the end of a long period of history in which a relatively small part of the human race, inhabiting first Europe and then the Atlantic basin, had been able to exercise domination over the great mass of the world's peoples chiefly by reason of its superior skill in mastering man's environment but also because of the uneven distribution of the earth's natural resources. Now Western man's own progress in science and technology had eliminated time and distance. No more revolutionary messages had ever been broadcast to the world than those which told all men everywhere that there *could* be relief from hunger, pestilence, poverty and oppression—that it was not an immutable fate which doomed men to degradation but ignorance and man's inhumanity to man. The revolutionary realization of this fact was not the product of communist conspiracy or Marxist propaganda; it was the product of the material progress of Western civilization.

The existence of a communist ideology serving Soviet interests, and seeking by its propaganda to capture the revolution of the oppressed, blinded Western leadership to the much

31

more important fact that this revolution would have taken place had there been no Soviet Union and no communist ideology. The unpalatable but inescapable truth was that the underprivileged two-thirds of humanity, composed largely of non-white peoples, was no longer willing to remain submerged and that Western man faced the alternative of allying himself with this revolution or being ultimately submerged by it.

The defeat of European power by Japan, followed by the elimination of Japan as a power factor, left the peoples of Asia more on their own than they had been since the first European ships had sailed into Asian ports. From the Far East the news that the end of the white man's rule was at hand spread to the remnants of the European empires in the Middle East and Africa. Here lay the great opportunity for constructive American leadership in providing help and guidance to the emerging peoples. For the United States had not been involved in the hated colonial past; it had itself broken the trail of revolt against European domination.

Only the United States was emerging from World War II stronger than ever before. Its lands and cities were unravaged. Its manpower and productive capacity had increased enormously while the resources of most other nations had been seriously impaired. While other people were scrabbling for the bare necessities of life, not only in the submerged areas but also in Europe and the Soviet Union, Americans had food, jobs, money and things to buy with their money. When Truman took office, only the United States possessed the resources to get the Old World started toward recovery and to help the emerging peoples in their efforts to catch up to the Twentieth Century.

In the first few months of peace, no one seemed less aware

32

of the responsibilities which had devolved upon the United States or of the opportunities open to it than the people of the United States and their government.

A fully employed population rushed to buy consumer goods which had been scarce or unobtainable during the war. The politicians and the mass media insisted upon the abolition of wartime controls and the government acceded. The picture of the world's wealthiest nation indulging itself in unrestricted luxury while the rest of the world was struggling for bare subsistence was not one to inspire confidence or respect. The world's doubts as to the American capacity for responsible leadership were heightened by Truman's abrupt cancellation of Lend-Lease assistance without any apparent awareness of the problems faced by America's recent allies. When the Soviet Union asked for a loan to finance the reconstruction of its devastated areas, the application was "lost" in the files of the Foreign Economic Administration and later brusquely turned down. And when the British asked for similar assistance, they were given only half of what they requested, and conditions for maintaining the convertibility of the pound were attached which very nearly wrecked the British economy.

All this played directly into Soviet hands. Throughout the continent of Europe and especially in those countries which had been occupied by the enemy, the communists had gained enormously in prestige and influence. In part, this was due to the reflected glory of the Red Army; but in large measure it was because, throughout enemy-occupied Europe, the communists had supplied the disciplined spearhead of the resistance movements. In addition, the demoralization of European middle-class leadership and the absence of a clear, pro-democratic Anglo-American political policy during the war had

33

permitted the communists to pose as the standard-bearers of liberation. Thus, the fifth column tools of penetration were ready to Moscow's hand. Apparent American indifference to Europe's needs filled the communist cup to overflowing.

As for the opportunity to aid and guide the worldwide revolution of rising expectations, Americans and their government seemed unaware that such an opportunity existed. Yet, for the time being there was no other country in the world which had the resources to enable it to provide the knowledge, the skills and the capital so urgently needed by the peoples emerging into freedom.

Perhaps even more shocking was the Truman administration's attitude toward the organization which Roosevelt had set up to provide postwar relief. The work of UNRRA had been scheduled to end in 1947. In 1946, its administrator, Fiorello La Guardia, the former mayor of New York, proposed that the work be continued through a Food Fund, internationally administered, like UNRRA, even though the United States provided the funds. His proposal was turned down in favor of an American proposal that relief be henceforth granted only to such nations as the donors might see fit to help. La Guardia was horrified and exclaimed:

> "Does the government of the United States intend to adopt a policy which will make innocent men and women suffer because of the political situation which makes their government unacceptable to the United States?" [1]

Truman's answer, unhappily, was "Yes."

This was the beginning of a turning away from interna-

[1] Quoted in Kenneth Ingram, *History of the Cold War* (London, 1953), pages 56–57.

tionally administered aid, as conceived by Roosevelt, to a system under which individual nations would decide which nations deserved their help and would extend that help on the basis of bilateral agreements motivated by political considerations.

It is true that there were many Americans, such as Paul Hoffman and New York's governor, Herbert Lehman, who disagreed with Truman's answer. But the world knew little of minority opinion in the United States; it judged America by the behavior of the American government, and that behavior during the immediate postwar period seemed heartless, selfish and irresponsible.

It is only fair to note that the Truman administration's indifference to world affairs in the immediate postwar period was in part at least due to the fact that the American people were in no mood to consider further involvement. American soldiers in Europe were rioting, demanding to be demobilized, and throughout the country there was a clamor to "bring the boys back home." In addition, there were widespread though unwarranted fears of a postwar depression, loud demands for the abolition of wartime controls and a rash of strikes and work stoppages. The domestic scene, in other words, was such as to preoccupy any administration.

But the sorely distressed peoples in other countries could scarcely be expected to understand this situation. From their point of view, the United States alone had emerged from the war stronger and more prosperous than ever; it alone was in a position to supply the world's backed-up and urgent needs —a fact which seemed clearly to guarantee the United States against a serious business recession and to make its self-centered anxiety incomprehensible.

4

The Cold War Begins—
Truman's Offensive

The effect upon Stalin of the Truman-Byrnes offensive was not, as its authors had hoped, to cause the Soviet leader to retreat. On the contrary, its immediate effect was to stimulate an all-out Soviet effort to break the American atomic monopoly through a combination of intense scientific effort and espionage—an undertaking which was to succeed in only a little over four years. Parallel to this military effort and pending its success, Stalin adopted a stubbornly unyielding diplomacy that could be summarized in a single word: "*Nyet.*" This negative diplomacy was applied by Molotov in his negotiations with Byrnes until he became known as "Old Stone Bottom," and by Vishinsky and Gromyko in the United Nations.

While the American Secretary of State was preoccupied with the peripheral issues of a European peace settlement, notably with the Balkan peace treaties, the central issue—Germany—was allowed to deteriorate.

Meanwhile, on March 5, 1946, Winston Churchill, now no longer Prime Minister, made his famous speech at Fulton, Missouri, with President Truman sitting by his side and apparently beaming approval. Shorn of its characteristic embellishments, the speech amounted to this:

The world is divided into communist and capitalist blocs. To check the expansion of the communist bloc, the English-speaking peoples—a sort of latter-day "master race"—must sooner or later form a union. They should immediately form an alliance and coordinate their military establishments. They must lead "Christian civilization" in an anti-communist crusade. They must hold on to the secret of the atomic bomb, for only thus, said Churchill, could a probable war be averted. Stalin, he said, respected strength and would probably come to terms with a powerful and determined alliance. What Churchill was really saying was that the United States must underwrite the British Empire—and this at the very moment when Clement Attlee's Labour Government had repudiated Churchill's old-fashioned imperialism.

The speech was immediately disavowed by London and was widely criticized here and abroad. There was much speculation as to whether, by his apparent sponsorship, the President had meant to convey his agreement or approval. The White House denied any such intention but the curious circumstances in which the speech had been delivered left a question mark. A year later, the question would be answered. At the time, Churchill's speech was considered an unfortunately disturbing factor in the then current effort to win Congressional approval for a loan to Britain.

It is a widely held belief that the Fulton speech prepared the way for the policy which Truman was to announce in

March 1947 (The Truman Doctrine). Actually, Truman was already thinking and acting in the manner Churchill recommended, except that he was not thinking of an anti-communist crusade conducted by the English-speaking peoples but, rather, of an anti-communist crusade conducted by the United States. Truman was no more interested than Roosevelt had been in preserving the British Empire.

While Byrnes was concentrating on the Balkan treaties, a Soviet attempt to maintain control of northern Iran was blocked by a prompt appeal to the United Nations which succeeded in forcing the withdrawal of Soviet troops in accordance with a wartime agreement. But the Western powers were able to do little more than protest against continuing Soviet penetration of the Balkans. The Rumanian treaty returned Bessarabia to the Soviet Union and ceded North Bukovina which had never been Russian. Western protests against Soviet-dominated governments lost much of their force because they were based upon the ambiguous promise of "free elections" obtained from Stalin at Yalta. What were "free elections" in countries like Rumania and Bulgaria where no such elections had ever been held? What, for that matter, was "freedom" or "democracy" where none had ever existed? The Big Three had used these words in their wartime agreements, but had left them undefined.

Similar semantic difficulties arose in the United Nations where the Soviet Union flatly rejected the already mentioned American proposal for the international control of atomic energy which the American press hailed as "generous" although it was formulated and presented in precisely the manner against which Stimson had warned.

*   *   *

Alarmed by the rapidly worsening conditions in Germany, the writer obtained the approval of the State and War Departments for a visit to that country in August 1946 in order to make a first-hand study on the spot. Working as an accredited war correspondent for the Chicago Sun Syndicate, he was able to visit each of the four zones of occupation and to talk with the zonal commanders as well as with German leaders and ordinary citizens. Conditions were even worse than expected. In the British and American zones, business and industry were at a standstill and near starvation prevailed. Things were not much better for the Germans in the French zone, where the French were taking away farm animals and vehicles, while in the Russian zone Soviet troops were not only shipping food from that rich agricultural area to Russia but also removing whole industrial plants with their equipment. The American and British authorities were working well together, and a surprisingly cordial relationship existed between them and the Soviet command, in spite of the disastrous disagreement about reparations. But the entire scheme of four-power government of Germany as a whole had broken down because of French refusal to let it operate.

In a report to the War and State Departments and in a series of newspaper articles, the writer described these conditions and put forward a number of suggestions for a revision of occupation policy. A suggestion for a new approach to Moscow in order to bring about greater harmony among the occupying powers was turned by Byrnes into an attempt to woo the Germans, and the result was a worsening of American-Soviet relations.[1]

By the end of the year, Truman had had enough of Byrnes,

1 See Warburg, *Germany—Bridge or Battleground*, pages 354–370.

not because he had been too tough, but apparently because the President thought he had not been tough enough, and also because he felt that Byrnes had not kept him sufficiently informed.

While the offensive against Stalin in Europe had been showing unsatisfactory results, a dangerous situation had been developing in the Far East. In spite of lavish American aid in the form of money, transportation and military supplies, Chiang Kai-shek's Nationalist troops were being steadily pushed southward by the Chinese Communists. In the hope of inducing both Chiang and Mao Tse-tung to end the civil war and to form some sort of coalition government, Truman sent General Marshall to try to mediate the conflict. The effort failed, partly because Mao already sensed complete victory and perhaps even more because Chiang refused to undertake a reform of his corrupt and oppressive regime which might have enabled him to arrest its loss of popular allegiance. There was at this time no evidence to suggest that Stalin had gone back on his treaty with the Nationalists by giving aid to the Chinese Communists. The latter were obtaining arms chiefly by capturing American weapons from Chiang's forces.

In the November elections of 1946, Truman lost majority control of the Congress to the Republicans. Partly because he now needed a Secretary of State who would command Republican as well as Democratic support and partly because of his great and well-merited confidence in the wartime Chief of Staff, Truman now asked for Byrnes's resignation and appointed General Marshall to take his place. His first assignment would be to attend the Moscow Conference on Germany

40

and Austria, scheduled to take place in early March 1947.

With Dean Acheson as Under Secretary, Marshall set about creating a more orderly procedure in a Department of State that had suffered from Byrnes's habit of "carrying around the department in his briefcase on his frequent travels." Marshall expressed the view that the United States must assume a "more military posture." The opportunity to do so was not long in presenting itself.

A communist-led revolt against the Greek monarchy—aided not, as was thought, by Stalin but by Tito's Yugoslavia[2] —had assumed proportions with which Britain was no longer able to cope. Simultaneously, the Soviet Union was making threatening gestures toward Turkey, demanding control of the Black Sea Straits and a cession of Turkish territory.

Just as Marshall was preparing to leave for Moscow, the British Government informed Washington that it would no longer be able to carry out the obligations assumed by Churchill in his spheres-of-influence deal with Stalin, and that both Greece and Turkey required military and economic aid beyond Britain's ability to provide. When Truman sent for the Congressional leaders to propose that the United States extend $400 million worth of aid, he was told that to obtain Congressional approval, he would have to "scare hell out of the Congress and the country." The task of drafting an appropriate message to Congress was assigned to Presidential assistant Clark Clifford and Under Secretary Acheson.

The message, delivered on March 12, 1947, set forth the need for aiding Greece and Turkey. Both were, at the time, governed by right-wing dictatorships. In Greece, the com-

[2] See Milovan Djilas, *Conversations with Stalin;* also David Horowitz, *The Free World Colossus*, pages 65–68.

munist-led revolt was against the military dictatorship resulting from Churchill's restoration of the monarchy. The Turkish government was the same regime which had declined to enter the war against the Axis and had, in fact, sold chromium to the Germans.[3]

Going far beyond a recommendation of the specific actions required, the President then proclaimed a global policy which quickly became known as "The Truman Doctrine." He declared that henceforth the United States would come to the aid of any country threatened from within or without by totalitarian conspiracy or aggression. Since it was obvious that the term "totalitarian" did not apply to the existing governments in Greece and Turkey, nor to the fascist governments of Spain and Portugal, nor to the dictatorships which ruled a number of Latin American states, it was clear that the Truman Doctrine amounted to a declaration of global ideological war upon communism.

Thus far, Truman's offensive against the Soviet Union had been confined to Europe, except for the American-sponsored United Nations action in Iran. Now, however, the new doctrine proclaimed the unilateral assumption by the United States of global responsibility for the containment of communism—a commitment undertaken outside of the United Nations and without the assured support of any allies. That "containment" was the right word became clear when the doctrine was spelled out by a high-ranking foreign service officer, George F. Kennan, writing anonymously as "Mr. X" in the April 1947 issue of *Foreign Affairs*.

While the containment policy under Truman and Eisen-

---

[3] See Howard K. Smith, *The State of Europe*, pages 92–185; also Denna F. Fleming, *The Cold War and Its Origins*.

hower became essentially a military policy designed to prevent physical encroachment, its author, Kennan, had in mind a somewhat different aim. Unlike Truman, he did not seek to extirpate communism but to hold the Soviet regime in check until, in the course of time, it would mellow and become less aggressive. Kennan did not share the view that the world could not exist "half-slave and half-free"; and his belief that the Soviet regime would mellow as Russia became more and more of a "have" nation was proved right by later developments.

Six days before enunciating the Truman Doctrine, Truman had made a little-noticed but important speech at Baylor University on the subject of foreign economic policy. "We are," he said, "the giant of the economic world. Whether we like it or not, the future pattern of economic relations depends upon us. The world is waiting and watching to see what we shall do." The President then discussed the need for freeing world trade from artificial barriers and restrictions and, having asserted that the pattern of world trade rested in American hands, proceeded to outline what he thought that pattern ought to be. The text warrants careful study. Briefly, what Truman said was this:

Political freedom is bound up with freedom of individual enterprise; that pattern of international trade which promotes individual enterprise and leaves the direction of the international movement of goods and services to private individual initiative is the pattern which leads to peace; that pattern in which governments direct or control the flow of goods and services between nations is the pattern which leads to war. Therefore, we, the economic giant, are going to use our power to set a world pattern of free-enterprise capitalism.

43

Mr. Truman was not merely reaffirming the American belief in the American system as the best system for America. He made it quite clear that he believed that the whole world should adopt the American system, first, because it was the best system and, second, because the American system could survive in America only if it became the world system.

This was an unequivocal challenge not merely to those governments and peoples who believed in the Marxist doctrine but also to the far greater number of nations which had come either to believe in or to accept as necessary some form of national economic planning and some degree of government control over their respective economies. The challenge, though little noticed or understood at the time in this country, was very much noted abroad and formed an important part of the background against which the more spectacular Truman Doctrine was interpreted.

As might have been expected, Stalin's reaction to the Truman Doctrine, announced on the eve of the Moscow Conference on Germany, was a reinforced policy of "*Nyet.*" Germany had now become merely one battleground in a global ideological conflict. It was all the easier for Stalin to take a negative attitude because the three Western powers had failed to arrive at a common policy regarding the political and economic future of Germany. Returning to Washington, Marshall dispassionately reported on the failure of his mission.

Marshall and Acheson now set about developing a new approach to the problems of Europe. They recognized, as Byrnes had not, that the basic threat to European stability resided not in Moscow's aggressive intentions but in the social and economic weakness of both Eastern and Western

44

Europe—a weakness that gave rise to mass discontent easily exploited by communist propaganda. In a speech at Cleveland, Mississippi, on May 8, 1947, Acheson outlined a policy of economic aid which was then more fully developed by Marshall in his famous speech at Harvard University on June 5. As stated by Marshall, the new American policy offered economic assistance to *all of Europe*, communist or non-communist. It was a policy "not directed against any country or doctrine but against hunger, poverty, desperation and chaos."

Coming only three months after the Truman Doctrine, the European Recovery Program, which was offered to all the European countries provided only that they would cooperate in mutual aid and self-help, seemed like an almost unbelievable reversal of American policy. It was enthusiastically welcomed by the nations of Western Europe which had been shocked and frightened by the belligerent Truman Doctrine, and it was hailed by many Americans, including the writer, as a return to sanity. Stalin's reaction, however, was one of skepticism. From his point of view, the Marshall Plan probably seemed merely a more intelligent (and therefore more dangerous) form of waging the Cold War. Nevertheless, he sent Molotov to the Paris meeting to explore what the Americans had in mind. Two East European countries, Poland and Czechoslovakia, accepted the American proposal. For a few days, it looked as if the Cold War might end and a new period of East-West cooperation might set in.

In Washington, there were mixed feelings. Some of the Administration advisers, including above all Secretary Marshall, hoped that the Russians would accept the unprecedented American offer. Others hoped that Stalin would reject it—some because they feared that the Congress would refuse to ratify a plan which involved aid to the communist countries; others because they were more sympathetic to the belligerent anti-communism expressed by the Truman Doctrine than to the conciliatory shift in policy sponsored by Secretary Marshall. Britain's Foreign Secretary, Ernest Bevin, who presided over the Paris meeting, made it clear that he, for one, had no desire to see the Russians accept the proposal. This, undoubtedly, was one reason why Molotov decided to walk out of the meeting on July 14; more importantly, Stalin probably realized that participation in the American program would require too great a disclosure of the Soviet economic weakness. Had Stalin decided to join the Marshall program, he might well have wrecked it, because it was more than likely that the Congress, inflamed by the Truman Doctrine, would have refused ratification. As it was, a sigh of relief emanated from many quarters in Washington when Molotov withdrew from the conference.

The fact that Poland and Czechoslovakia had joined the European Recovery Program (ERP) was now hailed by the American press as a breakaway on the part of these two East European countries from Soviet control. Shortly afterward, when the Foreign Ministers of Poland and Czechoslovakia visited Moscow and announced the withdrawal of their countries from the ERP, American headlines proclaimed that the Iron Curtain had descended upon these two countries, making them helpless satellites of the Soviet Union. (See Chapter 5.)

With Stalin's rejection of the unprecedentedly generous Marshall offer, Europe was now definitely divided into a Western and Eastern economic orbit, with the United States underwriting the rehabilitation of the Western countries and

46

the Soviet Union organizing the economy of those countries which lay east of the dividing line. This focused the Cold War even more sharply upon Germany, lying as it did between the two orbits and as yet not under the control of either camp.

Until early 1947, Washington's chief concern had centered on Eastern Europe, the security of the Western countries being taken more or less for granted in spite of mounting economic distress and the existence of powerful communist parties in Italy and France. Recovery from the devastation and dislocation caused by the war was extremely slow, not only because the food, fuel, machinery and tools urgently required could be obtained only in the United States in exchange for scarce American dollars but also because European recovery was severely hampered by the lack of German coal and steel, the production of which had all but ceased under four-power occupation.[4]

The Marshall Plan was developed primarily in order to meet the increasingly urgent needs of Western Europe and only incidentally as a modification of the anti-communist crusade launched by the Truman Doctrine. When participation was rejected by Moscow, it became a powerful adjunct to the Western prosecution of the Cold War, saving Western Europe from threatened starvation and economic chaos and thus

[4] After his previously mentioned visit to Germany in 1946, the writer called Washington's attention to the effect that the restrictions upon Ruhr production of coal and steel were having not only upon German recovery but upon all of Western Europe. He suggested lifting the level of industry regulations as well as the creation of a European Coal Authority under which coal production would be pooled and coal allocated to the various European users. The idea was rejected at the time but was revived, so far as Western Europe was concerned, by the Schuman Plan of 1950. See Warburg, *Germany—Bridge or Battleground*, pages 229–233.

locking the door against communist subversion or penetration. It is important to recall that, at this time, there was no fear of Soviet military action against Western Europe; that came only later, with the Berlin Blockade and the communist coup in Czechoslovakia.

However, by this time a powerful sentiment of distrust and hatred of the Soviet regime had been generated in the United States, nourished by official pronouncements. So far as is known, Truman himself had drawn little if any distinction during the early days of the war between Hitler's fascism and Stalin's communism. Both were totalitarian, oppressive, atheistic and aggressive. Both were our enemies and the enemies of Western civilization. It apparently made no difference to Truman that Stalin had been the first to oppose Nazi aggression (in the League of Nations and in the Spanish Civil War), had been eager to come to Czechoslovakia's assistance at the time of Munich, and had "ganged up with Hitler" only after he had failed to enlist Western support in stopping him. And when Hitler turned upon Russia in June 1941, Truman—then a senator from Missouri—was reported in the *New York Times* to have expressed the view that if Hitler seemed likely to win, the United States should help Stalin, and if Stalin seemed about to win, the United States should help Hitler. This sentiment was one that was widely held among Americans at the time.

On the other hand, once Russia had become an ally, her tremendous contribution to allied victory created a strong pro-Russian feeling in the United States. For the most part, this was not a pro-communist sentiment although a certain amount of actual pro-communism had been engendered in the 1930's by disgust at Western appeasement and admiration of Soviet opposition to the Axis, especially during the

Spanish Civil War. This pro-communist sentiment had de-
creased sharply when the American Communist Party and
its European counterparts performed their overnight somer-
saults on June 21, 1941, proclaiming that what had been a
"capitalist imperialist war" had now become a crusade for
freedom.

Roosevelt had never wholly equated Nazism and Communism, even during the period of the Molotov-Ribbentrop Pact.
Like most Americans, he loathed the totalitarian police-state,
deplored official atheism and rejected the Marxist dogma,
but he never lost sight of the fact that Hitler and Mussolini,
not Stalin, had begun a war of conquest. And, when the
Soviet Union emerged from the war as the strongest power
in Europe, having at great sacrifice made a tremendous contribution to victory, Roosevelt felt that the United States and
Britain must come to terms with the power-political realities
in the interests of preserving the hard-won peace. By persuasion and the extension of much-needed economic assistance,
he had hoped to lighten the lot of the East European peoples
whom the conduct of the war had brought under Soviet domination. Churchill, too, once he had failed to gain support for
his preferred strategy of invading the continent through the
Balkans, was reconciled to the need for coming to terms with
Stalin, and did so in his spheres-of-influence deal with respect
to Southeastern Europe. Neither Roosevelt nor Churchill seriously considered going to war with Russia in order to liber-
ate Eastern Europe. It was true that Britain had gone to war
over Poland, but, later, Churchill's primary concern had been
not so much the liberation of all Eastern Europe as the preservation of the British Empire and its lifeline through the
Mediterranean.

In contrast to the pragmatic idealism of Roosevelt and the

49

shrewd realism of Churchill, Truman combined a benevolent idealism with a cocky confidence that he knew what was good for the world and that he had the power to impose it. In addition, he possessed a short temper and a great capacity for moral indignation. The combination of these characteristics led him to take a simplistic view of the world somewhat like the dualistic theology of the ancient Persian philosopher Manichaeus, according to which the world was governed by Powers of Light and Powers of Darkness. During the war, the Axis Powers had represented the seat of all evil. As Truman saw it, the postwar world was polarized between a benevolent Washington and a malevolent Moscow.

The conviction that only the Soviet Union stood in the way of his imposing a benevolent design for peace upon the world created in Truman an angry hostility toward the Soviet Union. This, in turn, created counter-hostility in Stalin and a vicious circle of mutual suspicion, distrust and hatred. Thus, Truman and Stalin came to expect the worst of each other and thereby caused the worst to happen.

Unlike Roosevelt, Truman confused Russian nationalistic expansionism with what he conceived to be a worldwide communist conspiracy. As Truman saw it, the Devil who dwelt in the Kremlin was a spider in the center of a worldwide communist web plotting world revolution, whereas in reality Stalin was an old-fashioned, ruthless, Machiavellian nationalist using Marxist-Leninist ideology as a tool. To be sure, this ideology proclaimed the inevitable triumph of communism throughout the world, but this had been a prophecy rather than a program of conquest; and Stalin was far more interested in the power-political future and security of Mother Russia than in a realization of the Marxist dream.

The fact that Truman made communism, rather than Soviet imperialism, the target of his hostility had a number of fateful consequences. It automatically caused him to consider all communist governments and communist political parties as enemies of the United States; to identify socialism with communism; and to regard all anti-communist governments and political parties as friends and potential allies, including the most oppressive dictatorships and feudal oligarchies. It caused him to define as "free" any nation whose government was not communist-dominated, no matter how anti-democratic that government might be. And, finally, his identification of a worldwide communist conspiracy as the primary threat to American security caused him to issue a Loyalty Order aimed at discovering communists in the United States which reversed the established American principle that an individual shall be considered innocent until proved guilty, shifting the burden of proof upon the accused.

All these things were implicit in the two speeches which Truman delivered in March 1947. They were to become more explicit a year later.

5

The Cold War Continues— Stalin's Counter-Offensive

The psychological impact of the Marshall Plan inspired the peoples of Western Europe with new hope and energy, but a new psychological climate was not enough to start the wheels of recovery. Last-minute Washington agreement to permit Britain to reestablish currency controls, forbidden by the terms of the American loan, momentarily relieved Britain's position; but the British Treasury's reserves were all but exhausted, and a severe drought following an unusually harsh winter brought most of Western Europe close to starvation. In the face of these conditions, Truman was almost unbelievably slow to act. He went on a trip to Brazil to attend an Inter-American conference together with Secretary Marshall. When Marshall returned, he endorsed the warning of Under Secretary Robert A. Lovett: "It is later than we think." Truman, however, declared as he boarded the battleship *Missouri* for a leisurely trip home that there was "nothing on the horizon to require a quick return to the United States." Returning to

Washington, he announced that Austria, Italy and France would require interim aid to see them through until the Marshall Plan went into effect—presumably in March 1948—and that in the meantime he was asking the Congressional committees studying the plan to meet in October. The *New York Times* remarked editorially:

> The Marshall Plan, temporary aid, food conservation and price controls cannot be more than dreams without popular support and understanding. These cannot be enlisted without courage, conviction and leadership which, it appears, are not to be had from President Truman.

It was not until late October 1947 that the President finally made up his mind to call a special session of Congress from which he requested $597 million for interim aid and authority to apply price controls and rationing of scarce commodities, if necessary to curb the inflationary cycle. (Due to inflation, prices had risen to such an extent in the United States that European purchases of urgently needed food and fuel had become all but impossible.)

On December 19, Truman finally gave to Congress the recommendations of the study committees with respect to the operating plan prepared by the sixteen West European participants in the Marshall program. The recommended compromise called for a four-year program amounting to $17 billion.

While these leisurely moves were in progress at Washington, Stalin's counter-offensive got rapidly under way. A rival "Molotov Plan" was developed "to promote the recovery of Eastern Europe." At the United Nations, in September, Vishinsky launched into vitriolic abuse of the "imperialist designs" of the United States; and, on October 5, Moscow announced the organization of the "Cominform," a permanent coordinating committee of the communist parties in Western as well as Eastern Europe, thus signaling a return to an aggressive policy of fostering revolution.

In an atmosphere of mounting tension, the Council of Foreign Ministers met at London in late November to make one more half-hearted attempt to reach agreement on Germany and Austria. After three weeks of futile discussion, the Council adjourned without even setting a date for the next meeting.

The world was now divided into two openly hostile camps. The only question was whether the two rival orbits would compete by peaceful means, each trying to outstrip the other in reconstruction, or whether the competition would take a more dangerous form.

The failure to resolve the deadlock in Germany clearly foreshadowed events to come. Already, former President Hoover had suggested the creation of a separate West German state and the making of a separate peace. The idea was now rapidly gaining adherents and was soon to take form in action that would cause the permanent partition of Germany and precipitate a crisis over the maintenance of the Western sectors of Berlin.

The sudden communist seizure of power in Czechoslovakia, on February 17, 1948, rudely awakened the Western world to the realization that the Kremlin would now not rest content with tightening its hold upon its existing orbit of power but would seek to expand it wherever and whenever an opportunity might present itself. The writer had visited Czechoslovakia during the summer of 1947, shortly after Czechoslovakia had withdrawn its earlier acceptance of participation in the Marshall Plan. While there, he had heard about the circumstances surrounding that widely misinterpreted action from Jan Masaryk, the long-time foreign minister, and had also gathered much interesting information about the attitudes of the Czech people toward Russia and the West.

According to Masaryk, a strong anti-communist, the Russians had not ordered the Czechs to withdraw. The decision to do so had been precipitated by headlines in the American press hailing Czechoslovakia's acceptance of participation as a "break with Moscow." This had created great resentment in Prague because, while culturally Western-oriented, the Czechs vividly remembered how the West had betrayed them in 1938 and how the Russians, their fellow Slavs, had tried to come to their assistance. They remembered, too, that the American Army had sat at their border near Pilsen while the Nazis still occupied Prague and most of their country, and that it had been the Red Army which eventually liberated them. For these reasons, Masaryk said, the Czechs preferred to forgo American assistance if their acceptance of such aid would appear to the world as a break with Moscow.

The then existing Czech government had been freely elected in 1945, with the Communist Party gaining about 40 percent of the seats in Parliament; the oddly named National Socialist Party of Benes, to which Masaryk belonged, had won a like number, while the small Social Democratic Party held the balance of power with 10 percent of the seats. As a result, a coalition or popular-front government had been formed, with non-communists holding many of the important cabinet posts, including the presidency and the foreign ministry.

Masaryk was aware that this coalition was precarious although it worked fairly smoothly. The danger, as he saw it, was that the Social Democrats might some day form a "popular front" with the communists. This is precisely what happened six months later, undoubtedly with a nudge from a no longer passive Kremlin. It remains the writer's opinion, for what it may be worth, that it might not have happened if the American government and press had not first hailed Czech acceptance of Marshall aid as a break with Moscow and then prematurely written off Czechoslovakia as a Soviet satellite.

Be that as it may, the coup of February 17, followed by the murder or suicide of Jan Masaryk, shook Western Europe out of its preoccupation with its own affairs and altered the indifferent attitude of the Truman administration, the Congress and the American people, sharply increasing the tempo of foreign-policy development.

On March 17, 1948, Britain, France and the Low Countries signed at Brussels a treaty of mutual military and economic assistance. On the same day, President Truman appeared before Congress to demand prompt passage of the European Recovery Plan, more funds for Greece and Turkey, $500 million for Chiang Kai-shek, and the enactment of peacetime selective service.

Welcoming the signing of the Brussels Treaty, Truman implied that the United States would aid the signatories in case of need. As in the preceding year, it was not what he proposed but the context in which he put forward his proposals that was significant. Whereas in March 1947 the President had been imprecise in his statement of a belligerent attitude, he was now no less belligerent but more specific. His analysis of the world crisis was stated in four short paragraphs:

1. The situation in the world today is not primarily the result of natural difficulties which follow a great war. It is chiefly due to the fact that one nation has not only refused to cooperate in the establishment of a just and honorable peace, but—even worse—has actively sought to prevent it.

2. The agreements we did obtain, imperfect though they were, could have furnished the basis for a just peace—if they had been kept. But they were not kept. They were consistently ignored and violated by one nation.

3. One nation has persistently obstructed the work of the United Nations.

4. The Soviet Union and its agents have destroyed the independence and democratic character of a whole series of nations in Eastern and Central Europe. It is this ruthless course of action and the clear design to extend it to the remaining free nations of Europe that have brought about the critical situation of Europe today.

Truman had now persuaded himself and sought to persuade others that the Soviet Union alone had caused and was causing the critical state of world affairs.

The specific charges by which the President sought to buttress this devil-theory of the postwar world crisis were far from accurate.

The basis for a just and honorable peace had been laid down by Roosevelt and Churchill in the Atlantic Charter of 1941. It had been reaffirmed by the "United Nations Declaration" of January 1942. It had been destroyed not by Stalin alone but by Roosevelt, Churchill and Stalin in their wartime agreements made at Teheran and Yalta.

Truman contended that the agreements reached with the Soviet Union would have furnished the basis for a just and honorable peace if they had been kept, but that Russia and Russia alone had violated them. Could anyone seriously contend that the Yalta and Potsdam agreements had laid the foundations for a just and honorable peace? And had Russia alone violated them? What about French obstruction of the Potsdam Agreement? What about the later violations of the reparations clauses committed by all four signatories?

As for obstructing the work of the United Nations, it was true that Russia had argued, wrangled and vetoed until everyone's patience had been exhausted; but it was equally true that the United States, although it commanded a majority in the United Nations, had undermined the organization's authority by acting unilaterally in developing its own policies both in Europe and in Asia.

Finally, Mr. Truman charged that Soviet destruction of "the independence and democratic character of a whole series of nations in Eastern and Central Europe" had brought about the crisis. As a matter of historical record, none of these nations except Finland had ever been truly independent. Before World War I, only two of them had existed. Between the two wars, most of them had been members of the Little Entente, dependent for their security upon the French Army. Certainly, there was a vast difference between dependence upon a friendly power and subservience to a dictatorial overlord, but the Czechoslovakia of 1928 had been just as careful not to offend France as the Czechoslovakia of 1947 had been careful not to offend Russia. As for the destruction of the "democratic character" of these nations, this was tragically

58

true of Czechoslovakia; but most of the other Eastern and Central European nations had never had a "democratic character" to destroy; they had been ruled throughout their history by feudal squirearchies which exploited their oppressed peasant populations.

The inaccuracy and exaggeration of Truman's charges stultified the case that might justly have been made against the Soviet Union. The Kremlin *had* violated pledges, obstructed settlements, abused the United Nations and invaded the rights of neighboring peoples. The Kremlin *had* made dealing with a complicated world crisis infinitely more difficult. But the Kremlin had *not* originally caused the crisis; Russia had not been the prime mover in the endless quarrels which brought about the decline of Western Europe; it had not caused the anti-colonial revolt of Asia; it had made almost no contribution to the scientific and technological advance which had triggered the revolution of rising expectations.

The result of this scapegoat analysis of the complicated postwar world crisis was to blind American policy-makers to their own past mistakes; indeed, Truman's analysis implied that there had been no errors of any consequence.

Stalin was pictured as having illegally and immorally acquired a vast empire in Eastern Europe, whereas the truth was that most of this empire had been conceded to him by the wartime agreements. Roosevelt and Churchill had acquiesced in the absorption of the three Baltic states and had expressly sanctioned the annexation of parts of Poland, East Prussia, Finland and Rumania. Free elections had been held in Finland, Poland, Hungary and Czechoslovakia. Only in Bulgaria and Rumania had communist governments been imposed and maintained. Stalin had posed no serious threat to

West European security, much less a threat to American security, until after the Truman-Byrnes offensive, backed by the implied threat of the atomic bomb, had posed a threat to Soviet security. Then Stalin had reacted with a counter-offensive in which the first move had been to tighten his hold on Eastern Europe, the second to organize the Cominform including the West European Communist parties, and the third the coup in Czechoslovakia.

The consequence of Truman's distortion of recent history was the disastrous adoption by the United States of an essentially negative over-all aim of preventing Stalin from making any further inroads into what now began to be called "the free world." The adoption of this aim demanded that the United States devote its energies and resources, not to creative purposes such as reconstruction and economic development, but to building a physical wall manned by physical force around the periphery of the Soviet orbit.

This negative orientation of American policy placed the United States on the defensive—a posture recognized as both militarily and diplomatically unprofitable—a posture incompatible with the American temperament and wholly unsuited to the achievement of world leadership.

That was not all. The determination to forge a ring of steel around the communist periphery—which was soon to include China—committed the United States to a search for allies. In this search, the criteria were to become anti-communism, the possession of strategic bases, strategic raw materials and potential military manpower. The quest for allies that met these requirements was destined to push the United States into support of the remnants of European colonialism and into collaboration with corrupt dictators, feudal rulers, princelings

60

and puppets who opposed not only communism but any sort of revolutionary change. The policy which Truman and his successors would continuously proclaim a crusade for freedom and democracy would end up making the United States the chief defender of a *status quo* which the vast majority of mankind desired to change.

The Czechoslovak affair aroused fear that the Italian elections, scheduled for May, might produce another communist take-over, either through victory at the polls or by a *coup d'état*. Through its embassy in Rome, the United States poured in money and propaganda to help assure the victory of the Christian Democrats led by Alcide de Gasperi. As soon as this effort had succeeded, Britain, France and the United States turned their attention to Germany.

With Marshall aid now flowing into Western Europe, the one great brake upon recovery was the demoralized state of the West German economy. At a meeting in London, on June 2, Britain, France and the United States decided to merge their zones of occupation in order to bring West Germany into the European Recovery Program. The long-delayed writing-down of the inflated German currency set off a spectacular recovery, but the introduction of the new currency into the Western sectors of Berlin, combined with the merger of the Western zones, set off a predictable crisis over the future of Berlin.

The Kremlin took the view that the Potsdam Plan was now dead, that the Allied Control Council might as well be disbanded, and that the Allies should withdraw from the Western sectors of Berlin. To enforce their demands, the Russians instituted a blockade of West Berlin, shutting off

Western access by land and water. This move was countered by a quickly organized and ably maintained airlift and a Western counter-blockade of the Soviet zone.[1]

Meanwhile, Truman's intervention in Greece was narrowly saved from failure by the sudden revolt of Yugoslavia against Soviet domination and its expulsion from the Cominform. This brought about the closing of the Yugoslav-Greek frontier and deprived the Greek communists of their most valuable sanctuary, thus wrecking their chances of gaining control.

With Italy saved from a communist take-over, Greece and Turkey reasonably safe, the Berlin Blockade effectively stalemated, and with West European recovery proceeding rapidly, things looked rather well for the anti-communist cause in Europe. But these gains were offset by the political instability of France, where one cabinet crisis succeeded another, and by the inability of the Western powers to come to any real understanding with each other as to the future of Germany. Yet Germany was more and more becoming the focus of the struggle for the control of Europe.

Stalin's counter-offensive in Europe had been halted. However, in Asia the communist tide was in full flood. By the end of 1948, all of China down to the Yangtze River was in communist hands.

Prior to the presidential election of November 1948, practically everyone except Mr. Truman expected that he would be soundly defeated by New York's former governor, Thomas

---

[1] For a detailed account of this third move in the Soviet counter-offensive and the manner in which it was met, see Lucius D. Clay, *Decision in Germany.*

E. Dewey. At a United Nations conference in Paris, both Secretary Marshall and John Foster Dulles, who accompanied him as Dewey's representative, prepared for an interregnum in which Marshall expected to be a "lame duck" incumbent with Dulles occupying the position of Secretary of State designate. However, Truman's vigorous campaign, marked by a slashing attack upon the Republican-controlled "Do-nothing 80th Congress," gained him not only a personal triumph but recaptured for his party control of both houses of the legislature.

With his position now more secure, Truman gave impetus to the secret negotiations that had been carried on with Canada and the Brussels Treaty Powers toward the creation of a North Atlantic defense alliance. This project derived from Senator Arthur Vandenberg's resolution, passed by the Senate on June 11, 1948, authorizing the President to enter into defensive alliances consistent with the United Nations Charter and to extend military aid to nations willing to join the United States in seeking to preserve peace. This departure from the traditional American policy of avoiding "entangling alliances" put military teeth in the policy of containment.

At the end of the year, it was announced that ill health necessitated Secretary Marshall's retirement and that his former Under Secretary, Dean Acheson, would be appointed in his place.

6

The Partition of Europe is Frozen. The Cold War Heats Up

During his first year as Secretary of State, Acheson's major efforts were directed to Europe. The airlift and the counter-blockade had convinced the Kremlin that the Western powers could not be forced by any means short of war to give up their hold on the Western sectors of Berlin and that a continuation of the blockade would probably not prevent the West from consummating its plan for the creation of a West German state. With the Berlin crisis on the way to solution, Acheson and Truman faced two major decisions: *first,* whether to continue or reverse the trend toward the creation of two separate German states; and, *second,* whether to make the proposed Atlantic Alliance into a simple declaration of solidarity with Western Europe or to stretch it into a commitment to defend Western Europe's frontiers against a possible invasion.

In dealing with the first problem, Acheson quickly abandoned any thought of an all-German settlement and proceeded to carry the trend toward formal partition beyond the point of no return. During his first months in office, Acheson energetically fostered the creation of a new Federal Republic of West Germany. After the first free elections held on German soil since 1932, this new West German state came into being in August 1949, with its "provisional" capital at Bonn and with Konrad Adenauer as its first Chancellor, heading a coalition of Right and Center parties.

Two months later, as might have been expected, Moscow proceeded to convert the Soviet zone into a "German Democratic Republic" with a government allegedly elected but actually selected and imposed by the Kremlin.[1]

The West was now committed to a policy of subordinating its original aim of German unification to the aim of integrating West Germany into the Marshall Plan community. From the point of view of enabling Western Europe to compete successfully in economic progress with Eastern Europe, this was desirable, if not essential. In the writer's opinion, it had not been necessary to create a new political entity in order to achieve this purpose; to do so meant the indefinite postponement of a European peace settlement, for there could be no such settlement without a reunification of Germany, and there could be no German reunification as long as the West based its policy upon the inclusion of two-thirds of Germany in the Western half of a divided European community.

The Truman-Acheson policy, accepted with some misgivings by the British and with extreme reluctance by the French, presupposed that an eventual European peace settle-

---

[1] For a full account of the birth of the two German states and an analysis of the West German elections, see Warburg, *Germany, Key to Peace*, Chapter 6.

ment could be brought about only by making Western Europe—including West Germany—so strong and prosperous that its power of attraction for the peoples of Eastern Europe would become irresistible. (This presupposed that when and if such a point were reached, the Kremlin would bow to the wishes of the East European peoples.) In Acheson's own words, his policy was to create "situations of strength from which to negotiate."

Had this policy remained one of creating only economic strength and political stability, it might conceivably have succeeded. It could not possibly succeed if the integration of West Germany in Western Europe should come to involve military integration. In that case, no amount of "attraction" would cause the Kremlin to relinquish its hold upon the East. This was where danger lurked in the negotiations for a North Atlantic Treaty.

As laid before the Senate Foreign Relations Committee in April 1949, the treaty involved in essence nothing more than a declaration by the United States and Canada that, if any of the European signatories were attacked by an aggressor, the United States and Canada would consider such an act of aggression as an attack upon themselves. In other words, the United States was now undertaking to create a deterrent to aggression which, had it existed in 1939, might have prevented World War II. So far, so good.

However, what the Europeans and especially the French wanted was not merely an American undertaking to fight an aggressor, but an undertaking to fight an aggressor at the frontiers of Western Europe in order to prevent its being once more overrun and eventually avenged and liberated. Premier Henri Queuille of France had made this explicit when he said: "Next time you would be liberating a corpse."

66

In the writer's opinion, the only honest answer to this under-standable demand would have been: "You are asking for an unfulfillable promise. There is no way to protect you from invasion except by preventing that invasion from being launched. This we shall try to do by declaring that war against you means war against us and by making ourselves so strong that an aggressor will hesitate to embark upon an adventure which he knows will entail fighting us as well as you." No such reply was made.

Testifying before the Senate Foreign Relations Committee, Acheson made three statements from which it could be inferred that the treaty would not involve a commitment to defend Western Europe at its frontier in Central Germany:

1. Emphasizing that it was not intended to let rearmament impede recovery, he said that it was not proposed to create any substantial addition to existing West European forces but merely to modernize and equip the existing West European divisions, of which there were then about twelve.

2. He said that it was not intended to send any additional American troops to Europe beyond the two divisions already stationed in Germany.

3. He assured the Senators that in no circumstances would the United States acquiesce in the remilitarization or rearmament of West Germany.

This seemed to dispose of the question of stretching the treaty into a commitment to defend the line of the Iron Curtain. Senators Connally and Vandenberg, the Democratic and Republican leaders, publicly stated their conviction that the treaty would not commit the United States to defend any "new Maginot Line,"[2] and the treaty was ratified on that assumption.

2 See *New York Times*, May 11, 1949.

In his testimony before the Foreign Relations Committee on May 10, 1949, the writer ventured to question this assumption, warning that the commitment *would* be stretched and that this would inevitably involve both sending a substantial American garrison to Germany and the rearmament of the West Germans.

As it turned out, the promises not to divert Western Europe from recovery to rearmament, not to send additional American troops to Germany, and not to rearm the Germans themselves were all broken within less than two years. Their repudiation could not be reasonably attributed either to Russia's unexpected success in making an atomic bomb in the autumn of 1949 or to the outbreak of the war in Korea in June 1950. The announcement of the first atomic explosion in the Soviet Union in September 1949 was accompanied by an explicit White House statement that this event would cause no change in American policy. And, long before the North Korean aggression, plans for West German rearmament were being openly discussed in Britain and the United States.[3]

The decision to rearm West Germany sealed the partition of Europe, sounding the death-knell for any hope of German reunification.

Although it was announced that the first atomic explosion in the Soviet Union would not affect the development of United States policy, it did, as a matter of fact, lead almost immediately to the decision to launch a crash program for the development of a thermonuclear bomb. This matter had been under debate for some time. Among the scientists, there had been some reluctance to develop a means of mass incineration

---

[3] This whole matter remains a disturbing enigma for which no explanation was ever offered by the Truman administration.

far more terrible than the atomic weapons which already threatened civilization with extinction. The President, however, sided with those of his advisers who urged that the United States must at all costs perfect the new weapon before the Russians might succeed in doing so and thus acquire a blackmail power over the entire world; he overruled those who urged that another serious effort should be made at this time to bring all nuclear weapons under supranational control. The decision was publicly announced in January 1950.

In May, an event occurred in Europe which might have altered the whole course of the Cold War. The French Foreign Minister, Robert Schuman, disclosed to his British and American colleagues a plan conceived by Jean Monnet for the merger of Europe's coal and steel production under a supranational authority, designed primarily to bring France and Germany together in an economic union indissoluble by war. The plan was explicitly stated to be open to participation by any European country willing to place its coal and steel production under supranational authority.[4]

Unhappily, three developments occurred which undermined the great political potential of this proposal:

First: The United States demanded to know whether Schuman really intended to leave the plan open to nations in the Soviet orbit; "was he proposing to help win the Cold War or proposing to end it?" [5] Schuman replied that he doubted whether in the existing circumstances the Kremlin would permit any of its satellites to join but that, if it did permit participation, so much the better since this would tend to unify a

---

[4] See Warburg, *Germany—Bridge or Battleground*, pages 231–233, for the author's earlier and rather similar proposal rejected by Byrnes.
[5] Quoted by James Reston in *New York Times*, May 12, 1950.

divided Europe and bring a large part of its war potential under supranational control.

Second: The British Labour Government brusquely declined to participate—a decision the British were later to regret. West Germany, Italy, Holland, Belgium and Luxembourg enthusiastically accepted. In Germany's case, the reason for the enthusiasm was clear: the Schuman Plan provided Bonn with a short and relatively easy way back to a position of equality among the European nations.

Third: An almost fatal blow to the Schuman Plan came in September 1950 with Acheson's public demand for West German rearmament. From the moment when the United States declared a German military contribution essential to Western defense, the military cart was placed before the political horse and Konrad Adenauer sat in the driver's seat. He now had a bargaining position.

The decision to rearm the West Germans was the logical outcome of the American government's yielding to the French demand for a treaty commitment to defend Western Europe at its frontiers; nevertheless, France was profoundly shocked by the idea. In Britain, too, the decision aroused grave misgivings in the Labour Party. Even in West Germany, there was widespread dismay, especially among the opposition Social Democrats. Most Germans were not at this time enthusiastic over the proposal, partly because of a widespread postwar pacifism and partly because it was feared—and with good reason—that, if the Federal Republic were to become a military ally of the West, the Soviet Union would never agree to German reunification.

The Soviet reaction to Acheson's demand for West German troop contingents was an immediate, sharply worded protest, followed by a demand for a four-power conference to discuss an all-German peace treaty.

While these developments were transpiring on the European scene, the Chinese Communists were sweeping southward from the Yangtze Valley and rapidly gaining control of the entire Chinese mainland. The Nationalist armies were melting away, losing their American-supplied equipment to the Communists or defecting with it. In November 1949, Chiang Kai-shek fled to Formosa with the remnants of his forces and there established a government-in-exile.

The Department of State issued a White Paper, explaining in detail what had happened in China and placing the major part of the blame upon the corruption and incompetence of the Nationalist regime. This produced indignant denunciation by the pro-Chiang publicists in the United States, who not only insisted that a faulty American policy had produced the disaster but were beginning to suggest that this policy had been influenced, if not dictated, by communists or communist sympathizers in the Department of State. (In the writer's opinion, American policy had indeed been faulty—not because insufficient aid had been extended to Chiang Kai-shek, but because the United States had failed to disengage itself from the Chinese Civil War after the Marshall mission in 1946 had failed. The continuance of massive aid to a Nationalist regime foredoomed to overthrow by its own unwillingness to reform had not only constituted a futile waste of the American taxpayers' money but also had incurred the lasting enmity of a communist regime already certain of coming into power over one-quarter of the earth's population.)

It seems likely that, in spite of the outcry of the Chiang

71

sympathizers in the United States, the Truman administration would have disengaged itself from the forlorn Nationalist cause after Chiang had fled the mainland, had it not been for the outbreak, in June 1950, of the war in Korea.

Hostile critics accused Acheson of having "invited" the North Korean invasion by an ill-advised statement that Korea "lay outside the defense perimeter of the United States." It seemed to this observer more reasonable to blame the "invitation" upon the American military authorities who had withdrawn the American occupation forces from South Korea without first placing South Korea in a position to defend itself against the Soviet-trained and equipped North Korean army known to have been organized before Soviet occupation forces had been withdrawn. Actually, the original causes of the Korean conflict lay even further back in the past. The first mistake had been to leave American troops in an untenable position on a strategically irrelevant peninsula of Asia; this had been part of the early postwar strategy of the Truman administration aimed at keeping the Soviet Union out of East Asia after the Japanese surrender. The second mistake was to have permitted the 38th parallel to become a political boundary between two parts of a divided Korea. And the third mistake had been to agree with the Soviet Union upon a date of mutual withdrawal of occupation forces without making adequate preparations for the withdrawal. Instead of either insisting upon the disbandment of the North Korean army or postponing American withdrawal until at least its equivalent had been created in South Korea, the United States military authorities had half-trained and half-equipped a South Korean army and departed. When the chief of the American military mission was later asked why he had not supplied the South

72

Koreans with planes and tanks, he was reported to have said: "We did not dare give them offensive weapons for fear that Syngman Rhee [South Korea's president] might try to conquer North Korea."

In retrospect, it seems likely although by no means certain that Stalin triggered the North Korean invasion, either to forestall an attack by Syngman Rhee or, more probably, because it seemed a reasonably good gamble to assume that the Soviet-trained North Korean forces would overrun the entire peninsula before the United States would be able to take any effective action. As a matter of fact, this very nearly turned out to be the case. It was only because Truman took bold and immediate action, because there were some American forces in Japan with which action could be taken, and because a Soviet boycott of the Security Council enabled the United Nations to sanction the intervention that it was possible to save the Republic of South Korea.

There was a close parallel between the Berlin crisis of 1948 and the Korean crisis of 1950. Each was the result of blunders in judgment and timing. In each, prompt, courageous and gallant action prevented disaster. In neither case did gallant action solve the situation out of which the crisis had arisen.

Having, by the narrowest margin, maintained a foothold at the southernmost tip of the Korean peninsula, the United Nations forces were gradually built up to the point at which they could take the offensive. South Korea was cleared of communist invaders. The aggression had been repelled. Important prestige had been gained for the United Nations, even though the United States had provided most of the muscle for the operation undertaken in the name of the world organization. And then the incredible blunder was committed: the war was

73

carried across the 38th parallel and up to the Manchurian border. General Douglas MacArthur predicted that the war would be over by Christmas, with all of Korea in his hands. But, by Christmas, Communist China had entered the conflict and MacArthur's forces were in headlong retreat. Why and by whom the decision to invade North Korea was made, why repeated warnings of Chinese intervention were ignored, and why the United States failed to take counsel with its allies remained a mystery. The ultimate responsibility, however, was Truman's, both as President and as Commander-in-Chief of the United States armed forces.

Once the front was re-stabilized at about the 38th parallel, a stalemate ensued which lasted throughout the two remaining years of the Truman administration. Casualties continued to mount. The President and his advisers had worked themselves into a position from which they could neither achieve victory nor make peace. Neither the United Nations nor the principal allies of the United States could be counted upon to back a quest for victory which would almost certainly involve a full-scale war with China and perhaps with the Soviet Union. The Republicans would denounce, and majority opinion in the United States could not be counted upon to support, a peace at the 38th parallel.

The reason for this domestic political situation was to be found in a state of irrational suspicion and fear for which Truman himself was largely responsible. When accused of laxity with regard to communist espionage and infiltration, the Truman administration had, as already mentioned, sought to tighten up security by methods wholly incompatible with the basic principles of the free, democratic society it was trying to

74

defend. Under the Loyalty Order of 1947, the Attorney General prepared a list of organizations which he labeled "subversive," and membership, past or present, in any such organization became "evidence" that an individual's loyalty was doubtful. A few of these organizations were no doubt communist fronts; others, originally innocent, had become so; still others were wholly innocent. These distinctions mattered but little. If the Attorney General or, for that matter, anyone else said that such-and-such an organization was subversive, then anyone who had belonged to it, no matter when or for how long, became an object of suspicion. It needed only the fall of China to the Chinese Communists and the conviction for perjury of a high State Department official, Alger Hiss, to establish the widespread suspicion that the government had been thoroughly infiltrated and that American foreign policy was being shaped by a concealed communist fifth column in the Department of State. In this climate of suspicion and fear, it was inevitable that informers should flourish, that unsubstantiated denunciation should take the place of evidence, and that unscrupulous opportunists should reap a political harvest. In many respects, the condition of the public mind resembled that which had existed during the presidency of John Adams, when the notorious Alien and Sedition Acts had been passed. The danger arose that a free society might commit suicide out of fear of being subverted. For a time, the basic principles of freedom which the American people sought to defend were in greater danger from the irrational behavior of the American society than from the machinations of a relatively small number of communists and fellow-travelers subservient to Moscow.

The effect of this reign of suspicion and fear, if not of outright terror, upon the conduct of the nation's foreign policy was disastrous. The Truman administration began to compete with its critics in endeavoring to prove that it was more anti-communist than they. It accepted the thesis of its critics that any and all negotiations with its adversaries constituted dishonorable "appeasement" and thus worked itself into a position of frozen inflexibility. In Korea, this meant that a stalemated war would have to continue without hope of either victory or peace without victory. In Europe, it meant that the United States became deaf not only to anything that might be said by Moscow but also to the voices of its friends.

Britain and France had supported the original American intervention in Korea but were by no means satisfied with the policy which had brought China into the war; nor did they agree with Washington's continued support of Chiang Kai-shek. India, which had repeatedly warned against pushing up to the Manchurian border, was wholly out of sympathy with Truman's policies. Australia and New Zealand looked askance at the emerging American plan to rearm Japan, much as the European nations distrusted the Acheson proposal to rearm West Germany. The Truman administration treated these misgivings as if they were natural but childish aberrations and proceeded upon its inflexible course.

1951 was a year of stalemate in Asia and slow motion in Europe. Upon the recommendation of General Eisenhower, the newly appointed NATO commander, Congress authorized the dispatch of four additional American divisions to Germany. Truman had promised these reinforcements at the time when Acheson had demanded German rearmament. Alarmed by Acheson's call for German troops, the French improvised the so-called Pleven Plan for a "European Army," in which German contingents, limited in size and number, would be so

76

integrated with other NATO forces as to minimize the danger of resurgent German militarism. The ensuing debate as to the extent to which the Germans would be treated as equal partners in a "European Defense Community" (EDC) or as something less lasted throughout the rest of the year. The Germans bargained skillfully to obtain concessions and, by this time, were planning eagerly for their armed forces.

A lengthy exchange of notes between Moscow and the Western capitals led eventually to a meeting at Paris of the four Foreign Ministers from March 5 to June 21. It became increasingly clear during seventy-three futile sessions that, while France and Britain were anxious to reach an agreement with Russia over Germany, the United States had no such desire. Behind the scenes, Adenauer was now a powerful influence against any discussion of reunification.

The Bonn Republic, until now the passive object of East-West negotiations, was rapidly becoming a co-maker of Western policy. Adenauer realized that a four-power conference, even if inconclusive, would once more make Germany the object of negotiation; he was determined to prevent any discussion of the German future until he could be certain of exercising a dominant influence. Before the end of the year, he obtained most of the concessions he desired in order to make West Germany an equal partner in the planned European Defense Community; likewise, he worked out with the State Department the broad outlines of an agreement with the Western powers which would end the occupation and grant sovereignty to the Bonn Republic. Finally, he obtained an extremely favorable debt settlement. With its economy flourishing and its future position of power almost assured, the Federal Republic now found itself in a trading position such as no nation that

77

had wantonly broken the peace could ever have hoped to achieve just six years after it had suffered a crushing defeat.

Early in 1952, Acheson had to overcome a sharp crisis within NATO. Although the accelerated West European re-armament demanded by the United States was still largely in the planning stage, its impact upon the European economies was already evident; recovery halted and threatened to go into reverse. The Germans, confident in their bargaining position, were no longer asking but demanding that their conditions be met if the NATO powers desired their military assistance. These conditions included a return to Germany of the Saar (which Byrnes had permitted France to annex), full equality in the command structure of the proposed "European Army," and equal partnership in NATO. The French, with their best forces drained off into Indochina (see below), were more than ever insistent upon protection against German domina-tion of the Western alliance; with Britain refusing to join EDC, they were discovering to their alarm that, instead of in-corporating West Germany in a European Defense Commu-nity, they were about to be left more or less tête-à-tête with the Germans in a Little Europe in which the Bonn Republic would be by far the strongest partner.

To meet this crisis, Acheson met with his British[6] and French colleagues and Chancellor Adenauer at London and then with the NATO Council at Lisbon.

The results of these two meetings were:

1. Turkey and Greece were admitted as full-fledged mem-bers of NATO.

2. West Germany was technically denied membership in

---

[6] Churchill had been returned to power in late 1951 with Eden once more as his Foreign Minister.

NATO but was granted its equivalent by an arrangement under which EDC became a member of NATO and the North Atlantic Treaty's provisions were extended to cover EDC territory. This served to guarantee West German territory and to give the Bonn government its "equal voice" in NATO decisions.

3. The West German military contribution to EDC was fixed at twelve divisions—four armored and eight infantry— backed by a tactical airforce of 1,746 planes. This German contingent, almost exactly what the German generals had demanded, was to be integrated in a "European Army" of forty-three divisions and 6,000 tactical planes. The sole concession to the French was that integration would take place at the army corps level, thus denying the Germans their demand to command their own corps.

In addition, the Germans were promised the early signature of a West German peace treaty, the end of occupation, a reduction in their monetary contribution to Western defense and the right to manufacture certain types of arms. Finally, Adenauer won an agreement to have the cases of German war criminals reviewed by a six-man board of which three members would be German.

Thus, seven years after "unconditional surrender," the West Germans had achieved equality, independent sovereignty, and the function of serving as a major bulwark of Western defense. The force to be contained had become the instrument of containment!

On March 10, 1952, a Soviet note to the three Western powers put forward by far the most reasonable and most specific proposal for German reunification that had been made by Moscow in the long series of diplomatic exchanges. Neither the substance of the proposal nor the fact of its arrival was disclosed by Washington until after the Western reply had been sent on March 25.[7]

The Russian document was in some important respects ambiguous. It proposed German unification upon what appeared to be a basis of democratic freedom and independence, specifically providing for a guarantee of "the rights of man and basic freedom, including freedom of speech, press, religious persuasion, political conviction and assembly." On the other hand, it suggested the creation of an all-German government without specifically agreeing to free elections. This point required clarification.

The past obstacle of reparations was clearly removed by a provision suggesting that there be no further limitations of any kind on the development of Germany's "peaceful economy."

The Kremlin proposed that the new Germany should be permitted to have such armed forces as might be necessary for its defense, that the Oder-Neisse frontier be made permanent, and that Germany should not be permitted to enter into any kind of coalition or military alliance "directed against any power which took part with its armed forces in the war against Germany."

The Western reply raised four points:

1. Before there could be a peace treaty, there would have to be an all-German government freely elected by the German people. Did the Soviet government agree, and would the Soviet

---

[7] For the full text of the two notes, see *Tenth Quarterly Report of the U. S. High Commissioner*, John J. McCloy (Washington, D.C., U. S. Government Printing Office), pages 96–101.

government permit a United Nations Commission to investigate whether it would be possible to hold free elections in the Soviet zone? (The latter suggestion seemed rather absurd since, obviously, the question was not whether conditions permitting free elections existed in the Soviet zone but whether the Soviet authorities would permit them to be created.)

2. The Western powers could not accept the Oder-Neisse frontier as final. (Like Byrnes in 1946, Acheson made no specific proposal for revision.)

3. The Western powers considered the proposed remilitarization of the new Germany as a "step backwards," which might jeopardize the emergence of a "new era of peaceful cooperation."

4. Contradicting themselves on point three, the Western powers insisted that the new Germany be free "to enter into association with other countries," frankly admitting their intention to "secure the participation of Germany in a purely defensive European community."

Quite clearly, the one reason Moscow might be willing to give up its hold on East Germany and to permit unification on a basis of Western democratic principles was to prevent West Germany from becoming an armed participant in the Western military alliance. How far the Kremlin would actually go in permitting free elections remained to be discovered and could be discovered only if the West signified a willingness to forgo a German military participation in Western defense. But this was precisely what Acheson was unwilling to consider, although the French and British would probably have backed an exploration of the possibilities.

Whereas the Russians had indicated by the very ambiguity of their proposal that they *might* be willing to grant free all-

German elections, the Western reply stated flatly that the West would *not* give up German participation in the European Army.

On April 9, the Soviet reply rejected the proposal of a United Nations Commission but suggested that all-German elections be supervised by the four occupying powers. To this interesting proposal, the Western powers made no reply at all until May 13, when they said that the Soviet proposal would make the four powers "both judge and party," but they would consider any other "practical and precise" suggestion. By this time, Acheson had already completed his plans to get the West German treaties signed before the end of the month.

This final "triumph" of Acheson's inflexible diplomacy was not achieved without considerable difficulty. The Social Democratic Party in the Federal Republic openly demanded a four-power conference to explore the Russian proposal. Chancellor Adenauer, on the other hand, was as determined as Acheson not to delay the West German treaties. The British Labour Party Executive called upon the Churchill government "to take steps without further delay" for the calling of a four-power conference before signing the treaties. The *Times* of London commented that there could "quite obviously be no German unity if the Western powers were determined to insist that a united Germany should also be a member of the European Defense Community."

Acheson remained adamant. On May 26, the three Western Foreign Ministers signed at Bonn the contractual agreements which vested all but complete sovereignty in the Federal Republic. A day later, at Paris, West Germany, France, Italy, Holland, Belgium and Luxembourg signed the EDC Treaty; then, mutual guarantees were exchanged by EDC and NATO.

The United States and Britain declared that they would consider any threat to the integrity or unity of EDC as a threat to their own nations' security. (This was the guarantee against a German breakaway sought by France.) Acheson and Eden further promised to station on the continent "such forces as their governments deemed necessary and appropriate to contribute to the joint defense of the North Atlantic area." After the signing ceremonies, Acheson proudly declared: "We are standing on the threshold of a New Europe and a New World!"

To all intents and purposes the record of Truman's foreign policy with respect to Europe was now closed. The United States Senate promptly ratified the Bonn and Paris treaties without even discussing their two major implications: that the United States was now committed to vastly greater military and economic aid to EDC than had yet been contemplated; and that American troops would remain in Europe not as a stopgap but as a permanent feature of Western Europe's defense.

The ultimate fate of the treaties now rested in the hands of the European parliaments. Acheson's sole remaining task was to press for ratification and to stall off a conference with the Soviet Union until the ratifications could be obtained. Only British ratification was forthcoming before President Truman's term expired, and this was achieved at the expense of a wide-open split between the Conservative majority and a united Labour Party opposition. During the remainder of 1952, the prospects for French and German ratification grew more and more dubious. The weak French government made no effort to bring the matter before the Assembly. Adenauer's determined efforts to obtain Bundestag approval led to one postponement after another. The hesitancy and delay were not

83

surprising. The shotgun marriage of France and Germany which Acheson had so vigorously sought to bring about entailed great risks for both nations as well as for all of Europe and the United States.

Making West Germany the keystone in the arch of West European defense against the Soviet Union in effect placed the future of all of Europe in the hands of a truncated German nation which would never be satisfied until it achieved the liberation of 18 million compatriots still living under Soviet rule, even if it reconciled itself to the permanent loss of the trans-Oder-Neisse territories. The reunification of the two German states could be brought about only through war or by Soviet consent. Meanwhile, even a truncated West German nation with its 48 million inhabitants was certain to become the dominant power in the West European Defense Community. German ratification of the Bonn and Paris treaties would probably be obtained by the determined Chancellor of the Bonn Republic. The final fateful decision would have to be made by France.

So far as Asia was concerned, China was lost, but the United States still remained committed to the forlorn hopes of Chiang Kai-shek to recapture the mainland. The Korean truce negotiations dragged on. The French colonial war in Indochina continued to drain French manpower and resources. Through the Marshall Plan, the United States was extending aid to France in her effort to re-establish her Asian empire while, at the same time, it put pressure upon the Netherlands to grant Indonesia its independence. Only the peace treaty with Japan, negotiated by Dulles, denoted some degree of forward movement—whether it denoted progress toward peace remained to be seen. Since neither the Soviet Union nor the Peoples' Republic of China nor India signed the treaty, it signified little as to future peace in the Far East. In essence, it was a treaty between the United States and Japan, concurred in without enthusiasm by Britain and its Dominions. The United States obtained the right to maintain troops in Japan and to retain a base on Okinawa, while Japan itself was encouraged to rearm despite the prohibition against rearmament embodied in the American-imposed constitution. The policy of rearming Japan as a bulwark against Communist China encountered strong resistance in Japan as well as among the nations which had suffered from Japanese aggression, much as the policy of rearming the Germans was causing apprehension in Europe. The objections voiced by Australia and New Zealand were overcome by assuring them, through the ANZUS (Australia, New Zealand and the United States) mutual-aid treaty, that the United States would come to their assistance in the event of attack.

In the Near East, the Truman administration wavered between two conflicting policies. On the one hand, it sought to win Arab friendship and to create some sort of a dike against Soviet penetration from the north in order to protect the rich oil resources in the area. On the other hand, Truman favored the creation of Israel, which antagonized the Arabs, especially when Israel was allowed to retain the additional territory which it had won through its defeat of the Arab attack. Similarly, the Truman administration's ambivalence toward the maintenance of Britain's position in the Middle East served alternately to alienate both the Arabs and the British government. American fear of Soviet penetration created support for British control

85

of the area, thus antagonizing the Arabs, who were far more interested in ousting Western imperialism than afraid of Soviet incursion; while American anti-colonialism and disagreement with Britain's handling of the Palestine mandate infuriated Whitehall.

In March 1951, the newly installed Mossadegh government of Iran nationalized the Anglo-Iranian Oil Company, thereby sending a wave of shock and alarm through the Western capitals. (A year later, the secret operations of the American Central Intelligence Agency (CIA) brought about the overthrow of the Mossadegh government and the signing of a new international oil agreement. Quite possibly, although the facts are not known, the CIA operation was initiated before Truman left office.)

The last major efforts of the Truman administration in the Middle East were directed toward creating a Middle East defensive alliance, built around Egypt where the British still had their Suez base. King Farouk's government declined, partly because Washington was exerting pressure upon it to lift the illegal blockade of Israeli shipping. In the following year, Farouk was overthrown by a military coup.

All that can be said of the Truman policy in the Near East is that it was a strange mixture of conflicting aims and interests arising from disparate but deeply rooted forces in the American society, such as: a feeling of kinship for Britain contradicted by sympathy for the anti-British sentiment of colonial peoples; sympathy for Israel, because of the Nazi outrages and because of the large Jewish community in the United States; sympathy for the Arabs engendered chiefly by the work of Protestant missions reinforced by Roman Catholic courtship of what was believed to be a disintegrating Moslem world. (There were probably more Christian proselytizers of various sects in the Near East than there were communists, except in Iran where a strong communist-oriented Tudeh Party existed.) Over this mixture of disparate forces was spread the blanket of anti-communism which each group or lobby claimed as the rationalization for the pressures it exerted. But by far the strongest influence upon American policy in the Near East was silently exerted by the fabulously rich and powerful oil industry, closely linked to the armed services.

One could hardly expect anyone outside of the United States to understand this interplay of forces in the American society that shaped an amorphous and vacillating Near East policy.

7

Truman's Legacy

Harry Truman had come into office at the high tide of victory, with the nation at the summit of its power. He had had a choice of continuing Roosevelt's endeavor to hold together the victorious coalition or assuming that the continuation of this effort would be futile. He chose to try to force Stalin to accept the imposition of an American design for peace—a design that challenged not only the political power-position of the Soviet Union in Eastern Europe, which Roosevelt and Churchill had conditionally accepted, but also the economic organization of all socialist societies, the existence of which he considered hostile to the establishment of enduring peace.[1] The political offensive conducted by Truman against the Soviet Union, even though backed by the implied threat of the atomic bomb, failed to bring about Soviet acceptance of a *Pax Americana* and resulted, instead, in a Soviet counter-offensive that led to an atomic stalemate and the division of Europe into two hostile

[1] Baylor speech of March 6, 1946.

camps, with the opposing forces deadlocked in a struggle for the control of Germany. Truman's conviction that the post-war world crisis existed solely because of a Soviet-dominated worldwide communist conspiracy and the Kremlin's unwill-ingness to cooperate in making and preserving a just peace led him to devote the entire energies and resources of the United States to a worldwide effort to contain communism, involving an unsuccessful intervention in the Chinese Civil War and a stalemated war in Korea.

The simplistic scapegoat analysis of the postwar world crisis caused the Truman administration to overlook almost entirely the opportunities presented to the United States in connection with the worldwide revolution of rising expectations. Marshall Plan aid to Europe had been a major, unprecedentedly gen-erous and constructive contribution to reconstruction, but it applied only to a part of the world which was already highly industrialized. It was not until 1949 that the Truman admin-istration gave any consideration to the needs of the under-developed parts of the world. Even then, the so-called Point Four Program, announced by Truman in his inaugural ad-dress, consisted of little more than an offer to share technical advice and American "know-how"; it did not take into account the widespread need for capital assistance; and the whole subsequently developed foreign-aid program was distorted by political discrimination against countries which did not line up with the United States in the Cold War, and by the mili-tary strategy of the anti-communist crusade.

Worst of all, Truman left the American people in a state of mind in which there was little room for a calm considera-tion of national policy. He had convinced them that the one aim of United States policy must be to rid the world of the Soviet-

89

communist menace. All the pressure groups affecting the making of policy and the mood of Congress were operating within this oversimplified frame of reference. The devotees of Chiang Kai-shek and Syngman Rhee pressed for a policy of overthrowing the Mao regime in China. The East European nationality groups were demanding the liberation of the East European Soviet satellites. The Jewish groups demanded aid for Israel against the Arabs, and the pro-Arab groups urged aid for the Arabs against Israel; each claiming that its course of action was the only way to protect the Near East from Soviet-communism. Most of the enthusiastic anti-communist crusaders combined to arouse antagonism against India—and Indian hostility toward the United States—by fulminating against the "neutralism" of Jawaharlal Nehru. None of the pressure groups were observing George Washington's wise injunction against permitting either excessive sympathy for one nation or antipathy for another to submerge a reasoned consideration of the national interest. Nor was the President himself observing this injunction.

In a similar way, reasoned consideration of the national interest in domestic affairs was submerged in a nationwide struggle between two groups, both emerging from the generally accepted anti-communist frame of reference. On one side were those anti-communists who believed in fighting fire with water, desiring to combat the communist menace only with weapons consistent with the maintenance of a free society. On the other side were the authoritarian anti-communists who held that fire must be fought with fire—that a free society could not protect itself against subversion without adopting some of the methods of totalitarian tyranny. This conflict might have served to clarify the minds of the American people, had it arisen over

90

a clear disagreement in principle. This might have been the case if Truman himself had acted upon principle, instead of belatedly attempting to tighten up security by authoritarian procedures. With the government in Washington taking the lead in reaching for totalitarian tools, it was inevitable that a spirit of vigilantism should infect the entire nation and that an opportunity should be presented to unscrupulous informers and notoriety-seeking demagogues.

The fact that Truman had first been accused of being careless of security and had then betrayed the principles of freedom left his political opponents free to make the most of his alleged laxity while depriving his defenders of a principle to defend. The authoritarian anti-communists, led by the outstanding opportunist—Senator Joseph R. McCarthy of Wisconsin—thus were able to equate "Trumanism" with criminal negligence if not treason, while the liberal anti-communists could fight the authoritarians effectively only if they were prepared to admit that Truman himself had betrayed the liberal principle. Partly for reasons of partisan politics and partly because Truman had fought courageously for most of the other principles in which the liberals believed, few were willing to face the dilemma with which they were confronted. Among those who failed to do so was the Democratic candidate for the presidency, Adlai Stevenson. Thus, the basic issue between liberal and authoritarian anti-communism was never raised in the campaign of 1952; the question became quite simply one of deciding whether Joe McCarthy was doing more harm than good or more good than harm.

Nor were any real issues raised in foreign policy, although, during the early stages of the campaign, Stevenson gave some indications that he would depart from the Truman-Acheson inflexibility and be more willing to explore the possibilities of negotiation. Neither General Eisenhower, the Republican nominee, nor his opponent questioned the idea with which Truman had indoctrinated the entire nation—that the sole threat to the world's peace resided in the existence of a communist conspiracy. Nor was there any serious debate about how that conspiracy should be met. The policy of military containment had become an article of faith.

In the writer's opinion, Truman, a typical American, reacted to the world situation as he found it when he entered the White House just as the majority of Americans would have reacted at that time.

By no means an ineffective President in domestic affairs, as witness his legislative program and especially the Full Employment Act of 1946, he seemed, in dealing with the world, to exemplify the smug self-satisfaction, the partisan point of view and the ignorance of other countries and other civilizations characteristic of most of his fellow Americans. But, even if this were true, it would leave unexplained why the majority of Americans were smugly self-satisfied, why they tended toward partisan rather than judicial attitudes and why they knew so little about the outside world. It would leave unexplained why the American people, at the pinnacle of their nation's military and economic ascendancy, should have felt frightened and threatened.

The cause of smug self-satisfaction is not hard to identify; due to their possession of a spacious and extraordinarily rich part of the earth's inhabitable surface and the protection afforded by two oceans, the American people achieved a material prosperity unequaled in the world, And, thanks largely to the wisdom of an extraordinary group of Founding Fathers, this unrivaled prosperity was more widely shared than in any other country. On Sundays, holidays and in Fourth of July orations, the American people gave thanks to God for these blessings; in their daily life, they credited their own industry, resourcefulness and intelligence.

Partisanship had its roots in a pioneer society composed at the outset of various religious sects and nationality groups. Sectional partisanship developed between the North and the South and between the Eastern Seaboard and the rapidly expanding interior. Contrary to the hopes of the Founding Fathers, a political cleavage resulting in a two-party system developed over the centralization or decentralization of power. As industrialization took place, cleavages developed between capital and labor and between farmers and industrial workers. The whole history of the United States is a history of gradual accommodation between strongly partisan groups fighting for their respective interests. It is as natural for Americans to be partisans in politics as it is for them to be passionate partisans in sports. The American who refuses to affiliate himself with a church, an economic group or a political party is a maverick. The United States is not known for its wealth of independent thinkers, except in science and technology.

Social scientists would probably say that the average American feels insecure unless he is a member of a group to which he can give his loyalty and from which he can expect loyalty in return. This may be true and may partially explain the apparent need to conform, which in most European societies seems to disappear with maturity, but which in this country continues through adult life.

In no country is there an equivalent of the word "un-

American," which describes in the United States a noncon- formist attitude or behavior deemed to be inconsistent with "Americanism" as defined by the majority and, therefore, hos- tile and subversive.[2] There is no such concept of "un-English- ness" in England, or of "un-Frenchness" in France. The near- est approach to the American distrust of "un-Americanism" is to be found in totalitarian societies where conformism is de- manded, not by the people but by dictatorial governments.

It is easy to explain American ignorance of other countries and cultures on the grounds of a faulty educational system; and it is true that the American educational system is still to a large extent the one which was developed in the nineteenth century to fit the mental patterns of a self-satisfied, self-centered parochial society, concerned with "Americanizing" immigrants and more or less immune to outside influence or interference. But this does not explain why the American people have been satisfied with such an educational system, nor why it took the shock of a Soviet Sputnik in 1957 to touch off a wave of reform and improvement. Ever since then, reform has con- sisted chiefly in providing better physical facilities—more teachers and higher teachers' salaries—all of which were urgently needed; but the average American child still is taught very little about the world and ill-equipped for anything like responsible world citizenship.

From the point of view of this study, it is sufficient to recog- nize that the self-centeredness of American education has pro-

[2] This may be due to the fact that the United States was and is a nation of immigrants in which each successive wave of newcomers has sought quickly to attain a status of equality with the older residents by dropping its foreign language, customs and culture. The drive for Americanization may be both a partial cause and a partial result of a xenophobia which dates back to the earliest days of the Republic.

duced in most Americans an almost infantile resentment of "outside" interference and a resistance to any development which might conceivably affect the domestic scene.

Much the same thing was true of the American press, which both reflected and catered to the self-centered parochialism of the American society at the conclusion of the war. With few exceptions, the mass media backed the outcry for "bringing the boys back home," for abolishing wartime controls and for returning to something like Harding's "normalcy." And, with few exceptions, the mass media joined in fostering the idea that the only real threat to a return to "normalcy" was posed by the existence of an ideology that challenged democracy, religion, free enterprise and "the American way of life."

To the extent that he had thought about the postwar world before he became President, Truman undoubtedly had thought of it as a world of divided power in which the United States, Britain, France, China and the Soviet Union would exercise the dominant influence. This had been Roosevelt's expectation and Churchill's, although Roosevelt had overestimated the role that would be played by China, and Churchill had overestimated the importance of France.

However, when the war ended, Truman found himself as chief of state in a nation which unexpectedly possessed paramount military and economic power. China was torn by civil war and ravaged by inflation; France was prostrate; an exhausted Britain was in dire financial need. Only an apparently hostile Soviet Union posed any threat to American hegemony, but Russia, too, was bled white, weakened by the ravages of war and in need of economic assistance. For a short moment in history, the United States was actually in a position to

95

impose a *Pax Americana* and to realize the neo-imperialist dream of what publisher Henry Luce called "The American Century."

That moment was lost. Before Truman realized his opportunity and while he was still preoccupied with Eastern Europe, he permitted the great armies of the United States to be demobilized, the fleet to be put into mothballs and the American military machine to be dismantled, while the economic power of the United States was immobilized by a domestic orgy of self-indulgence. It was not until two years after the war had ended that Truman began to think in terms of a global *Pax Americana*. By this time, British power had unexpectedly collapsed, the Soviet Union had regained much of its strength, and the world had again become a world of divided power, polarized now between Russia and the United States. The only peace now possible had again become a peace by agreement. But this fact the Truman administration was unwilling or unable to recognize.

However one may judge the wisdom of Truman's foreign policy—and there are many who judge it less harshly than the writer—there can be no question of his courage and his power of decision. The little sign on his desk reading *"The Buck Stops Here"* accurately expressed both qualities, as did his often quoted saying: "If you can't stand the heat, get out of the kitchen." There was nothing weak about President Truman; the companion quality of a capacity for implacable enmity toward a foe was unhesitating loyalty to a friend.

8

The Eisenhower Years

John Foster Dulles had played a considerable part in developing the foreign policy of the Truman administration. As Secretary of State under President Eisenhower, he took over that policy lock, stock and barrel, bringing to its implementation no little skill and a large measure of self-righteous conviction. Since the pattern of anti-communist crusading remained essentially unchanged under his management, it is not necessary for the purposes of this essay to trace in detail the developments that took place during his stewardship, except to note those occasions when United States policy might have been, but was not, modified.

The first such opportunity for modification was inherent in the deteriorating condition of the Western alliance and the low state of West European morale in the winter of 1952–1953.

The Russian threat to Western Europe had almost certainly never been a threat of military conquest. The danger of com-

97

munist subversion had been met by the restoration of Western Europe's economic health and political stability through Marshall Plan aid. Even if one assumed that the intention to invade had ever existed, the deterrent had been provided not by the wholly inadequate conventional forces of NATO but by the certainty that an attack upon Western Europe would bring on a suicidal war with the United States. There was only one logical explanation for the fateful American decision, in 1949, to undertake the erection of a shield at Western Europe's frontier—namely, to bolster European morale and to create solidarity and a will to resist. If such had been the reason, its purpose had been defeated by the psychological effect of the decision to rearm West Germany, for this decision had caused dissension and alarm throughout Europe.

The decision to rearm Germany did, however, have one unforeseen virtue: it had created a bargaining counter. As noted in Chapter 6, it had caused Moscow to make a number of overtures which, if explored, might have led to an all-German settlement on terms acceptable to the West at the price of abandoning German participation in the NATO alliance.

When General Eisenhower was elected President, having previously served as NATO commander, it seemed reasonable to hope that he would re-examine a policy which, far from creating "a position of strength," was rapidly producing a situation of serious weakness.[1]

However, Dulles and General Lucius D. Clay, Eisenhower's chief adviser on Germany, strongly urged a continuation of

[1] Hopefully, the writer submitted a paper to the President-elect shortly before his inauguration, first analyzing the German deadlock and the rapidly declining morale of Western Europe, and then outlining in detail a plan for negotiating an all-German settlement, with both sides giving up their attempt to gain control of all of Germany. See Warburg, *Germany, Key to Peace*, pages 251–356.

98

Acheson's European policy and, for four years, the Eisenhower administration continued to insist upon the creation of West German armed forces which neither the French nor a great many Germans wanted. More than a year elapsed before Chancellor Adenauer could persuade the reluctant Bundestag to ratify the Bonn and Paris treaties. Stalin's death in March 1953 and the adoption of a somewhat softer policy by Georgi Malenkov slowed French progress toward ratification. In June and July, East German uprisings signaled the beginning of a satellite rebellion directed not so much against Soviet domination as against the harsh terms of existence imposed by local communist rule. After Britain, France and the United States had reaffirmed their belief in NATO as the foundation of Western policy at a conference in Bermuda, Dulles threatened an "agonizing reappraisal" of United States policy if French ratification should not be forthcoming. This was in December 1953. In January 1954, Vyacheslav Molotov proposed and Dulles rejected a General European Security agreement at a four-power conference held in Berlin. On August 30, the French Assembly finally voted upon the Bonn-Paris treaties and rejected EDC. On October 3, a substitute plan for bringing West Germany into NATO through the back door of the West European Union was adopted and, surprisingly, accepted by France—surprisingly because, whereas the EDC plan had provided for the integration of German contingents in a "European Army," the substitute device permitted the Germans to have their own armed forces subject only to an integrated NATO command. On December 21, Dulles declared that the NATO forces would be armed with "tactical" atomic weapons.

French rejection of the European Defense Community set

back the hope for political and economic union of the West European countries; and, with the postponement of this hope, there vanished most of the enthusiasm for "Europeanism" that had existed in Germany. Reunification, rather than European-ization, now became the West German goal; and, soon, it was to become evident to most thinking Germans that reunification and partnership in NATO were mutually exclusive. Thus, there was a growing danger that, if the Germans did not soon achieve reunification through a settlement negotiated by the West with the Soviet Union, they would be tempted to make their own deal with the Kremlin on terms not neces-sarily consistent with Western interests.

Malenkov's fall, in February 1955, and the partial return to rigid controls under the duumvirate of Bulganin and Khru-shchev momentarily suppressed incipient satellite rebellion. On March 21, Moscow announced the formation of the Warsaw Pact, an anti-NATO East European defense alliance. And, on May 15, the Soviet leaders finally agreed to an Austrian peace treaty which made Austria into a neutral, demilitarized state. This was undoubtedly the pattern which Soviet leadership had in mind for a reunited Germany. However, at a meeting of the chiefs of state held at Geneva on July 18–23—the first such meeting since the Potsdam Conference of 1945—no progress was made toward solving the German problem. Eden proposed a plan for the demilitarization of East Germany which the Soviet leaders rejected, although it might have led to a similar plan for all of Germany. Eisenhower put for-ward his "open skies" proposal which the Russians rejected as a pretext for espionage. Nevertheless, the mere fact that Eisenhower had gone to Geneva in a conciliatory spirit raised hopes for peace. Unfortunately, they were short-lived.

100

* * *

While he was stubbornly clinging to the Acheson-Adenauer policy in Europe, Dulles was extremely active in other parts of the world, setting out to extend the containment policy to Asia and the Middle East.

The achievement of an inconclusive truce in Korea was not followed, as might have been expected, by any disengagement from the Chinese Civil War. On the contrary, American ties to Chiang Kai-shek were strengthened and hostility was deliberately maintained toward the Peking regime which, as Dulles saw it, had committed unprovoked aggression in Korea. Moreover, Dulles was certain that the Peking regime would crumble and fall because of its own iniquity, just as he repeatedly assured the American people that the Soviet regime would soon be overthrown.

To hasten the end of the Sino-Soviet menace and, in the meantime, to prevent any further communist encroachment upon "the free world," Dulles set out to build a ring of military bases and alliances around the whole vast periphery of the Sino-Soviet orbit. When the French effort to reimpose colonial rule upon Indochina threatened to collapse in spite of massive American aid in money and war material, Dulles tried to get Britain to agree to a joint intervention. Eden's refusal to take part in this adventure earned him the lasting enmity of his American colleague. At the last minute, Dulles, along with Vice President Richard Nixon, wanted to intervene with nuclear weapons to save the French from defeat at Dien Bien Phu, but was wisely restrained by Eisenhower.[2] And when France accepted defeat, conceding independence to Laos, Cam-

[2] For a carefully researched account of this whole episode, see Chalmers M. Roberts in *The Reporter*, September 14, 1954, reprinted in Marcus G. Raskin and Bernard Fall, *The Viet-Nam Reader*, pages 57–66.

bodia and Vietnam, Dulles refused to sign the protocol of the Geneva Accords which provided for the neutrality and independence of Laos and Cambodia and for the temporary division of Vietnam at the 12th parallel—the northern part to be under the rule of the communist-dominated regime of the victorious Ho Chi Minh, while South Vietnam was to hold free elections. Within two years, it was provided, all-Vietnamese elections should be held and the two parts should be reunified. Although not a signatory of the accords, the United States agreed to respect them. (A promise which Dulles violated two years later by backing the refusal of the American-sponsored South Vietnamese government of Ngo Dinh Diem to permit all-Vietnamese elections.[3])

To close the gap left in the anti-communist defense of Southeast Asia by French defeat, Dulles promptly moved to create a Southeast Asia Treaty Organization (SEATO), intended to function like NATO in Europe. Pakistan, Thailand and the Philippine Republic were the only Asian nations willing to sign this treaty along with the United States, Britain, France, Australia and New Zealand. India, Burma and Ceylon declined membership; the policy of non-alignment in the Cold War pursued by these three countries was denounced by Dulles as "immoral neutrality."

Having constructed an Asian perimeter from Okinawa to Pakistan, Dulles lost no time in turning his attention to the Middle East. Egypt flatly declined to become the center of a Middle East alliance, even after Dulles had persuaded the British to evacuate their great Suez base well ahead of the schedule set by the Anglo-Egyptian treaty of 1936. Egypt's

[3] See Raskin and Fall, *The Viet-Nam Reader;* also Robert Shaplen, *The Lost Revolution.*

new president, Gamal Abdel Nasser, wanted no part of an alliance with the West. Dulles then set about constructing with Britain a so-called Northern Tier Alliance, linked (through Turkey's membership) with NATO, linked (through Pakistan's membership) with SEATO, and with Iraq and Iran as its Near Eastern members. Having done this, Dulles had, as he thought, completed his ring of containing military power from the Baltic to Japan.

The results of this frantic alliance building were disastrous. Pakistan was interested in obtaining American military equipment not because it feared a Soviet invasion but because it wished to strengthen its position as against India and Afghanistan. Rearming Pakistan added little if any strength to the anti-communist coalition, but it dangerously upset the balance of power between Pakistan and its neighbors, alarming India and driving Afghanistan toward alignment with the Soviet Union. Similarly, Iraq, unlike Turkey, did not want arms to defend itself against the Soviet Union; it wanted arms to establish its hegemony in the Arab world and, eventually, to drive Israel into the sea. Rearming Iraq and linking it with Britain in the Baghdad Pact hopelessly alienated Egypt, which also sought hegemony in the Arab League. Thus the Northern Tier Alliance split the Arab world without erecting even the shadow of a barrier to Soviet expansion into the Middle East. On the contrary, the rearming of Iraq caused Egypt to seek and to obtain arms from the Soviet bloc, thus opening the door to Soviet penetration of the whole Middle East area. Soviet rearmament of Egypt, in turn, threatened to upset the balance of military power and endangered Israel.

Faced with the collapse of his Middle East policy, Dulles tried to forestall further Soviet penetration of Egypt by hastening American aid toward building the Aswan High Dam. In this, he was hampered by a reluctant Congress. However, when it appeared that the Soviet Union was in no hurry to outbid the United States for this costly and in some respects dubious project, Dulles reversed his course, abruptly withdrawing the offer of American aid and justifying his aboutface by a statement which would have offended even a chief of state far less proud and sensitive than Nasser. Nasser's answer was to seize and nationalize the Suez Canal, which was owned by Anglo-French interests.

If Dulles wanted a showdown, he certainly got it. The strange thing about this episode was that the American government was totally unprepared to meet the crisis which it had predictably precipitated. According to C. L. Sulzberger's article of April 7, 1957, in the *New York Times*, "the State Department's Policy Planning Staff didn't even have a position paper covering this eventuality."

What followed is well known. After weeks of futile negotiations during which Dulles infuriated Britain and France, Israel suddenly invaded Egypt's Sinai Peninsula and Britain and France launched an operation to seize the Canal Zone "in order to separate the belligerents." We are not concerned here with the rights and wrongs of Israel's action, nor with the justification—if any—for the Anglo-French intervention. We are concerned solely with the effects of Dulles' diplomacy; these were more far-reaching than the unhappy but temporary split in the Western alliance resulting from American condemnation of the invasion as a breach of the United Nations Charter.

Apart from the resentment aroused on both sides of the Atlantic, the results of the Egyptian fiasco were:

104

1. The restoration of the very conditions which had provoked the explosion, plus the blocking of the Suez Canal for about six months.

2. The strengthening of Nasser's position in spite of the overwhelming defeat of his forces.

3. The destruction of British influence in the Arab world and the endangering of what remained of Britain's preferential position in Iraq and the Persian Gulf area.

4. The creation of a serious cleavage within the British Commonwealth, the resignation of Eden and the realization on the part of the British public that Britain was no longer a power capable of independent action.

Even more far-reaching, however, were the effects upon the Cold War between the Soviet Union and the West.

Tito's breakaway from Soviet domination in 1948 had marked the beginning of a slowly spreading satellite rebellion which, after Stalin's death, had been evidenced by the East German uprising of 1953, a similar outbreak in the Polish city of Poznan in 1955 and a strike of Czech workers in the same year. What really set off the fireworks, however, was the de-Stalinization program announced by Khrushchev in his now famous secret speech to the 20th Congress of the Soviet Communist Party in February 1956. The denigration of the demi-god who had for more than thirty years ruled with a rod of iron and the sudden destruction of the myth of his infallibility shook not only the structure of the satellite empire but also the foundations of the dictatorship in Russia itself. Overnight, the hitherto unchallengeable dogmas of Stalinism were thrown open to challenge. Small wonder, then, that this unforeseen development should have a profound effect upon the satellite peoples.

105

The Polish and Hungarian revolts of October 1956 for the first time combined resentment against indigenous communist rule with nationalist rebellion against Russian domination. In Poland, the revolt was staged by a government responsive to popular sentiment and, hence, no longer willing to take orders from Moscow. For this reason, Moscow was forced to seek a compromise; it could not use force without risking the outbreak of a full-scale war. In Hungary, the Russians could and did resort to brutal force because the government asked Moscow for help in maintaining itself in power against the will of its own people.

In both countries, the revolt was spearheaded by what might almost be called a new type of middle class—not the traditional capitalist bourgeoisie but a new largely propertyless and distinctly socialist-minded intelligentsia that included not only students, scholars and writers but soldiers, factory workers and peasants as well. The revolt was not against socialism but against the mismanagement of socialism by communist dictatorship. It was a revolt against bad planning, inefficient administration, inflexible adherence to dogma and the suppression of dissent. Ironically, this new revolutionary attitude had been created by communist-inspired and -directed mass education. The spread of literacy and the dissemination of scientific knowledge had undermined the foundation of mass ignorance and mass acquiescence in leadership decisions upon which the "dictatorship of the proletariat" had been erected.

The Eisenhower administration wisely refrained from intervening in the Hungarian revolt, although there was considerable pressure-group demand for intervention. In the United Nations, where the United States and the Soviet Union had voted together to condemn the invasion of Egypt, the Soviet

106

Union vetoed a similar condemnation of its own brutal action in Hungary. Partly because of the coincidence of the Egyptian and Polish-Hungarian crises, American diplomacy missed a great opportunity presented by the East European revolt—namely, that the revolt gave the Western powers a wholly unearned second chance to escape from the dead-end street into which the Acheson-Adenauer-Dulles diplomacy had led them with respect to Germany.

The satellite revolt presented the West with an entirely new situation with regard to the future of Europe. Poland and Hungary were no longer outposts of Soviet power. They had suddenly and dramatically become areas of resistance to Soviet power dangerous to leave in the rear of any Soviet westward move. A Soviet note of November 17, 1956, to the Western powers showed that the Kremlin was acutely aware of this altered situation. The note proposed a mutual withdrawal of Russian and Anglo-American troops from Europe. While unacceptable in the form presented, the proposal showed that the Kremlin might now be ready to seek a face-saving device by means of which it might be able to withdraw its coercive power from positions which had become ultimately untenable.

Washington failed lamentably to seize upon the opportunity thus presented. The State Department brushed off the Soviet note as "insincere propaganda" and no counter-proposal was made to test its sincerity. The Cold War warriors had not wanted to negotiate a European settlement until they had a formidable bargaining position; now that they had it, they counseled against negotiation because Russia's unexpected weakness in Eastern Europe had been exposed.

On December 7, 1956, the writer sent a letter to President Eisenhower the substance of which was subsequently endorsed by a distinguished group of citizens assembled at a conference held at Arden House, Ardsley, New York, a week later. The Arden House resolution was personally taken to the President by three of its participants: Senators Ralph Flanders (R) of Vermont and John Sparkman (D) of Alabama, both members of the Senate Foreign Relations Committee, and Congressman Brooks Hays (D) of Arkansas. This was the substance of the suggested reply to the Soviet note:

If the Soviet Union is now prepared to begin a withdrawal of its own forces from Eastern Europe and to grant the East European countries an increasing measure of independence, the United States will welcome such action and do everything in its power to encourage and facilitate it, giving due consideration to the interests of Soviet security.

Specifically:

1. The United States will respect the independence of the East European nations and will in no way try to influence their political or economic development or to loosen such bonds as they may voluntarily wish to maintain with the Soviet Union. Should any of these countries request economic assistance and should the United States comply with such requests, any such aid will be given without political conditions.

2. The United States is willing to consider favorably the Soviet proposal for a mutual withdrawal of troops from Europe. Such withdrawal can, however, be accomplished only by a step-wise procedure.

As a first step, the United States is prepared to recommend to its allies a withdrawal of Anglo-French-American forces to the West bank of the Rhine, provided that Soviet forces are withdrawn to the East bank of the Oder and Western Neisse rivers, with suitable arrangements for aerial and ground inspection and adequate provision for the maintenance of the *status quo* in Berlin pending the reunification of Germany.

3. The United States is further prepared to recommend to its allies an agreement with the Soviet Union whereby the Federal Republic of Germany would be released from NATO and the German Democratic Republic would be released from the Warsaw Pact. Thus the ground would be prepared for the reunification of Germany as a nation without military commitments to East or West, and with its neutrality guaranteed by both the Soviet Union and the Western powers.

It would be the hope of the United States that the first step, above outlined, could be followed by further steps leading to a general security agreement for all of Europe lying between the Soviet borders and the Atlantic seaboard, ultimately involving the withdrawal from this area of all Soviet, American and British forces.

Should this hope be realized, the NATO alliance will ultimately be reduced to a simple declaration by the United States that it would regard any attack upon the nations of Western Europe as an attack upon itself, while the Warsaw alliance would be reduced to a similar declaration by the Soviet Union that it would consider any attack upon the nations of Eastern Europe as an attack upon itself.

When this proposal was presented to him, President Eisenhower expressed interest but told the delegation which presented it that he was afraid neither Dulles nor Adenauer would like it.[4]

Thus the unearned second chance to reach a European peace settlement was lost.

An important step toward the consolidation of Western Europe took place at Rome, in May 1957, when France, West Germany, Italy, Belgium, the Netherlands and Luxembourg signed treaties providing for the political and economic integration of their countries. The treaties created a supranational commission with its seat at Brussels, charged with integrating the economies of the signatories and with ultimately bringing about their political merger. The first result was the creation of the European Economic Community (EEC) which established what became known as a "Common Market" for industrial products, with plans to integrate agricultural production as well. Having declined to join the European Coal and Steel Community, and being disinclined to subject their nation to any form of supranational authority, the British organized a rival "Free Trade Area," comprising the Scandinavian countries, Austria, Portugal and Switzerland which, along with Britain, desired to reduce barriers to international trade without forming a closed customs union. Thus Western Europe was divided into the Inner Six (EEC) and the Outer Seven (EFTA).

In the summer of 1957, a new impetus toward European disengagement came from an unexpected source. The Polish Foreign Minister, Adam Rapacki, put forward a plan for the

---

[4] For a fuller account see Warburg, *Agenda for Action: Toward Peace Through Disengagement.*

creation of a denuclearized and perhaps eventually demilitarized zone in Central Europe—a zone which would include not only the two German states but also Poland and Czechoslovakia. This proposal had the virtue of avoiding a discriminatory treatment of Germany. Moscow endorsed the Rapacki Plan but Washington promptly rejected it as mere "communist propaganda."

However, the concept of disengagement as an approach to disarmament and peace could not so easily be brushed aside. Support came from none other than George F. Kennan, the original author of the containment policy, who was now no longer a State Department official. Kennan's Reith Lectures, delivered over the British Broadcasting Corporation's transmitters to a worldwide audience, aroused widespread interest in an approach toward peace that had previously not been fully understood by most Europeans and Americans. The State Department remained silent, but Acheson, Kennan's former superior, promptly denounced the whole notion of disengagement as "fuzzy-headed thinking."

In October 1957, Washington was shaken out of its complacency by the sudden launching of the first Soviet *Sputnik* and the subsequent testing of an intercontinental missile. Doubt was now cast upon the adequacy of the whole American defense effort and upon the quality of American education and scientific research. Abroad, friends of the United States began to question both its ability and its willingness to hold a protective nuclear umbrella over them, now that American cities had suddenly become vulnerable to Soviet attack. (Until now, the vast superiority of the American Strategic Airforce over Russia's comparatively small fleet of long-range planes had lent credibility to the American nuclear deterrent.)

The anxiety of the newly elected 82nd Congress was heightened by renewed turbulence in the Middle East, where Nasser was seeking to inflame Arab nationalism and to establish Egyptian leadership in the Arab world. As usual, Washington tended to equate Arab nationalism with communism and to suspect that Nasser's moves were Soviet-inspired. (Actually, the shrewd Egyptian leader was already recoiling from the uncomfortably close relations with Moscow that had resulted from the crisis of 1956.) The establishment in 1957 of a pro-Nasser regime in Syria, a threatened revolution in Lebanon and anxiety over the future of the two anti-Nasser Hashemite kingdoms in Jordan and Iraq led to the final fiasco of the Eisenhower-Dulles policy in the Middle East.

The proclamation, in January 1958, of the "Eisenhower Doctrine," a unilateral American declaration promising military aid to any Middle East state threatened by aggression, and the subsequent landing of American troops in Lebanon and of British troops in Jordan touched off the crisis. As might have been expected, these moves evoked angry denunciation and the threat of counter-action from Moscow, but the noises emanating from the Soviet capital were drowned out by a totally unforeseen event in the Middle East itself. While the British and American governments, having landed their troops, were wondering what to do next, a revolution overthrew the anti-Nasser government of Iraq; King Faisal and his pro-British premier, Nuri-as-Said, were slain; and the new Iraqui government repudiated the Baghdad Pact, thus tearing a gaping hole in the Northern Tier Alliance. In Lebanon, the pro-Western government of Camille Chamoun resigned, leaving only Jordan among the Arab states with a government friendly to the West.

* * *

With its Middle East policy in ruins, the Eisenhower administration's attention was now drawn to the Far East. In May, the long-smoldering crisis in the Taiwan Strait erupted in a Chinese Communist attack upon the Nationalist-held off-shore island of Quemoy which the United States had unwisely permitted Chiang to fortify and garrison. This brought the United States within a hair's breadth of involvement in a major conflict. Eisenhower asked for and obtained from Congress a resolution authorizing him to do whatever he might think necessary to defend Formosa. Fortunately, it soon became evident that the attack on Quemoy had not been the opening move in an attempt to recapture the main Nationalist stronghold. However, the episode emphasized once more that the continued ties to Chiang Kai-shek left the United States in a position from which it could at any time be forced into a major war by the rash action of either side in the unliquidated Chinese civil conflict.

The fact that Khrushchev had successfully overcome the satellite revolt and that his moves toward disengagement at the time when he had been in deep trouble had been rebuffed, plus the collapse of American policy in the Middle East, now presented the Soviet leader with a tempting opportunity to resume the offensive. His own position had been strengthened while that of the Western powers had been weakened not only by the Middle East fiasco but by the dissension within the Western alliance brought on by the decision to rearm West Germany. Six years after Acheson's demand for West German troops, not a single German soldier had yet taken the field, but West Germany was now rearming and it would not be long before NATO would be stiffened by a powerful West

113

German army. Meanwhile, the existence of a Western enclave in the heart of the Soviet's East German satellite remained, as Khrushchev put it, "a bone in his throat." In November 1958, he decided to remove it.

In a sharply worded note to the Western powers, Khrushchev demanded that they withdraw the Western garrisons from Berlin within the next six months and agree to convert West Berlin into an "open city" under United Nations protection. The predictable Western reply was a refusal to consider any proposal whatever under the threat of an ultimatum. There the matter rested throughout the winter of 1958–1959.

While the United States was practicing its "brinkmanship" in the Far and Middle East, France was in the bitter throes of losing a second colonial war. She had freed Tunisia and Morocco from their semi-dependence as French protectorates but refused to grant independence to Algeria, partly because Algeria was technically a part of metropolitan France, but chiefly because there were over a million colons, most of them French, in Algeria. One might have expected that the sad lesson of Indochina, where a trained conventional army had bled itself white fighting guerrillas supported by the native population, would prevent the French from engaging in another such war—but such was not the case. While the majority of the French people detested "*la sale guerre*," a series of weak governments had proven unwilling to buck the powerful colon lobby and, above all, the French generals and colonels who were unwilling to face another humiliating defeat. In 1954, a young Massachusetts senator had spoken up strongly against the war and had incurred the enmity of the French government. His name was John F. Kennedy.

Finally, in May 1958, the tottering Fourth Republic was overthrown and, with crowds shouting *"De Gaulle au pouvoir!"* Charles de Gaulle re-emerged upon the European scene, ostensibly to keep Algeria French, but actually to end the war in spite of the "ultras" and the generals and to grant Algeria independence. This act of statesmanship was soon to be followed by an amazingly rapid "de-colonization" of France's African empire.

In the early months of 1959, Dulles was fighting a losing battle against a cruelly painful recurrence of abdominal cancer which had first attacked him in 1956. During the last of his many trips abroad, he was living on a bare subsistence diet of liquids and soft foods. Shortly thereafter he was hospitalized but, for a few weeks, nevertheless directed American policy from his sickbed.

Fortunately, Harold Macmillan, who had succeeded Eden as Prime Minister in 1956, fully understood the danger of the situation and, entirely on his own initiative, journeyed to Moscow to explore the possibility of opening negotiations without doing so under the threat of an ultimatum. A Macmillan-Khrushchev communiqué, issued on March 3, indicated that the exploratory talks had ranged beyond the question of Berlin and had set that question into the broader context of Germany's relation to the problem of European security. It was agreed that the subject should be further pursued at an early meeting of the Big Four Foreign Ministers.

Macmillan's reconnaissance at once aroused the angry suspicion of Chancellor Adenauer and the jealous resentment of President de Gaulle, both of whom feared an Anglo-American deal with the Soviet Union. Their greatest ally in pursuing an intransigent policy, John Foster Dulles, died on May 24 and was buried at Arlington. Eisenhower, who had trusted his Secretary of State implicitly and had left foreign policy largely to his direction, was now on his own.

Dulles had not essentially changed the Truman-Acheson policy. Accepting and firmly believing in the scapegoat analysis of the world crisis, he had extended the containment policy to Asia and the Middle East. In so doing, he over-extended American military power and placed reliance upon a number of dubious allies. Where Truman and Acheson had been concerned primarily with the containment of Stalin's expansionism and, after Chiang's defeat, had been ready to disengage the United States from any further commitment to the Chinese Nationalist cause (until the Korean war and Peking's intervention made that impossible), Dulles had been as much concerned to contain Red China as he was to contain the Soviet Union. Dulles, in fact, saw the Peking regime as indissolubly linked to Moscow. His Assistant Secretary of State for Far Eastern Affairs, Dean Rusk, went even further, asserting as late as 1952 that the Peking regime was "not Chinese"—that it was, in fact, "a sort of Soviet Manchukuo!" (This referred to the puppet regime which Japan had installed in Manchuria during the late 1930's.) While it was true that the Soviet Union extended considerable aid to Communist China after Chiang Kai-shek's defeat, subsequent revelations indicated that one of the original causes of the later Sino-Soviet rift had been Moscow's refusal to back Peking's attack upon Quemoy in May 1958.

Finally, whereas Acheson, in dealing with the allies of the United States, had been a polite diplomat of the old school, Dulles had been overbearing in his treatment of Britain and

116

France, inconsiderate of Asian and Middle Eastern sentiment and, perhaps worst of all, insupportably sanctimonious.

Eisenhower, on the other hand, was a man of great personal charm and a native inclination to listen to the opinions of others. He, too, accepted the simple scapegoat analysis of the world crisis; he, too, was a devout anti-communist crusader; but his experience as a soldier made him hate war, and his wartime collaboration with the Red Army tempered his antipathy toward communist Russia. On at least two occasions —at Dien Bien Phu and Quemoy—he had restrained the brinkmanship of Dulles. And in view of his expressed feelings about dropping the first atomic bombs upon Japan, one may doubt whether he ever wholeheartedly approved of the Dulles doctrine of "massive retaliation"; in all probability he acquiesced in it only because his fiscal ultra-conservatism made him agree to a policy which promised "more bang for a buck."

On the domestic scene, Eisenhower had been more interested in "modernizing" and reunifying the Republican Party than in repairing the damage done to American prestige abroad by the anti-communist hysteria of the McCarthy era. His failure to denounce McCarthy's outrageous charges against General Marshall, and his later unwillingness to face a showdown with the unscrupulous Wisconsin demagogue destroyed much of the esteem in which he had been held abroad. (At home, it left the Republican Party saddled with the incubus of McCarthyism.) Nevertheless, except in Paris and Bonn, there was an almost audible worldwide sigh of relief when Eisenhower for the first time directly took over the conduct of American foreign policy. This feeling seemed justified when Eisenhower extended and Khrushchev accepted an invitation to visit the

United States.[5]

It is scarcely necessary to recall how the world's hopes for peace were raised by Khrushchev's visit to the United States in the autumn of 1959, nor how these hopes were shattered in the tragic anti-climax of the Summit Meeting at Paris, in May 1960. For a short time, it appeared that the suspicious Soviet leader had become convinced that neither the American people nor their government wanted war; and Khrushchev's ebullient, earthy humor seemed to have convinced most Americans that he was something less than the devil incarnate. In spite of his much-quoted remark—"We shall bury you!" [6]—it seemed to most Americans that Khrushchev sincerely wanted to transfer the Cold War out of the dangerous military arena and into a political and economic competition which he called "peaceful coexistence"—a competition which he was supremely confident of winning but in which Americans had every reason to feel equal confidence.

The proposal for "general and complete disarmament" which Khrushchev placed before the United Nations seemed to bear out the impression that "peaceful coexistence" meant competition without war. This somewhat vague but important proposal touched off the first serious discussions of how the arms race might be halted—a subject which had hitherto received little attention in Washington.[7]

[5] It was not known until after the publication, in 1965, of the second volume of Eisenhower's memoirs that the invitation had been extended through a misunderstanding on the part of one of Eisenhower's representatives at the Berlin meeting of the Big Four Foreign Ministers which had resulted from Macmillan's initiative. See Dwight D. Eisenhower, *Mandate for Change*, pages 312–313.

[6] The Russian word for "bury" was used in the sense of "outlive" rather than in the sense of digging a grave.

[7] For a detailed account of postwar disarmament initiatives and negotiations, see Warburg, *Disarmament, the Challenge of the Nineteen Sixties*. For the 1959–1960 period, see pages 76–122.

When Khrushchev departed, he extended an invitation to Eisenhower to visit Moscow later in the year which, in the happy atmosphere of "the spirit of Camp David," the President accepted.

Both Adenauer and de Gaulle insisted upon coming to Washington before the chiefs-of-state meeting in Paris now scheduled for May. Adenauer was grimly determined that there should be no change in the Acheson-Dulles policy. The myth that German reunification could be achieved through a "policy of strength" without sacrificing the German partnership in NATO had become the doctrine upon which his political life depended. De Gaulle, too, wanted the inflexible Western policy continued, not because he desired German reunification but because he needed Adenauer's cooperation in establishing French hegemony in Europe; if there was to be an East-West settlement, he—de Gaulle—wanted to be the one to negotiate it.

The German Chancellor's almost mesmeric influence at the State Department appeared to have survived the death of Dulles. Shortly after his departure, Eisenhower's new Secretary of State, Christian Herter, speaking at Chicago, strongly indicated a change in mood from the spirit of Camp David. His foreshadowing of an unyielding policy with respect to Berlin was echoed by a speech in New York by Treasury Secretary Douglas Dillon. That Khrushchev was not unaware of this change in mood was evident when he, too, reverted to Cold War polemics in a speech at Baku, on April 25, 1960. In all likelihood, the shrewd Soviet leader already suspected that the Summit Meeting would fail to produce any constructive result. His suspicion must have turned to certainty when an American U-2 spyplane was shot down over Sverdlovsk only a few days before the scheduled meeting. The fact that

119

high-altitude spyplanes had for some time been flying over Soviet territory confirmed Khrushchev's belief that Eisenhower's "open skies" proposal of 1955 had, in effect, been motivated by espionage; and the scheduling of such a flight *after* his visit to Camp David must have come as a considerable shock.

Nevertheless, the failure of the Summit Meeting might not have turned into a catastrophe for Eisenhower, had it not been for the miserable and disingenuous handling of the U-2 affair by the State Department and the Central Intelligence Agency. The President's courageous assumption of responsibility served only to make any negotiations impossible.

Eisenhower's greatest personal asset had been the confidence which he had inspired in the sincerity of his desire for peace. This was all but destroyed by the U-2 affair. It was a foregone conclusion that Khrushchev would make the maximum propaganda use of the episode and angrily withdraw his invitation for Eisenhower to visit the Soviet Union.

An added humiliation was in store for the discomfited President. He had planned to visit Japan on his return from Moscow, but anti-American demonstrations in that country now assumed such proportions that the friendly Japanese government felt compelled to ask Eisenhower to cancel the visit.

It was clear that any further progress toward peace would have to await the election of a new American President. Unfortunately, however, Eisenhower's term of office would not expire for another seven months, during which the world could not be expected to stand still. Crises were brewing in Southeast Asia, in Africa and in the Caribbean. The crippled Eisenhower administration would have to endure a session of the General Assembly of the United Nations and there face

120

a Soviet onslaught upon the structure of the world organization.[8]

The Eisenhower years left more than deadlocked and dangerous confrontations in Europe and Asia, turbulence in the
Middle East and an unpredictable future in Africa. They also
left a critical situation in the Western Hemisphere. The
domestic economy was stagnating after eight years of a "fiscal conservatism" which had placed a balanced budget ahead
of public needs in health, education, housing and medical care.
Negro citizens were demanding rights long unjustly denied to
them. The American people were still obsessed with a fear of
communism which blinded them to the realities of a rapidly
changing world. The long-neglected countries of Latin America were in a state of incipient revolution.

In their preoccupation with the containment of communism
in Europe and Asia, neither Truman nor Eisenhower had given
much thought to nearby Latin America. Except for an isolated
instance,[9] they had not been aware of any communist threat
in the Western Hemisphere prior to the Cuban revolution.

Neither Truman nor Eisenhower had shown any understanding of the worldwide revolution of rising expectations among
the underprivileged peoples of the world; nor did they display
any marked appreciation of the danger to world stability and
peace arising from the growing gap between the conditions
of life in the relatively rich industrial nations of the northern
half of the globe and the conditions of ignorance, poverty and
degradation prevailing in the less developed countries situated

[8] This matter will be discussed in Chapter 13.

[9] In 1954, when Dulles suspected the Arbenz government of Guatemala
of communist leanings, he and his brother Allen, head of the CIA, had
launched a clandestine operation to overthrow the legitimately elected
Arbenz regime and to supplant it with a military dictatorship.

mostly south of the equator and inhabited largely by non-white races.

Most Latin Americans, like most Asians, lived on agriculture, husbandry and the production of raw materials. Argentine wheat, Chilean copper and nitrates, Brazilian coffee and Venezuelan oil had been in worldwide demand during World War II. So had Central American bananas and Caribbean sugar. With the sudden cessation or diminution of this demand, wartime Latin American prosperity had come to an abrupt end. At the same time, due to the primitive methods of agriculture imposed by a feudal system of land ownership, the growing movement of people into the cities and a phenomenal population growth, most of Latin America became dependent upon imports of food. The fall in raw material prices and the upward trend in the cost of manufactured goods, the drop in exports, the need for foreign foodstuffs and the importation of luxuries by wealthy Latin Americans created a situation in which most Latin American governments urgently required financial assistance. But no United States Marshall Plan relieved their distress. In many of the countries, inflation and unemployment created smoldering unrest.

The vast majority of the Latin American populations had always lived on a bare subsistence level, sharecropping the lands of wealthy landowners, working in the mines or performing menial labor wherever there was an opportunity. The wealthy few, many of them educated in Europe, contributed little to investment in economic development, either sending their money abroad or using it to acquire more land, much of which remained idle.

Industrialization came about largely through profit-seeking foreign investment. Foreign investors, most of them from the

122

United States, gradually acquired control of banks, mines, oil fields, railroads and air lines, as well as power plants and communication facilities. In the tropical regions, they acquired vast sugar, coffee and banana plantations. In many cases, these foreign investors worked closely with the indigenous ruling cliques which controlled the local governments, combining with the oligarchs to suppress any change that might endanger their privileged positions. As the technological revolution brought increased literacy and knowledge of the outside world, the oppressed masses began to realize, as they had in Asia, that they were not condemned forever to a miserable condition of want and servitude by some immutable fate. Once this happened, revolution was inevitable.

The Latin American ferment was not caused by communist propaganda, but the incipient revolutions leaned strongly toward socialism since they were directed against capitalist exploitation. And, since capitalist exploitation was due to both domestic and foreign power groups, the revolutions tended to become strongly nationalist—i.e., anti-North American.

Neither Truman nor Eisenhower understood that a country which desired to be independent would naturally resent foreign ownership of its means of production. Nor did they understand that the absence of indigenous capital accumulation would naturally cause a trend toward some degree of socialism in any poor country impatient to catch up to the twentieth century. Both of the postwar Presidents considered socialism a step toward communism, or, as Truman had put it, "a pattern that leads to war." In their crusade for "freedom," capitalism was more important than representative government or social justice. When Truman declared war on "totalitarianism," he was not thinking of the anti-democratic dictatorships of Péron in Argentina, Batista in Cuba, Trujillo in the Dominican Republic or Somoza in Nicaragua. Under Eisenhower and Dulles, the United States even showed a positive concern and respect for such strong-man governments. Their top military personnel was trained in the United States, and they were furnished modern military equipment, not to meet any external threat to their countries but to use in maintaining themselves in power.

It was a significant fact that the cruel and corrupt Perez Jiminez, dictator in Venezuela, was received with honor and awarded a decoration by Eisenhower only a short time before his enraged countrymen drove him into exile; and that when Fidel Castro came to Washington after overthrowing the Cuban tyrant Fulgencio Batista, he was accorded no such honors, although he was not at that time suspected of being a communist.

The Eisenhower administration was clearly more concerned over the fate of private North American investments in Cuba than interested in the liberation of the Cuban people from corrupt and tyrannical rule. There was ample reason for such concern. Private investment by United States citizens had made Cuba into little more than an economic colony. Inevitably, any social revolution, even if under impeccably anti-communist leadership, would proceed to nationalize the one-crop island's sugar industry as well as the banks, factories and public utilities owned by United States citizens or corporations. It was only a question, as it had been in the earlier Mexican revolution, of whether the expropriated owners would be fairly compensated.

Given Castro's highly emotional and volatile personality, it will probably never be known whether he was alienated by

124

Washington's tit-for-tat policy or whether he had made up his mind before he came to Washington that he needed to use the United States as a foreign enemy to fan the revolutionary ardor of the Cuban population. It has been said that Washington's coldness drove Castro into the arms of the Soviet Union; and it is true that cutting off the Cuban sugar quota and restricting exports to Cuba in reprisal for the seizures of property did put Castro in a difficult position. But it is also true that Castro reacted without enthusiasm to the suggestion of aid to enable him to offer adequate compensation for expropriated property; and, from his own subsequent utterances, one may doubt whether he turned to Moscow because he had no place else to go or because of an originally concealed communist orientation.

What might have happened, had the United States enthusiastically welcomed the Cuban revolution, is less important than what did happen. Convinced that Castro had become a threat to the security of the United States and that, through him, communism was now menacing the entire hemisphere, the Eisenhower administration began to plot his overthrow. Training camps for anti-Castro refugees were secretly set up in Guatemala and a staging area for an invasion of Cuba was prepared in Nicaragua. Almost the last act of the Eisenhower administration was to sever diplomatic relations with the Castro government.

Both the secret CIA intervention in Guatemala in 1954 and the planned clandestine operation against Castro violated the Charter of the Organization of American States and the Charter of the United Nations. They set in motion a chain of events destined to undo the work of thirty years under

Roosevelt's Good Neighbor Policy, to reawaken Latin American hostility toward the "Colossus of the North," to cast doubt upon the sincerity of the United States in seeking to establish a world of law and to create more communists and communist sympathizers throughout Latin America than might ever have been created by Fidel Castro.

President Eisenhower had come from much the same type of Middle Western family background as his predecessor. In his case, however, weak eyesight did not prevent his realizing his ambition to attend the West Point Military Academy, even though he did so over the strong objection of his mother, who was a member of the pacifist sect of River Brethren. While this maternal influence was not strong enough to keep Eisenhower from becoming a soldier, it probably accounted for his hatred of war and his unquestionable desire to lead the world toward peace. Unlike Truman, Eisenhower had no liking for the hard work of political leadership. Having spent his life in a disciplined chain of command, he never felt quite at home as Chief Executive in a political structure that recognized only a limited command authority. Where Truman had made every effort to assert the power of the Presidency, Eisenhower was content to reign rather than to rule.

President Eisenhower left no legacy of memorable state papers, except for a valedictory address which may some day be ranked with George Washington's famous farewell. Surprisingly, its subject was an earnest warning against the growing influence and power of what he aptly called "the military-industrial complex." Noting how the defense establishment had become linked to the suppliers and manufacturers of weapons and how it was pre-empting not only the nation's material resources but its scientific brain-power, this soldier President hoisted a danger signal that his successors might perhaps have heeded, had they not inherited from him a position of vastly over-committed American military power.

9

Kennedy—A Break
with the Past

John F. Kennedy brought to the conduct of the nation's foreign affairs an attitude, a spirit and an outlook radically different from that of his two predecessors. Unlike Truman and
Eisenhower, Kennedy did not see the world in blacks and
whites. In his unemotional, rational realism, he did not believe
that any nations or people were inherently "good" or "bad."
He did not believe that the communist bloc was, or probably
ever had been, a monolith, nor that all communist governments were necessarily aggressive. As early as 1954, he had
written a magazine article decrying the myths which surrounded American foreign policy, such as "the untouchability
of national sovereignty"; or the belief that "the democratic way
of life" would "inevitably be the victor in any struggle with an
alien power"; or the idea that other nations owed "homage and
gratitude to the United States and all of its views at all times."
Having, as a young man, lived through the period of Anglo-
French appeasement in England, where his father was United

States Ambassador to the Court of St. James, he recognized the need for firm opposition to aggression. But he neither associated aggression with the internal ideological or economic arrangements within nations so long as they did not seek to impose these arrangements upon others, nor did he think that "the American way of life" was necessarily suitable to all nations, especially to those lacking in private capital. In the fall of 1961, after he had become President, he said at the University of Washington:

> We must face the fact that the United States is neither omnipotent nor omniscient . . . that we cannot impose our will upon the other 94 per cent of mankind . . . that we cannot right every wrong nor reverse each adversity and that, therefore, there cannot be an American solution to every world problem.

Earlier, in his Inaugural Address, he had referred to the communist nations not as "our enemies" but as "those who would make themselves our adversaries." And, on the same occasion, he promised that he would never "negotiate out of fear," but would also never "be afraid to negotiate."

It was in this spirit that Kennedy tackled the almost incredible collection of world problems that he inherited, most of which demanded immediate attention. These included a crisis in the United Nations over the intervention in the Congo and over the future organization of the Secretariat; a dangerous deadlock over the future of Berlin and Germany; a Western alliance in disarray; an ill-advised involvement in Laos and Vietnam from which withdrawal with honor would be extremely difficult; and—unbeknownst to the American people and to Kennedy himself until he entered the White

129

House—a well-advanced plan for secretly aiding and directing an invasion of Cuba by a brigade of anti-Castro refugees already training in Guatemala. In addition, Kennedy inherited a vacuum in clearly defined American policy with respect to arms control and disarmament, and an involvement in the unliquidated Chinese Civil War which posed a roadblock to bringing China into the United Nations and, hence, to universal disarmament.

On the domestic scene Kennedy inherited a business recession, a stagnating economy and a balance-of-payments deficit which by inattention and inaction had been allowed to develop into a major gold crisis, undermining confidence in the dollar and arousing fears of devaluation and international monetary chaos.

Never in the history of the United States had the inauguration of a new President coincided so precisely with the coming home to roost of so many chickens.

How Kennedy dealt with these problems has been told in admirable detail by his close associate Theodore Sorensen, and much additional light has been thrown upon the inner workings of the administration by another intimate, the historian Arthur Schlesinger, Jr.[1]

For the first twenty-two months of his all-too-short presidency, Kennedy was too preoccupied with his inherited domestic and foreign problems to go very far toward articulating a new approach to foreign policy. Nevertheless, at least four important forward steps were taken during this crisis-laden period.

The Foreign Trade Expansion Act set the scene for both a

[1] See Sorensen's *Kennedy* (New York, Harper & Row, 1965) and Schlesinger's *A Thousand Days* (Boston, Houghton Mifflin Company, 1965).

worldwide reduction of barriers to international trade and for an Atlantic Partnership between the United States and a united Western Europe. At Kennedy's urging, a new organization was set up to increase West European participation in development aid and to coordinate it with the American effort.

The announcement of the Alliance for Progress showed Latin America that the days of its neglect were over. More importantly, the projected plan tied economic aid to social, fiscal and land reform, thus putting the United States squarely on the side of the progressive movements that were trying to break the power of the oligarchies, to bring about reform and to install governments responsive to the needs and aspirations of the people. The Alliance promised to be a deliberate break from past policy, but it remained to be seen whether the promise would be fulfilled.

The creation of the Peace Corps provided the opportunity for Americans—particularly for young Americans—to help in the development of the less developed countries, to learn to understand the problems faced by two-thirds of mankind, and to see their own country in world perspective. Hopefully, it would give the inhabitants of various parts of the world a better understanding of what Americans were really like.

The third major step was taken in the field of disarmament. Before his election, Kennedy had noted with dismay that, in the huge government bureaucracy, there were less than one hundred men—and these scattered throughout different government agencies—who were devoting their time and energy to a serious study of how the arms race might be halted and brought under control. The task of setting up an organization devoted solely to this purpose, and the further task of obtaining the approval and the necessary appropriation from an unenthusiastic Congress were given to that able and versatile public servant John J. McCloy, who later negotiated with the Soviet Union the first important agreement on the basic principles of disarmament.[2]

Apart from these four major steps in the direction of developing a new approach to world affairs, Kennedy devoted his energy to the immediately pressing problems.

The most immediate of these was the American entanglement in Laos. Few Americans were familiar with the wretchedly reported story of the Eisenhower administration's self-defeating intervention in that distant Asian country, although much of it had been revealed by the June 15, 1959, report of the Congressional Committee on Government Operations. It was a shocking tale of incompetence, corruption and, above all, of incredibly bad judgment.[3] Instead of stiffening the neutrality of the Souvanna Phouma government, some $300 million of American money had served to corrupt it and to make it vulnerable to subversion. Under the pretext of helping the French to carry out the training mission assigned to them by the Geneva Accords of 1954, the United States had sent in a military mission disguised in civilian garb and had supported the installation of General Phoumi Nosavan as the openly pro-Western dominant figure in a new Laotian government. This was in direct violation of the Geneva Accords and led to the counter-action of communist-led and Soviet-armed Pathet Lao guerrillas from the North who, in the last days of the Eisenhower administration, were rapidly overrunning the country. The peaceable Laotians were disinclined to fight for a govern-

2 Sorensen, *Kennedy*, pages 517–519.
3 See William Lederer, *A Nation of Sheep* (New York, W. W. Norton & Company, 1961).

ment which seemed to them corrupt, oppressive and dominated by foreign interests.

This was the situation which Kennedy inherited. With coolness and courage, the barely installed President proceeded to reverse a course which, besides alienating most of America's allies, would almost certainly have led to war. Renouncing the intention to make Laos a Western stronghold, he declared that the United States wanted a peaceful solution resulting in the establishment of an independent neutral Laos, as provided by the Geneva Accords of 1954. At the same time, however, he declared with greater firmness than the previous administration had ever shown that the United States would tolerate no foreign interference and would, if necessary, fight to preserve Laotian independence and neutrality. This statement was backed by no threat of "massive retaliation" but by a coolly conceived demonstration of conventional air, sea and land power.

By this action, Kennedy inaugurated a new American policy of standing for the protection of the independence and neutrality of nations which desired a neutral status, in place of the Dulles brothers' policy of seeking to make anti-communist allies out of neutral states. Thus, he began to extricate the United States from a morally indefensible position in which it would have stood alone, while making it clear that its new and morally impeccable position would be backed by force, if force were required.

To carry out this policy by negotiating a settlement, Kennedy enlisted the able services of W. Averell Harriman. Harriman, who had held various high positions under Roosevelt and Truman and had recently served as Governor of New York, now, at the age of seventy, was eager to take any task assigned

133

to him and did not hesitate to accept the relatively low-ranking position of Assistant Secretary of State for Far Eastern Affairs. It was largely due to the firmness, pragmatic sense and diplomatic skill which he had shown on so many previous occasions that an agreement on Laos was finally reached. This, however, was not to be accomplished until after Kennedy himself had obtained the agreement of Nikita Khrushchev.

Before setting out to meet de Gaulle in Paris and Khrushchev in Vienna, Kennedy committed a blunder which tarnished his rapidly rising prestige abroad. Yielding to the unanimous advice of the Joint Chiefs of Staff and the top men in the Central Intelligence Agency, he permitted the clandestine invasion of Cuba to proceed as planned by his predecessor. The reasons why he did so have been fully described by Schlesinger and Sorensen, who have also fully documented the considerations which caused Kennedy to doom the operation to failure by refusing to permit any direct involvement of the armed forces of the United States. Failure, painful as it turned out to be, was almost certainly less disastrous in the long run than would have been the "success" of an unwise, illegal and dishonestly conceived operation. This Kennedy quickly realized, and he gallantly assumed full responsibility for the fiasco. Much to his own surprise, the young President's popularity at home suffered very little from this misadventure, but it was not a happy prelude to his first encounter with de Gaulle and Khrushchev.

Largely due to the charm of his French-speaking wife, the President's visit to Paris was a social triumph,[4] but his private

---

[4] With characteristic self-deprecating humor, Kennedy introduced himself to a French audience as "the man who came to Europe with Jacqueline Kennedy."

talks with the French leader, while polite and friendly, left Kennedy with little hope that de Gaulle's uncompromising nationalism would change.

The meeting with Khrushchev in Vienna was another story. Kennedy quietly and persistently set forth his belief that an armed encounter must be avoided and that it could be avoided if Russia and the United States would respect each other's points of view. While Khrushchev agreed that war would be a disaster, he was rough and unyielding with regard to his demand for a reorganization of the United Nations Secretariat (the famous "troika" proposal), and even more grimly determined to eliminate the West Berlin enclave in the heart of the East German state. His concurrence in the neutralization of Laos indicated to Kennedy that the greatest danger of a confrontation existed not in Asia but in Europe. Kennedy came away from the meeting saying: "It's going to be a cold winter." He was determined to make clear to the Soviet leader that he would firmly resist any Soviet attempt to alter the *status quo* in Central Europe. This he proceeded to do by calling up certain reserves and ordering a rapid build-up of American forces in Germany—an undertaking which caused him to realize how small a strategic reserve of conventional forces was at his disposal and how ill prepared were the armed forces of the United States for fighting anything less than a nuclear war.

Throughout the summer, an atmosphere of crisis prevailed in Washington, with Kennedy vainly trying to get the State Department to work out a negotiating position with respect to Germany. For a short time, Acheson seemed to dominate the discussions, displaying his old intransigent attitude toward any negotiation and his predilection for planning military procedures to meet any overt Soviet move. The State Department could think of nothing better than to dust off old proposals for the reunification of Germany under free elections—proposals which Kennedy knew had been and would again be rejected by Khrushchev. Meanwhile, there was something close to panic in East Germany, with a steadily mounting stream of East Germans defecting to the West. It was estimated that two million East Germans had "voted with their feet" against the Ulbricht regime, among them some of the people whom the German Democratic Republic could least afford to lose.

And then the crisis was suddenly resolved in a wholly unexpected way. West Berlin was sealed off from the East by the notorious wall and the East Germans were locked into the Soviet satellite state by barbed wire. The West was completely taken aback and reacted uncertainly. By this brutal method, Khrushchev had solved the immediate problem of stopping the drain, although at the cost of an admission that the German Democratic Republic was anything but a "workers' paradise."

Kennedy dispatched a series of emissaries to assure the West Berliners of continued American protection, among them Vice President Johnson and Attorney General Robert F. Kennedy.

The tension appeared to simmer down, but Kennedy was under no illusions. The real showdown was still to come. What most troubled the President was that the state of the armed forces left him so few options as to the way in which firmness could be combined with a search for peaceful solutions. With General Maxwell Taylor as Chief of Staff and Defense Secretary McNamara's able assistance, rapid progress was made in reorganizing and re-equipping the armed forces and providing them with adequate air transport.

It is this writer's belief that, had it not been for the domestic repercussions of the Cuban fiasco and the tension over Berlin, Kennedy would have pursued a course in Vietnam similar to

136

the disengagement he had successfully brought off in Laos. Whether or not this impression is correct, Kennedy certainly realized that a new policy would have to be pursued in Vietnam, a policy quite different from that which he had inherited from his predecessor. The Eisenhower-Dulles policy had not only relied too much upon military and too little upon political means, but the military policy itself had been wholly unsuited to the achievement of its ends. It had consisted in helping to train and equip a World War II type of South Vietnamese army, fit to fight set-piece battles but not to cope with the hit-and-run guerrilla tactics that were tearing the country to pieces. Realizing that there was presently no viable way to get out of the Vietnamese entanglement without casting doubt upon the value of all United States commitments, Kennedy laid the emphasis upon re-training the South Vietnamese army for guerrilla war, giving it mobility through airlift, and helping by political means to gain greater allegiance to the government on the part of the largely disaffected peasant population. In the first part of this program, he achieved considerable success, but his political efforts were frustrated by the obduracy of the dictatorial police-state regime which Dulles had installed and with which a timid United States diplomatic mission was disinclined to argue.[5]

President Ngo Dinh Diem had been hand-picked by Washington to head the government of South Vietnam after the Emperor Bao Dai's resignation. The story of how he happened to be chosen was interestingly revealed by Robert Scheer and Warren Hinkle in a magazine article written in 1965.[6]

Diem was undoubtedly a sincere patriot and anti-communist

[5] See David Halberstam, *The Making of a Quagmire*, and John Mecklin, *Mission in Torment.*

[6] "The Viet-Nam Lobby," *Ramparts* (July 1965), reprinted in Marcus G. Raskin and Bernard Fall, *The Viet-Nam Reader*, pages 66–81.

but proved totally incapable of winning the allegiance of the South Vietnamese people. The mandarin, urban clique with which he surrounded himself not only had little understanding of the predominantly peasant population but actually alienated popular sentiment by installing what amounted to a police-state regime under which all dissent was suppressed. Diem himself, a verbose and somewhat inscrutable figure, proved utterly unwilling to undertake the reforms proposed by his American advisers, with the result that matters in the country-side went from bad to worse. At the same time, the morale of the Vietnamese armed forces was all but destroyed by political favoritism in the appointment of high officers and the unwillingness of local commanders to risk a defeat which might deprive them of their preferred positions.[7]

Kennedy's substitution of a tough-minded Republican, Henry Cabot Lodge, as United States Ambassador, in place of the gentle career diplomat Frederick Nolting, was followed by the overthrow of the Diem regime by a military junta and the wholly unplanned murder of Diem and his Rasputin-like brother, Ngo Dinh Nhu. But the military junta proved no more capable of winning popular allegiance than the regime it had overthrown. The succession of military coups which followed destroyed what was left of the fiction that the United States was advising and supporting a government responsive to the will of the people of South Vietnam.

Almost all of Kennedy's advisers tried to persuade him that the only way to save the situation would be to send in American combat troops—not because the South Vietnamese forces were outnumbered by the Vietcong and the steadily increasing

[7] See Robert Shaplen, *The Lost Revolution*, and Raskin and Fall, *The Viet-Nam Reader;* also Sorensen, *Kennedy*, pages 629–633, 648–661.

infiltration of North Vietnamese regulars (they were not), but
for reasons of morale. Almost without support, he voted "No."
As Sorensen points out,[8] the key to his refusal could be found
in his Senate speech of April 6, 1954, in which he had said:

> . . . unilateral action by our own country . . . without
> participation by the armed forces of other countries of
> Asia, without the support of the great masses of the
> people [of Vietnam] . . . and with hordes of Chinese
> troops poised just across the border in anticipation of
> our unilateral entry of their kind of battleground . . .
> such intervention would be virtually impossible in the
> type of military situation which prevails in Indochina
> . . . an enemy which is everywhere and at the same
> time nowhere, an "enemy of the people" which has the
> sympathy and covert support of the people.

Making what he knew to be an unsatisfactory choice between unacceptable alternatives, Kennedy refused to send in
combat troops but gradually increased the number of American "advisers" from 2,000 to 16,000; these "advisers" included helicopter pilots and combat support troops, a number
of whom were killed or wounded in action. The writer thought
at the time that this was a mistake. Kennedy had inherited a
foreign policy which, in Sorensen's words, "identified America
in the eyes of Asia with dictators, CIA intrigue and a military
response to revolution." His efforts to change that policy had
failed through no fault of his own. Yet he increased the commitment even while insisting over and over again that the war
in Vietnam was not "our war" but a struggle which the people
of South Vietnam would have to win or lose.

8 Sorensen, *Kennedy*, pages 653–654.

Khrushchev had apparently come away from the Vienna meeting in June 1961 determined to find out whether his new young adversary was a real or a paper tiger. To do this was not easy because the rapid progress made by the United States during 1961–1962 in the development of Polaris and Minuteman missiles made it impossible to risk a direct confrontation without accepting the probability of devastating retaliation. His own stock of ballistic missiles consisted predominantly of intermediate-range weapons (IRBM's) which could not reach the United States and were targeted mostly on Western Europe. His long-range bomber force was greatly inferior to that of the United States.

Probably in order to alter this unfavorable balance of nuclear power, although possibly also for other reasons, Khrushchev took the bold gamble of attempting secretly to install IRBM's in Cuba, from where they could reach a considerable portion of the United States. He would then be in a position to risk a confrontation. If the gamble succeeded, and if Kennedy backed away from a confrontation, the American guarantee of Western Europe's security would be shown to be valueless, the confidence of Latin America in the United States would be destroyed, and the Soviet Union would be left with a strong political and military foothold in the Western Hemisphere. Soviet prestige throughout the world would be enhanced, especially in Asia and Africa where China was challenging Moscow's leadership against "capitalist imperialism."

If, on the other hand, Kennedy should stand up to the confrontation, Khrushchev would be in a position to bargain a withdrawal of the missiles from Cuba against Western withdrawal from bases in Europe which threatened Soviet security.

It was a shrewd plan whose success depended upon its being carried out through deceit and secrecy until the weapons should be in place.

The fascinating story of how the missiles were first suspected and then discovered, how Kennedy skillfully pretended to be deceived, and how the counter-action was debated, planned and carried out is dramatically told by Sorensen and Schlesinger.[9]

Discovery of the first few IRBM's in Cuba before they were operable and quick, resolute action by the United States before Khrushchev knew that his perfidious plan had been discovered produced the confrontation in circumstances wholly unfavorable to the Soviet Union. Soviet ships carrying more men, missiles and equipment were still at sea when Kennedy's ambassadors informed the world of Khrushchev's deceitful aggression and of the counter-actions being taken. The fact that Kennedy brilliantly chose a naval quarantine of Cuba, instead of an air strike or an invasion of Cuba, demanding the immediate removal of the missiles and the turning back of the Soviet ships at sea, gave time for negotiation and, above all, gave Khrushchev a chance to retreat—a chance made easier for him by Kennedy's wise magnanimity in agreeing to a face-saving promise on his part not to invade Cuba.

Thus, Kennedy learned that Khrushchev would recoil from nuclear war with the United States at least unless Soviet vital interests were threatened or Russia itself were attacked; while Khrushchev and the whole world learned that Kennedy would not shrink from nuclear conflict—no matter what the cost—if the vital interest of the United States or the United States itself was threatened. This dramatically changed the whole world

[9] See especially Sorensen, *Kennedy*, pages 667–719.

picture in a number of ways, enabling Kennedy to embark upon a re-shaping of American policy.

Soviet troops were gradually withdrawn from Cuba while Castro screamed that he had been betrayed, refusing to allow the on-site inspection of Soviet withdrawal by the United Nations to which Khrushchev had agreed. Kennedy made no great issue of this but ordered continuous aerial reconnaissance over the island and, when, in spite of Castro's threats, no American planes were shot down over Cuba, the whole Cuban issue subsided for the time being.

Throughout Latin America, the prestige of the United States soared to a new high and the Bay of Pigs was all but forgotten. For a short time at least, the same was true in Europe, although many Europeans suffered a delayed reaction of resentment over having been taken to the brink of holocaust without being consulted.

On the other hand, Khrushchev's prestige was diminished both at home and abroad, though there were many who praised and were grateful for his sane realism in accepting defeat instead of plunging the world into an atomic holocaust. In China, Khrushchev was excoriated as a coward and the split between Moscow and Peking widened.

All this added up to creating a favorable setting for Kennedy to launch his new over-all approach to foreign affairs. He had been extremely careful after the Cuban showdown never to refer to this episode as a victory for the United States or as a defeat for the Soviet Union. He viewed it as a joint escape from catastrophe, and this attitude was greatly appreciated in Moscow. In Peking, it was viewed as the beginning of a joint Soviet-American attempt to dominate the world.

Kennedy's hands were now freed for the tasks of developing

142

his "strategy of peace." His first aim was to achieve a treaty banning the further testing of nuclear weapons, progress toward which was being blocked by Soviet resistance to inspection and by French insistence upon creating an independent nuclear striking force.

In calling Khrushchev's hand, Kennedy had performed a great service for his European allies, but he had also taken them, without consultation, to the edge of the abyss. He had sent Acheson to inform the European leaders of the situation in Cuba and of his intended action, but he had not asked their advice. Thus he had served notice upon the European powers, who were not accustomed to such treatment, that, where its own vital interests were at stake, the United States would no longer allow itself to be immobilized by consultation with partners who could rarely agree with one another and who were reluctant, if not unwilling, to assume their full share of responsibility for the preservation of peace and the promotion of freedom and justice throughout the world.

This implied declaration of independence might have meant —as the writer hoped it would—that the President was determined to overcome the obstructionism of Adenauer and de Gaulle and that, together with Britain, he would now take the initiative in seeking to negotiate a German settlement with the Kremlin.

Until now, de Gaulle and Adenauer had blocked every approach to a relaxation of East-West tensions. In return for de Gaulle's support of his own refusal to permit even a discussion of Germany's future, Adenauer had supported the French leader's insistence upon building an independent nuclear striking force, thereby blocking progress toward a test-ban treaty. Both men dreamed, not of an Atlantic partnership between a united

143

Europe and the United States but of a Franco-German-dominated Carolingian Little Europe. De Gaulle's hostility toward the "Anglo-Saxons" had been evident ever since his return to power in May 1958. It derived to some extent from the cavalier treatment accorded him during World War II by Roosevelt and Churchill but probably even more from his having been rebuffed by Washington and London when he sought, after his return to power, to establish an Anglo-French-American directorate of the Atlantic alliance. Since then, he had shown a marked lack of enthusiasm, if not outright contempt, for the NATO alliance. He had withdrawn his Mediterranean fleet from NATO command, refused to permit nuclear installations on French soil, and, when the Algerian war was settled, had transferred no French forces to reinforce his under-sized garrison in Germany.

Kennedy's concept of an Atlantic partnership was based upon the assumption that the European Economic Community would be expanded to include Britain and the countries associated with Britain in the Free Trade Area. His Trade Expansion Act of 1962 had been explicitly predicated upon that assumption. It therefore seemed reasonable to expect that his next action would be aimed at smoothing the path toward its realization.

Unfortunately, Washington's first demonstration of its independence consisted of a move which seriously embarrassed the one allied government which could be counted upon to back a constructive Atlantic policy. Defense Secretary McNamara's decision to discontinue manufacture of the Skybolt missile, however sound in itself, suddenly deprived the British of the weapon upon which they had based their independent bomber-borne nuclear deterrent and placed the Macmillan gov-

144

ernment before an extremely awkward choice. It would have to abandon the independent striking force to which it was committed, or assume the cost of continuing the development of Skybolt, or accept the American offer of Polaris missiles for an as yet nonexistent fleet of nuclear-armed submarines. In effect, this action forced Britain to make a choice between accepting greater dependence upon the United States or turning away from the United States toward Europe—and this at the exact moment when Britain's belated efforts to join the European Economic Community had reached a crucial stage of negotiation.

Macmillan's acceptance of the American offer at a meeting with Kennedy at Nassau presented de Gaulle with precisely the evidence he wanted in order to prove that, if Britain were to enter the European Economic Community, she would do so as a Trojan Horse for the United States.

Up to this point, de Gaulle had not revealed the depth of his anti-"Anglo-Saxon" feelings, gambling upon the likelihood that the negotiations at Brussels would come up against insuperable economic obstacles. At the very moment when it seemed that these obstacles might be overcome, the Nassau agreement provided the suitable context for the veto against British entry which de Gaulle had no doubt been determined in any case to interpose. At his press conference of January 14, 1963, the imperious French leader demolished in a few elegant sentences both Britain's hope of entering the Common Market and Kennedy's "grand design" for an Atlantic partnership. In doing so, de Gaulle also wrote "finis" to a fourteen-year-old NATO policy which, whatever its original merit, had outlived its usefulness.

A few days later, Adenauer came to Paris to sign the

Franco-German Treaty of Friendship which he considered the crowning achievement of his long career. When he returned to Bonn, however, all the political parties in West Germany united in demanding that a preamble be added to the treaty making clear that it would in no way interfere with the Federal Republic's relations with Britain and the United States or with West German loyalty to the NATO alliance.

To reinforce this attitude on the part of the West Germans and to fortify NATO solidarity, Kennedy decided to make a flying visit to Bonn, Berlin, London and Rome, but not until after he had made a major pronouncement of his new over-all foreign policy.

In his historic speech of May 10, 1963, at the American University in Georgetown, the President was able to make two important announcements: (1) He and Macmillan had proposed, and Khrushchev had agreed to, a July meeting of their representatives at Moscow to endeavor to reach agreement on the long-stalled test-ban treaty; and (2) the United States had decided that it would not resume testing in the atmosphere. (This had been his own personal decision.)

Kennedy began by defining his concept of the kind of peace to be sought as a peace "based not on a sudden revolution in human nature but on a gradual evolution in human institutions." Such a peace, he said, was not impossible, nor was war inevitable. The American aim, he said, was "not a *Pax Americana* enforced on the world by American weapons of war . . . not merely peace for Americans, but peace for all men; not merely peace in our time but peace for all time."

Then he challenged the widely held view that it was useless to think of world peace until the Soviet leaders adopted a more pacific and enlightened attitude. "I hope they do," he said. "I believe we can help them do it. But I also believe that we must re-examine our own attitude." Then he asked Americans to take a new look at the Soviet Union and the Cold War, to forget past prejudices and disagreements and to concentrate upon the common interests shared by both great powers.

Quoting from a Soviet text to illustrate how misconceptions and distortions created a false image of the United States, he warned Americans not to "fall into the same trap as the Soviets, not to see only a distorted and desperate view of the other side."

> History teaches us that enmities between nations do not last forever. . . . Among the many traits the peoples of our two countries have in common, none is stronger than our mutual abhorrence of war. Almost unique among the major world powers, we have never been at war with each other. [This was not quite correct; the United States had for a short time participated in the attempt to overthrow the Soviet regime at its birth.] We must deal with the world as it is, not as it might have been had the history of the last eighteen years been different.
>
> We must conduct our affairs in such a way that it becomes in the Communists' interest to agree on a genuine peace . . . to let each nation choose its own future, so long as that choice does not interfere with the choices of others. . . . If we cannot now end our differences, at least we can make the world safe for diversity. For, in the final analysis, our most basic common link is the fact that we all inhabit this planet. We all breathe the same air. We all cherish our children's future. And we are all mortal.

147

Then came the announcement of the Moscow meeting and the decision not to resume testing in the atmosphere, carefully prefaced by a reaffirmation of American commitments to our allies' security in order not to arouse European apprehensions. And finally:

> The United States, as the world knows, will never start a war. We do not want a war. We do not now expect a war. This generation of Americans has already had enough—more than enough—of war and hate and oppression. We shall be prepared for war, if others wish it. We shall be alert to try to stop it. But we shall also do our part to build a world of peace where the weak are safe and the strong are just. We are not helpless before that task or hopeless of its success. Confident and unafraid, we labor on—not toward a strategy of annihilation but toward a strategy of peace.

The speech was hailed in most of Europe but made no immediate great impression in the United States, partly because it was blanketed by the President's great television address on civil rights delivered the following evening. The Georgetown speech was attacked, as might be expected, by adherents of the Cold War policy which Kennedy had discarded. Khrushchev, however, accepted it as a sincere overture, permitted it to be broadcast all over the Soviet Union and told Harriman later that it had been "the best speech by any President since Roosevelt." (Its direct result would soon be seen in Soviet agreement to a partial test-ban treaty.)

Kennedy's trip to Europe was undertaken for the specific purpose of assuring the always suspicious Germans that a

148

test-ban treaty and a *détente* between the United States and the Soviet Union would in no way prejudice their chances of achieving reunification. The alliance, he said, had been formed to prevent war. Its aim must now be to "find the way to a new peace." He told a Berlin audience, which remembered only his famous *"Ich bin ein Berliner!"* that the path to a united Germany lay through a united Europe.

Although the President achieved tremendous popularity among the German people, Chancellor Adenauer was far from pleased and made it clear that, in his view, Dulles had been the best friend Germany had ever had.

On his way home, Kennedy received word that Khrushchev had agreed to the test-ban meeting and had set the date for July 15. This meant that, if a successful negotiation should result, Khrushchev would have accepted American nuclear superiority.

A team of American negotiators led by the veteran trouble-shooter W. Averell Harriman, went to Moscow and, in daily cabled consultation with the President, successfully concluded a treaty banning test explosions in the air, under water and in space. Underground tests were, for the time being, not prohibited because of disagreement over the number of on-site inspections required for enforcement.[10]

In rapid succession, nation after nation signed the Moscow Treaty. The President left no stone unturned to obtain rapid ratification by the Senate. Only France and the People's Republic of China refused outright, but the Adenauer govern-

---

[10] The writer, among others, had suggested making a start with a partial test ban. See *New York Times*, April 17, 1962, for a letter published with Kennedy's approval; also the writer's testimony in favor of ratifying the treaty before the Senate Foreign Relations Committee on August 23, 1963.

ment indulged in long debate and distressing delay. The test ban should have been the first important step in an East-West *détente*—a *détente* which the Russians needed in order to be able to face eastward toward the rising menace of China, and which the West needed because of the disarray brought about by the Paris-Bonn axis and because of the precarious position of the Anglo-American military forces deployed in Germany at the end of a line of communications which ran through a disaffected France. A real *détente* was possibly only if this moment were seized to override both de Gaulle and Adenauer and to take the initiative in proposing a German settlement.[11]

But this moment was lost. Worried by the possibility that the Bonn government might completely ally itself with France and thus disrupt NATO altogether, the Kennedy administration sought to patch up the NATO alliance by resuscitating a proposal for a multilateral nuclear striking force (MLF) that had been developed by the State Department in the last days of the Eisenhower administration. This was a proposal to paper over a political problem with a military device designed to give the European members of NATO—and particularly the Germans—a sense of equal participation in the control of the Western deterrent, without giving them an actual finger on the trigger.

Perhaps Kennedy was right in postponing the crucial issue. Elections loomed ahead in Britain and Germany. The Conservatives in Britain might be supplanted by a Labour government more inclined toward disengagement in Europe. Adenauer was on his way out and his successor, whether a man

11 The writer once more proposed grasping the nettle of an all-German settlement in a memorandum to the White House under date of September 25. See Appendix B.

of his own Christian Democratic Party or the Social Democratic leader Willy Brandt, would almost certainly be less obdurate than the aging Chancellor, and less inclined to follow de Gaulle in his quest for European hegemony. But the fact remained that an ideal moment to approach Khrushchev with a proposal for an all-German settlement that would eliminate the chief bone of contention between the Soviet Union and the West had been lost. It might or might not recur again.

The decision to try to patch up an obsolete Atlantic alliance by one means or another, instead of eliminating the confrontation in Europe, did not prevent Kennedy from taking further small steps toward fortifying the *détente*.

The test-ban treaty was followed by the establishment of a direct "hot line" system of communication between the White House and the Kremlin, specifically intended to prevent any miscalculations or misunderstandings.

A further U.S.-U.S.S.R. agreement banned the military use of outer space. (Kennedy had actually suggested a joint exploration of outer space.)

Finally, Kennedy overrode opposition and put through a sale of American wheat to the Soviet Union.

On September 20, in his address to the United Nations, Kennedy summed up what had been accomplished and stressed once more his conviction that war could and must be avoided and that a peace of mutual accommodation could and must be achieved. Concretely, he proposed the banning of underground testing, controlling the dissemination of nuclear weapons, cooperation in outer space and a freer flow of people and information from East to West and from West to East.

Then, at the zenith of his popularity, Kennedy set out on

151

a number of trips to various parts of the United States during which he hoped to convince the skeptical among his countrymen that a new era had dawned in international relations. . . .

In the midst of that effort, he was assassinated at Dallas, Texas.

Kennedy left the nation with a new set of beliefs which he had not had time to implant firmly—the belief that the tools existed to prevent cyclical depressions—that public needs in health, housing, education and transportation were more important than a bookkeeper's view of the national budget—that Negroes were entitled to equal rights now, not at some future date—that war was not inevitable and that the Devil did not reside solely in the Kremlin—that the Cold War was obsolete and that the world could be made "safe for diversity."

He left the world with the feeling that the people of the United States might not be as intolerant, imperious and inconsiderate as they had in recent years appeared to be—that the youthful zest and universal sympathy which had once characterized America, and for a time had seemed to be lost, had been restored by a youthful leader whose eyes were on the future instead of on the past—and that, throughout the world, hope was in the process of replacing fear.

John Kennedy had not solved all the world's problems. He had not found the way to a European settlement. He had made the problem of China, if anything, more troublesome by his policy in Vietnam. He had, in fact, solved few of the problems surrounding the establishment of enduring peace, but he had done something infinitely more important—he had pointed the way toward their solution.

Perhaps the most impressive thing about this youthful President was the way in which he had grown and matured in office. He had come upon the scene as something of a young Roman emperor. Before he died, he had become a statesman who recognized that the problems of survival and peace were not soluble by far-flung legions.

10

LBJ: Recessional?

Lyndon B. Johnson inherited a country lifted out of the economic doldrums, cured of complacent euphoria, and requiring not very much more than the steering through Congress of the Kennedy programs to assure a continuation of social and economic progress. In this, Johnson was spectacularly successful during his first year in office, obtaining the passage of most of the Kennedy program, including the highly controversial Civil Rights Bill. In addition, he launched his own "war on poverty" and undertook the creation of what he called the "Great Society."

In the field of foreign affairs, Kennedy had achieved at least the beginning of a needed *détente* between the Soviet Union and the West by changing the whole direction of United States foreign policy; but most of the specific problems left by the Eisenhower administration remained unsolved and the *détente* itself remained precarious.

The deadlock over Berlin and Germany had not been broken,

remaining as the greatest single obstacle to a real *détente* in Europe.

The Western Alliance was in even worse disarray than it had been before Kennedy became President—not through any fault of his but because of Bonn-Paris obstructionism and because a resurgent Western Europe no longer fearful of invasion had become restless under American leadership.

The dangerously obsolete Truman-Eisenhower China policy remained unchanged and was breeding implacable hostility toward the United States in one quarter of the world's population.

Kennedy had skillfully disengaged the United States from his predecessor's attempt to convert Laos into a Western bastion, but he had become more rather than less deeply involved in the defense of South Vietnam.

Latin American relations had been vastly improved by the Alliance for Progress, but progress had been slow; and Castro remained a problem.

Revolutionary turmoil in Africa and latent conflict in the Middle East continued to pose threats to world peace.

In contrast to his amazing record of domestic accomplishment during his first year in office, President Johnson undertook few moves in foreign policy beyond pledging a continuance of the Strategy of Peace. This was about as much as could be expected from a man who, within less than a year, would have to seek a continued mandate and whose experience had been chiefly in the field of domestic politics.

During the 1964 election campaign, specific issues of foreign policy were scarcely discussed, but Johnson conducted a powerful and sustained attack upon his opponent's proposal that control of nuclear weapons be given to field commanders.

155

Again and again, in all parts of the country, he emphasized the need for restraint and responsibility in the handling of nuclear power, pledging himself to a patient quest of lasting peace. "The world you save will be your own," he told his audiences, repeating everywhere Kennedy's warning that 100 million Americans, 100 million Russians and 100 million Europeans might die in the first hour of a nuclear war. He forcefully defended the test-ban treaty, which his opponent had opposed, and conducted a much broader peace campaign than was generally realized because arguments over "extremism" preoccupied so great a part of public attention.

On October 29, at Salt Lake City, a citadel of ultra-conservatism, Johnson told his audience:

> All political systems change; they are forced to by historic circumstances. It would be dangerously foolish to say that Soviet Russia or Communist China will soon become open societies. But it would be equally foolish to think that they will never change.
>
> Inside the Communist Bloc powerful currents are surging against the dam. We cannot sit idly by . . . we must work to guide the inevitable changes that lie ahead.

This was the most emphatic assertion yet made by an American President of the belief that American action could encourage hopeful change within the communist orbit. Significantly, the President mentioned Communist China as well as the Soviet Union.

In an earlier speech (September 28 in Manchester, New Hampshire) Johnson made a statement which might well have been recalled to his mind five months later. Rejecting rash action in Southeast Asia such as he felt that his opponent advocated, Johnson said:

> As far as I am concerned, I want to be very cautious and careful and use force only as a last resort when I start dropping bombs that are likely to involve American boys in war in Asia with 700 million Chinese.

Prior to his election, Johnson tried unsuccessfully to prevent Congress from indulging in a last spasm of blind, undiscriminating anti-communism by cutting Poland and Yugoslavia out of the Food-for-Peace Program. But, after his overwhelming victory at the polls, it was clear that the Chief Executive had received an unprecedented mandate for moderation and a patient pursuit of peace. Barry Goldwater, with his undiscriminating anti-communism and his confidence in military power, had performed a noteworthy service to peace by sharply presenting the American people with an unmistakable choice.

So far as domestic affairs were concerned, the issue during the campaign had never been one of liberalism versus true conservatism. "Conservatism" had been distorted into something more like an angry and frustrated nostalgia for the past. This, too, the American people overwhelmingly rejected.

Johnson's victory gave him majorities in both Houses of Congress such as had not been seen since the days of Roosevelt. He was as untrammeled as any American President had ever been by political opposition or past dogmas.

The situation abroad was also promising.

On October 15, 1964, Nikita Khrushchev had suddenly been ousted and a new regime installed in the Kremlin, with Alexei Kosygin as Premier and Leonid Brezhnev as Party

Chairman. The change had taken place quietly, probably caused by several domestic and at least two foreign factors. Internally, the failure of Khrushchev's agricultural policy and a growing dissatisfaction not with socialism but with its mismanagement were apparently the major factors. In foreign affairs, it seemed that Khrushchev was deemed to have gone too far in his polemics against the Peking regime and to have been too reckless in the Cuban adventure. Whatever the reasons for Khrushchev's ouster, the new regime appeared to be moving cautiously and reaffirmed the desire to fortify the East-West *détente*.

The British and West German elections held in the autumn of 1964 favored the assertion of strong American leadership.

In Britain, the Labour Party was returned to power by the narrowest of margins. The legacy which the new Prime Minister, Harold Wilson, inherited from the Macmillan government was such as to make it imperative for him to establish the closest possible relations with the United States.

In Germany, Ludwig Erhard succeeded Adenauer as Chancellor, heading a somewhat unruly coalition of Christian Democrats, Bavarian Socialists and the Free Democratic Party. Erhard and his foreign minister, Gerhard Schroeder, were strong "Atlanticists" favoring close ties with the United States and Britain, but within the coalition there were powerful dissidents grouped about Adenauer and Franz Josef Strauss, leader of the Bavarian Christian Socialist Union (CSU). These dissidents, while not full-fledged Gaullists, were nevertheless suspicious of any *rapprochement* between the United States and the Soviet Union and determined to acquire for the Bonn Republic an equal voice in the shaping of alliance policy. Majority sentiment in the Federal Republic had shown itself definitely more interested in Atlanticism than in following

158

France into a Carolingian Little Europe, and strongly determined to carry out the Rome Treaties which would create a united Western Europe under supranational institutions—a concept which de Gaulle opposed. Nevertheless, the margin was small and could easily be reversed.

Johnson, like Kennedy before him, had the choice between taking a bold initiative toward a European settlement or attempting to rebuild the Western alliance without France and with West Germany as the keystone on the continent. Whether wisely or unwisely, Kennedy had postponed the decision in order to await the results of the British and German elections. Now with a Labour Government in Britain anxious to reach a European settlement which would reduce its commitments on the continent, and with the stubborn Adenauer at least for the time being a minority dissenter, the time seemed ripe for an American initiative that would seal the *détente*. Tensions in Europe could never be expected to relax so long as two hostile alliances, each depending for its life upon continued tension, remained confronting each other in Central Germany. To this observer at least, it seemed that the time had come for an effort to end the confrontation by an all-European security agreement in which the two German states would be released from adherence to military alliances and given a period of time in which to decide, without outside interference, whether or not they wished to reunite. A specific proposal for action along this line was submitted to the White House and later published in a letter to the *New York Times*, dated November 4, 1964.[1]

Instead of assuming leadership toward nailing down the *détente*, the President chose the course of attempting to patch up the NATO alliance by reviving the proposal for a multi-

[1] See Appendix B.

lateral nuclear-armed force of submarines and, possibly, surface ships (MLF). Although this project was pursued in a rather half-hearted manner, it served to alarm the Kremlin and to weaken the *détente*.

A far more serious blow to the *détente* was yet to come.

On January 4, 1965, in his State of the Union message, the President stated:

> In Asia, communism wears a more aggressive face. We see that in Vietnam. Why are we there? We are there, first, because a friendly nation has asked us for help against Communist aggression. Ten years ago, we pledged our help. Three Presidents have supported that pledge. We will not break it. Second, our own security is tied to the peace in Asia. Twice in one generation we have had to fight against aggression in the Far East. To ignore aggression would only increase the danger of a larger war. Our goal is peace in Southeast Asia. That will come only when aggressors leave their neighbors in peace. What is at stake is the cause of freedom. In that cause we shall never be found wanting.

This was a disturbing statement for a number of reasons.

1. The "friendly nation" which had asked us for help and to which we had "pledged" our help ten years ago was not a nation at all but part of a temporarily divided nation which was to be reunited, under an agreement which we had agreed to respect but had violated.

2. The Diem government, which we had installed and supported, and to which we had pledged nothing more than aid in establishing "a viable regime," had failed to establish a viable regime and no longer existed.

160

3. It was true that American security was "tied to the peace in Asia" in the sense that American security was tied to peace throughout the world. But, surely, the implication that American security was at stake in the preservation of a South Vietnamese government that lacked support by the majority of its own people was a debatable proposition.

4. Finally, to assert that the "cause of freedom" was at stake in South Vietnam implied that freedom existed there, whereas the Vietnamese people had never had any freedom in the Western sense of the word and certainly did not have it under the government which we had established, nor under the government we were currently supporting. The President's statement implied that "freedom" meant nothing more than the absence of communist control.

The whole statement sounded more like Truman or Dulles than like the man whose "strategy of peace" Johnson had promised to continue. It ignored the fact that the rebellion in South Vietnam and the support given to it by the North were part of the same drive for Vietnamese independence that had motivated both the resistance to Japanese occupation and the revolt against the re-imposition of French colonial rule. It was true that the drive for independence had been captured by communist leadership. Was that sufficient reason for a great country, which had itself been born through a revolution for independence, to consider that its security was threatened?

The President's answer was "Yes."

On February 7, 1965, he gave the order to escalate the war by bombing roads, railroads and bridges in North Vietnam to interdict the flow of men and materiel to the South. The rationalization for this decision was that North Vietnam

161

had committed and was committing aggression. If so, it was much the same sort of aggression as that committed by France when it helped the thirteen colonies to establish their independence.

On February 27, the State Department published a White Paper attempting to prove that North Vietnam had from the outset triggered the rebellion in the South, had armed the rebels and was, in fact, directing Vietcong operations.[2] A week later, *I. F. Stone's Weekly* published a deadly and well-documented analysis of this flimsy justification.[3]

The escalation of the war created consternation throughout most of the world and evoked sharp criticism from both Moscow and Peking. Alexei Kosygin, the recently installed Premier of the Soviet Union, had happened to be in Hanoi when the first raids on North Vietnam took place. If any American move had been deliberately taken to undermine the *détente* and to bring Moscow and Peking together, it could scarcely have served these purposes better than a move which both communist capitals would regard as an attack upon "a socialist sister republic."

In the United States, too, many informed citizens voiced their misgivings and urged the President to clarify the aims of his policy. The American public as a whole began to suspect that, instead of winning the war as the people had been led to believe by repeated optimistic statements, the United States was actually losing it.

Largely in response to expressions of concern at home and abroad, the President delivered a speech at Baltimore, on

[2] For the text, see Marcus G. Raskin and Bernard Fall, *The Viet-Nam Reader*, pages 143–155.
[3] Reprinted in Ibid., pages 155–162.

April 7, in which he affirmed that the aim of the United States was peace in Southeast Asia—peace which could be had if only countries would "leave their neighbors alone." He offered the Hanoi government "unconditional discussions" as to how such a peace might be achieved, without mentioning any such discussions with the leaders of the South Vietnamese revolt. In addition, he offered a $1 billion aid program for the development of the Mekong Delta which would benefit all the countries of the area.

On April 14, Soviet Premier Kosygin and North Vietnam's Premier Pham Van Dong jointly outlined a four-point program for negotiations involving the withdrawal of foreign troops and bases from both Vietnams and their reunification through free elections at a later date.

(It was not known at the time, and it was not disclosed until seven months later, that the United States had turned down two offers by Hanoi to hold discussions at Rangoon, both of which were transmitted to Washington by U.N. Secretary-General U Thant, the first shortly before and the second shortly after the presidential election in November 1964. The disclosure came through a conversation with Ambassador Adlai Stevenson, two days before his death, which his friend Eric Sevareid subsequently reported in the November 30, 1965, issue of *Look*. Until this disclosure, the American people and the world were given the impression that Hanoi was unwilling to talk peace. This was certainly the impression left by the White House and the State Department throughout the winter of 1964–1965 and the following summer and spring.)

Acting on the assumption that the Baltimore speech meant that the President really wanted to start peace negotiations, the writer submitted a suggestion for three modifications of his policy:

1. Willingness to include South Vietnamese rebel leadership in the negotiations for a cease-fire and a peace settlement.

2. Willingness to support all-Vietnamese free elections on the sole condition that the sovereign independence and neutrality of an all-Vietnamese government—no matter what its ideological complexion—be guaranteed by the major powers, including the Soviet Union and the People's Republic of China.

3. Cessation of the attacks upon North Vietnam. It was pointed out that even if the bombing succeeded in stopping the flow of men and materiel to the South, it would not end the insurrection because the insurgents had ample manpower and would continue to capture American weapons from the Saigon government's forces as long as that government remained unrepresentative and foreign-supported.

On the other hand, it was pointed out that continued bombing would alienate our friends, would probably stiffen communist resistance and solidarity and prevent the Soviet Union from playing its part in keeping Southeast Asia free from Chinese domination.[4]

It was soon to become clear that these suggestions were unacceptable for the simple reason that the President's offer of "unconditional discussion" was, in fact, not unconditional;

[4] The memorandum of April 25, embodying these suggestions, was sent to the White House and, later, to each member of Congress as well as to a list of leading citizens. The White House reaction was noncommittal, but a number of Senators and Congressmen expressed interest. The paper became one of the documents used by the organizers of the teach-in protests.

that it intentionally excluded the National Liberation Front from the proposed negotiations, and that the administration intended to exclude the communists of both the North and the South from participation in any coalition government. This was not openly stated at the time, but was implied by the attitude taken by the White House when several Senators and Congressmen made speeches asking for clarification.

As if one controversial act in the field of foreign policy had not been enough to cause doubt and misgiving, the President suddenly announced in the last week of April that he was sending 20,000 United States Marines to Santo Domingo, where a rebellion had broken out against the military junta which had, a few months earlier, overthrown the legitimately elected government of President Juan Bosch. The President stated that the purpose of the intervention was to protect the lives and property of United States and other foreign citizens in the Dominican Republic and to prevent a threatened communist take-over of the rebel movement.

It so happened that the writer had been asked to testify before the Senate Foreign Relations Committee in support of a Senate Concurrent Resolution[5] asking the President to move more energetically toward arms control, disarmament and the establishment of a law-abiding world community of nations.

The following were the main points made by the writer's statement to the Committee on May 11, most of which were later substantiated by the evidence obtained by the Committee in secret hearings.[6]

[5] S.R. 32, introduced by Senator Joseph Clark (D) of Pennsylvania on behalf of himself and twenty-five other Senators.

[6] See *Congressional Record*, May 11, 1965, and the speech delivered on the floor of the Senate by the Committee's Chairman, Senator J. W. Fulbright (D) of Arkansas, on September 15, after a careful study of the evidence obtained.

1. The escalation of the war in Vietnam has arrested progress in the relaxation of tensions between the United States and the Soviet Union, thus making it unlikely that any meaningful progress toward disarmament or arms control can be made. It has exacerbated our already hostile relations with the People's Republic of China, thereby raising new obstacles toward bringing China into the disarmament talks and into cooperation in establishing a world of law.

2. Our intervention in the Dominican crisis has raised new doubts as to our government's determination to establish enduring peace through the creation of a law-abiding community of nations.

This action clearly contravened Article 15 of the Charter of the Organization of American States which forbids any member to send its armed forces into the country of another member for any reason whatsoever. This violation might have been overlooked by our Latin American neighbors and by other nations, had the action been taken solely to protect foreign residents, but the frank avowal of an additional political purpose raises the question:

How does the United States intend to relate to the world?

Does the United States intend to rely upon law and the creation of legal institutions to preserve the peace? Or does it assert the right to use its military power to defend what it conceives to be the national interests whenever it considers these interests to be threatened?

The Charter of the United Nations permits any nation to take unilateral action when its own security is endangered, as United States security was clearly endangered by the emplacement of Soviet missiles in Cuba in 1962.

166

It is by no means clear that the presence of a small number of communists in a heterogeneously assorted uprising for the purpose of restoring a legitimately elected government in the Dominican Republic constituted a direct and immediate threat to United States security justifying unilateral action.

3. The decision to intervene in Santo Domingo seems clearly to have been based upon doubtful intelligence and was certainly taken without adequate understanding of Latin American sentiment and the conditions which make for social revolutions in the Caribbean.

Our ill-advised intervention has predictably aroused deep resentment throughout Latin America, even in those countries which have reluctantly agreed to sanction our action; it has alienated the governments of such advanced democracies as Mexico, Uruguay and Chile. Instead of strengthening the OAS, it has split and weakened it.

Communism is not native to Latin America. It feeds upon the desperation created by repressive dictatorships serving the interests of feudal oligarchies—dictatorships such as the United States has supported in Cuba, Nicaragua and Santo Domingo. Sending the Marines to quell a popular uprising against a military dictatorship in the Dominican Republic has probably created more communists and communist sympathizers throughout Latin America than previously existed in its various progressive movements. We are doing Castro's work for him better than he could do it himself.

In discussion with a number of Senators a point was brought out that was later much more fully developed by Senator Fulbright in his notable speech of September 15th—namely, that

167

the Dominican intervention tended to demonstrate that the United States had become, or at least was becoming a *status quo* power—opposed to the very kind of revolutionary change which the Alliance for Progress had been designed to foster.

A study of the world press showed that the Dominican intervention was interpreted in many quarters as the revival of something like the Monroe Doctrine, plus an amplification of Theodore Roosevelt's Corollary[7]—a declaration that Latin America lay within the sphere of vital interest of the United States and that the United States would use force, if necessary, to prevent any social revolution in Latin America from being inspired or taken over by communist leadership.

It was, of course, quite possible to make a case for the contention that diplomacy aimed at reducing tensions in the world must recognize that all major powers have vital interests in areas close to their own borders and that, in such areas, they will not tolerate the existence of hostile governments. Churchill and, to some extent, Franklin D. Roosevelt had recognized the legitimacy of such spheres of influence with respect to the

---

[7] In 1902, the European powers, under the leadership of Germany, sent warships to Venezuela to enforce collection of debts owed to them. They informed the United States of their intention and disavowed anything more than "a temporary occupation of Venezuelan territory." Roosevelt told both Germany and Britain that he "expected a peaceful solution" and, by way of a hint, sent Admiral Dewey's fleet to Puerto Rico. In order to prevent a repetition of this sort of incident, Roosevelt then sent a treaty to the Senate under which the United States assumed custodianship of Dominican revenues, declaring that it was "incompatible with international equity for the United States to refuse to let other powers take the only means at their disposal of satisfying the claims of their creditors and yet to refuse, itself, to take any such steps." The Senate took two years to ratify the treaty.

This "Roosevelt Corollary" to the Monroe Doctrine amounted to the extension of a semi-guardianship over the entire area and led to Latin American charges of "dollar diplomacy" and "Yankee imperialism." The Corollary nevertheless dominated the United States' Latin American policy until it was repudiated by the second Roosevelt's "Good Neighbor Policy."

168

Soviet Union. But if President Johnson meant to assert such a doctrine with regard to Latin America, how was this to be reconciled with his clear determination to establish a government hostile to China in a country actually contiguous to Chinese territory?

Taken together, the escalation of the war in Vietnam and the intervention in Santo Domingo seemed to indicate a reversion to the unilateral assumption of global police power which Kennedy had explicitly renounced.

Was the costly lesson of the Bay of Pigs fiasco forgotten when the Marines were sent into Santo Domingo?

Was the costly lesson of General MacArthur's march to the Yalu River forgotten when a limited commitment to help the people of South Vietnam was permitted to blossom into an undeclared war against a country on China's doorstep? For that matter, had President Johnson forgotten General MacArthur's warning to President Kennedy, frequently quoted by the latter, against becoming involved in another war on the Asian mainland?

These were the questions which troubled many people in many parts of the world in the spring of 1965.

If any proof was required of the unwisdom of United States policy in Asia, it was supplied in September 1965, when war broke out between India and Pakistan—a war fought by each side with American weapons. Pakistan had been rearmed in the Dulles era as a supposed bastion against Soviet Russia and Red China. But when China attacked India in 1962, during the Cuban missile crisis, Pakistan had engaged in a flirtation with Peking and had held a large part of Indian fighting strength facing the Pakistani border, while both the United

States and the Soviet Union had rushed to help India rearm. And now, here were India and Pakistan, the presumed barriers to Chinese domination of Asia, fighting each other with American arms in a war which threatened to lay them both open to Chinese invasion!

In this instance President Johnson wisely left it to the United Nations to demand a cease-fire. For the first time since the Suez crisis of 1956, the United States and the Soviet Union acted together in backing the United Nations demand for a cessation of hostilities, to which both sides somewhat reluctantly agreed. This clearly showed that the United States and the Soviet Union had, and that each recognized, a common interest in preventing Chinese domination of Asia. One might have hoped that Soviet-American cooperation might now be extended to halting the war in Vietnam, but this was clearly impossible so long as American bombing of North Vietnam continued.

All through 1965, the build-up of American forces in Vietnam continued—from 25,000 to 50,000 and, finally, up to some 200,000 men. On June 9, the White House stated that American air and ground troops were now openly committed to combat but that this implied no change in American policy!

All through 1965, the White House and the State Department kept repeating that the United States earnestly desired to talk peace, but that no "signal" had been received from Hanoi. On July 10, the President declared that in Vietnam we had "committed our power and our national honor and that has been reaffirmed by three Presidents." [8]

[8] The fact that no such commitment had been made by either President Eisenhower or President Kennedy was carefully documented by Don R. and Arthur Larson in *Vietnam and Beyond* (Durham, N.C., Duke University Press, 1965), an excerpt from which is reprinted in Raskin and Fall, *The Viet-Nam Reader*, pages 99–108.

As a matter of fact, there had been several "signals" from Hanoi, and not only the overtures through U Thant in 1964 which had been belatedly revealed in November 1965 by the Sevareid story. In February 1965, after months of protest demonstrations in Saigon against the military dictatorship, a civilian government headed by Phan Huy Quat had been installed. Quat, an anti-communist who had opposed the tyranny of the Diem regime, apparently wanted to end the war. On April 16, the responsible Paris newspaper *Le Monde* had published an interview with Quat's deputy premier, Tran Van Tuyen, who had been imprisoned by Diem, in which he said:

> What counts for us is the people who are suffering from the war—the women and children who are being murdered. This war must be stopped. We will need several months to consolidate our regime, to create finally a national front *including all Vietnamese national currents* [emphasis added] in order to build a real force capable of negotiating with the adversary on a footing of equality.

The Quat regime, whether or not it was, as alleged, negotiating or preparing to negotiate with the National Liberation Front, did apparently release hundreds of prisoners who had been arrested for neutralism or pacifism and did apparently put in jail a number of extreme anti-communists. In June 1965, the Quat regime was replaced by another military government, headed by Vice Air Marshal Nguyen Cao Ky. What role, if any, the United States government played in this overturn was not made known to the American people.

Ky made no bones about his attitude toward peace negotiations. In an interview on August 31, he said that his government was "not ready now" to enter peace talks. On November 1, speaking at Seoul, he said flatly that he would never bargain with the communists. "If we want to achieve a genuine victory," he was reported as saying, "then we must begin to annihilate all the capabilities of the communists both north and south of the 17th parallel."

Washington neither rebuked Ky nor dissociated itself from these remarks. On the contrary, on November 5, William P. Bundy, the Assistant Secretary of State for Far Eastern Affairs, told the Chicago Council on Foreign Relations: "The United States rejects Hanoi's demand for acceptance of communists in a coalition government."

There were other reports of "signals" from Hanoi that were difficult to evaluate because of the lack of information given to the public. Sid Lens, a free-lance reporter, assembled bits and pieces of evidence in an article which he entitled "A Policy of Deceit," claiming that the administration was deliberately misleading its own people as to its intentions. If this was unfair, the President had no one to blame but himself for his lack of candor, the secrecy with which he shrouded his purposes and the fiery resentment with which he reacted to disagreement or criticism. Typical of this attitude was the President's reaction to the restrained and thoughtful critique of the Dominican affair by the Chairman of the Senate Foreign Relations Committee, an old personal friend, whom he punished by exclusion from the White House invitation list for dinners honoring visiting dignitaries.

At the invitation of President Johnson, the writer attended the White House Conference on International Cooperation, held in Washington on November 28–December 1, 1965.

The stated purpose of the conference was to obtain constructive suggestions from informed citizens interested in various aspects of foreign affairs. Reports had been prepared by thirty panels of such citizens on thirty subjects which had been designated by the administration. The subjects did not include relations with China or Southeast Asia (specifically, the war in Vietnam), nor did they include the future of Germany, the future of the NATO alliance or the question of a *détente* with the Soviet Union.

It was a pity that some of America's critics abroad could not have seen the wealth of constructive criticism with which the administration was presented at the White House Conference, although it was just as well that foreigners did not witness the negative manner in which suggestions were received by the representatives of the State and Defense Departments.

The outstanding report was that made by the Committee on Arms Control and Disarmament, headed by Dr. Jerome B. Wiesner and composed of experts all of whom had served as advisers to the government. In addition to making a number of suggestions in the field of arms control, this panel explicitly recognized that progress toward disarmament constituted an essentially political problem, rather than one of technique, and then proceeded to put forward a number of challenging ideas in the political field.

1. The committee recognized that a *détente* between the United States and the Soviet Union was the first essential for halting the arms race and the proliferation of nuclear weapons. To achieve a *détente*, it recommended:

a) that the United States seek to achieve a non-aggression pact between the NATO and Warsaw Pact alliances, and the manning of fixed and mobile observer posts in both groups of countries.

b) that a joint study be undertaken with the Soviet Union of possible troop reductions in Germany.

2. The Committee asserted that "an unsettled and divided Germany" constituted the greatest obstacle to a *détente* and urged that steps be taken to bring about German unification, implying that West Germany should be released from NATO and East Germany from the Warsaw Pact.

3. The report called for a comprehensive test ban and a non-proliferation treaty and urged President Johnson to abandon any project that would increase the number of nuclear forces.

All these proposals were characterized by the State and Defense Department representatives as either "not new" or "impractical," implying that most of them had been considered and rejected.

4. Turning to the question of providing conventional armaments to other nations, the Committee urged greater restraint in dealing both with Latin America and with presumed allies in other parts of the world. The arming of Pakistan was cited as an example of unwise policy.

Sales of war materiel were defended by the government representatives both as necessary aid to allied nations and as a major factor in reducing the United States balance-of-payments deficit.

5. The Committee urged that an attempt be made to open bilateral talks with China on arms control and to ascertain the conditions upon which China might qualify for and accept the responsibilities of U.N. membership and thus be brought into

174

the discussions on disarmament.

The response of the government representatives was pained boredom. When members of the audience brought up Vietnam, they were told that they were out of order. (The same thing happened in the panel discussions on Peace-Keeping and Peaceful Settlements.)

Talking to a considerable number of the invited delegates, the writer found that most of them shared his own impression —namely, that the conference had been called not so much for the purpose of obtaining suggestions for the improvement of the nation's conduct of its foreign relations as for the purpose of justifying current policies. Almost everyone at the conference wanted to hear a discussion of Vietnam, but it was apparent that the administration desired no such discussion. In their addresses to plenary sessions, four top administration officials all assured the delegates that the United States wanted peace throughout the world, attributing the failure to achieve peace in Vietnam to Hanoi and Peking.

Nevertheless, the administration appeared to have learned one thing from the White House Conference (and from the Peace March on Washington which had preceded it, though the two events had no connection): it apparently learned that public belief in its candor and sincerity had been badly shaken.

A Christmas truce in Vietnam brought about a suspension of air raids on its Northern neighbor. When these were not immediately resumed, it soon became apparent that the American government was going to make a major effort to prove its sincerity both to "the other side" and to the world. The first sign of this "peace offensive" was the sudden appearance of the indefatigable Averell Harriman in Warsaw, Poland

175

being one of the three members of the International Control Commission (ICC) that had been set up at Geneva in 1954. From Warsaw, Harriman flew to Yugoslavia to see Marshal Tito, and thence to New Delhi. (India, which was also a member of the Control Commission, had practically given up its policy of non-alignment after it had been attacked by China.) Simultaneously, Canada, the third member of the ICC, was visited by presidential assistant McGeorge Bundy. U.N. Ambassador Goldberg flew to Rome to see the Pope, whose New Year's message had urged peace, and then held high-level conferences with the Italian, French and British governments. Vice President Humphrey flew to Japan, the Philippines, Taiwan and South Korea. Ambassador Kohler conferred with Soviet officials. Assistant Secretary of State G. Mennen Williams explained the United States position to African leaders. And Under Secretary of State Thomas Mann visited Mexico City. One newspaper referred to this orchestrated demonstration as "megaphone diplomacy"; another described it as being carried out in a typically Texan "anything-is-possible, can-do spirit of an oil speculator."

The peace proposals which the emissaries carried around the world contained nothing startling. The fourteen points reaffirmed willingness to accept the Geneva Agreements of 1954 and 1962 as a basis for peace; willingness to discuss Hanoi's four-point program as well as any other program; support of free elections in South Vietnam and free decision of the Vietnamese people as to reunification and as to neutrality or non-alignment. It was specifically stated that the United States wanted no bases in Southeast Asia and would withdraw its troops once peace was assured.

The proposals did not accord the National Liberation Front

176

belligerent status but repeated the President's earlier somewhat ambiguous statement that "the Vietcong would not have
difficulty being represented and having their views represented
if for a moment Hanoi decided she wanted to cease aggression.
I don't think that would be an insurmountable problem."

On the question of communist participation in a coalition
government of South Vietnam, or in an eventual all-Vietnamese government, the statement was silent.

There was, in fact, nothing new in this approach except
the manner of its presentation and the fact that it was put
forward in connection with a suspension of air attacks upon
North Vietnam.

Both Peking and Hanoi denounced the whole peace offensive as propaganda. A broadcast from Hanoi on January 4
called it "a large-scale deceptive peace campaign coupled with
the trick of temporary suspension of air attacks as a sign of
goodwill." If the administration received any private response,
it was not disclosed.

Soviet diplomacy was becoming increasingly active in Asia.
It had gained considerable prestige through Premier Kosygin's
success in bringing President Ayub Kahn of Pakistan and
Premier Shastri of India together at Tashkent and there inducing them to withdraw their forces from each other's territory and to undertake mutual efforts to end their countries'
hostility. This peace-making intervention where two non-
communist countries were concerned constituted an interesting departure from past Soviet policy. Whether Moscow
would now work actively for peace in Vietnam seemed to depend chiefly upon whether the United States permanently
ended its attacks upon communist North Vietnam or resumed

177

them. It seemed clear that Moscow wanted the war in Southeast Asia to end, and to end in such a way as to deny the United States a "victory" while at the same time preventing Southeast Asia from falling under Chinese domination. Thus, if the United States would be satisfied with less than what would appear to the world as a victory, it seemed that Soviet and American interests would coincide, as they had coincided in the Pakistan-India affair.

While Soviet prestige in Asia was rising, Chinese influence appeared to be diminishing. Peking had alienated a formerly friendly India, and Chinese diplomacy had suffered a number of setbacks, notably through the recent failure of the attempted communist *coup d'état* in Indonesia and the near-destruction of the Indonesian Communist Party. It seemed likely that Peking's influence at Hanoi had been diminished and that the one thing most likely to restore it would be a resumption of bombing and a further escalation of the war by the United States.

A well-reasoned warning against escalating the conflict was contained in a full report to the Senate Foreign Relations Committee presented on January 3, 1966, after a visit to Southeast Asia, by Senators Mansfield, Aiken, Muskie, Boggs and Inouye.

Nevertheless, as the days passed and no sign came from Hanoi, the President was subjected to increasing pressure, by the warhawks in Congress and by certain quarters in the Pentagon to resume bombing.

On January 21–22, at the invitation of eight worried Democratic members of Congress, the writer took part in a thorough discussion of the Vietnam problem together with a dozen experts on Southeast Asian affairs, at least half of them with

178

direct experience in Vietnam.[9] The group was unanimous in feeling that the government's peace proposals lacked clarity and precision. It felt that the American peace proposals should be clarified and that bombing should not be resumed until every means of reaching a peace settlement had been explored. (This did not imply that the group would necessarily favor a resumption of bombing in the event that all efforts to reach a peace settlement should fail.)

As to clarification of the American proposals, there was agreement that:

1. The United States should unambiguously accord the National Liberation Front belligerent status and the right to sit at the peace table.

2. The United States should make it clear that it would not object if free elections in South Vietnam (or eventually in all of Vietnam) should result in a coalition government with communist participation.

3. The United States should take steps to broaden the base of the Saigon government and to bring about a change in its intransigent attitude toward a coalition representing all the elements in the population of South Vietnam.

The Mansfield report and speeches by Senators Fulbright, Aiken, Clark, Church and McGovern during the latter part

9 The sponsoring Congressmen were:
 Benjamin S. Rosenthal (D-L) N.Y., Chairman
 Charles C. Diggs, Jr. (D) Michigan
 Don Edwards (D) California
 Leonard Farbstein (D) New York
 Donald M. Fraser (D) Minnesota
 Robert W. Kastenmeier (D) Wisconsin
 Henry S. Reuss (D) Wisconsin
 William F. Ryan (D) New York
The report of the Ad Hoc Congressional Conference on Vietnam was printed for distribution to all the members of Congress and released to the press on February 15, 1966. See Appendix A.

of January aroused a large part of the Senate membership and resulted in a request to the President for full consultation. A similar plea against the resumption of bombing was signed by seventy-six members of the House.

Analyzing the situation with his usual clarity, Walter Lippmann forecast the failure of the peace offensive on the grounds that the President had been "trying to obtain by propaganda the victory he had not been able to obtain on the battlefield—that is to say, the acceptance in the whole of South Vietnam of a government which has lost control of a large part of South Vietnam." The Mansfield report showed, Lippmann said, "that Mr. Rusk's objective—the rule of General Ky or his successor over the whole of South Vietnam—is unattainable, no matter how much the war is escalated." This led to the conclusion, with which the writer agreed, that "our war aims should be reduced and our strategy revised."

Such a revision of strategy had just been suggested by Lieutenant General James M. Gavin (retired) in the February 1966 issue of *Harper's*. The former paratroop commander advocated a strategy of holding Saigon and other enclaves and bases in South Vietnam, while giving up the attempt to search out and destroy the Vietcong throughout the interior. A holding operation of this nature, pending the working out of a peace settlement, would require neither the bombing of North Vietnam nor any further substantial increase of American ground forces. On the other hand, Gavin warned that further escalation would almost inevitably lead to a war with China and that, if that was what the warhawks in the Pentagon and State Department wanted, the place to fight China was in Manchuria and certainly not in Vietnam. (He might usefully have added that, while the place in which to hurt China was

180

Manchuria, there could be no surer way of precipitating a war with both China and the Soviet Union than by attacking that sensitive province.)

Would President Johnson see that what the warhawks were asking him to do would eventually lead to the utter isolation of the United States, if not to a catastrophic major war? Would he have the wisdom and the fortitude to do what the proud and imperious General de Gaulle had done in Algeria—to withdraw, in spite of the generals, colonels and civilian "ultras," from an adventure that should never have been undertaken? Certainly, de Gaulle's prestige had suffered neither at home nor abroad from his action in pulling out of a land in which France had far greater national interests than the United States ever had or has in Vietnam. Would Lyndon B. Johnson realize that his own and the nation's prestige would be enhanced, rather than diminished, by liquidating a mistake made by his predecessors?

Unhappily, the answer was negative.

The President refused to consult the Senate leaders on the grounds that Congress had already given him full authority to do whatever he deemed necessary by passing the so-called Tonkin Resolution on August 10, 1964. On January 31, 1966, he announced that he had reached the decision to resume bombing attacks upon North Vietnam, while simultaneously instructing Ambassador Goldberg to ask for an immediate meeting of the U.N. Security Council to act upon a United States resolution asking the Council to bring about a cease-fire. Prior to this time, the Johnson administration had rebuffed all suggestions for bringing in the United Nations; but now that the great peace offensive had failed, the administration decided to drop the matter into the lap of the world

181

organization. It was difficult to imagine a less auspicious way of doing so than by preceding the request with an announcement that bombing North Vietnam had been resumed.

When the administration presented the Congress with a request for additional funds to finance its operations in Vietnam, the Senate Foreign Relations Committee had an impeccable reason for doing what a number of concerned citizens, among them the writer, had for months urged it to do— namely, to hold public hearings on the administration's Vietnam policy. In the full glare of the television cameras, Foreign Aid Administrator David Bell and Secretary of State Dean Rusk were subjected to rigorous questioning. While the Senate hearings were in process, the President suddenly announced, on February 6, that he and a retinue of his chief aides were going to Honolulu to meet Ambassador Lodge, General Westmoreland and the leaders of the Saigon government, in order to review both the military and the political aspects of the war. The effect of their three-day conference was to give a strong boost to the morale of the Ky government and also to tighten the commitment of the United States to that government. In view of the Saigon leaders' frank statements that they were not ready for peace talks and their flat refusal to deal with the National Liberation Front, this appeared to be a step away from peace. If the President expressed any disagreement with the Saigon viewpoint, no hint of it appeared in the communiqué.

While the Presidential party was in Honolulu, the Senate Foreign Relations Committee continued its open hearings. The two star witnesses were General Gavin and the veteran diplomat George F. Kennan. Both strongly urged a de-escalation of the war. Kennan's carefully prepared statement revealed a point of view very similar to that of the group in whose deliberations the writer had participated a fortnight earlier. This point of view seemed to be shared by Chairman Fulbright and a majority of his colleagues on the committee.

The President's reaction to the testimony was not encouraging. His public statements at Honolulu left the impression that he thought all his critics were "special pleaders" who "counsel retreat" and that "only the callous or timid" could ignore the just cause of the Saigon government. James Reston commented in the *New York Times:*

> Everything in the Johnson strategy seems to be done in twos; something for the hawks and something for the doves; bomb North Vietnam and go to the Security Council; step up the military forces and increase the pacification program; criticize the Saigon government in private and commit American power and prestige to it in public; assert that America cannot police the world but proclaim simultaneously that tyranny in the jungles of Southeast Asia is just as much America's concern as tyranny and subjugation of the peoples of Europe. . . . Does half a war offensive and half a peace offensive, excluding the enemy that is doing most of the fighting, add up to a whole policy or to no policy?

The next two witnesses were General Maxwell Taylor and, for the second time, Secretary of State Rusk, both of whom defended the administration policy. Taylor said that the amount of further escalation, if any, would depend upon "the other side." He did not want or expect the war to spread to China but said that Gavin's proposal for de-escalation and holding the coastal enclaves would be tantamount to surrender. Rusk went through the whole dreary and familiar ritual of blaming "the other side" for the original violation of the Geneva Agreements and of insisting that the National Liberation Front was nothing but a creature of Hanoi. Rusk based his justification of United States intervention upon the SEATO Treaty, rather than upon any commitment to the Saigon government; this was a highly debatable position and one which was immediately challenged by Senator Wayne Morse of Oregon. The impression left by the two chief administration witnesses, and especially by Rusk, was one of complete inflexibility.

The great virtue of the hearings was that the American people could at long last hear the issues debated. For the first time in many years, there would be something like "government by discussion."

Both Taylor and Rusk refused to set any limits upon what forces or what weapons the United States might "be forced" to employ. Both said that this would depend upon what "the other side" might do.

In addition, Rusk developed the extraordinary theory that the United States was committed under the SEATO Treaty (and apparently under any defense alliance) to resist communist attack, no matter what the other signatory powers might do. Not even Dulles had gone so far as to suggest that the United States was committed to act, if necessary alone, to redeem the promises of the worldwide alliances that he contracted. This Rusk Doctrine—a sort of global Monroe Doctrine—stood in odd contrast to the fact that most of the allies of the United States, in Europe, the Middle East and even in Japan, were extremely critical of American action in Vietnam. It was hard to reconcile this global unilateral assumption of responsibility with the Secretary's denial of the frequently heard assertion that the United States had appointed itself as the world policeman.

It was becoming more and more difficult to escape from the feeling that a military juggernaut had taken control of national policy and that this juggernaut was rolling with increasing momentum toward a confrontation if not a war with China. The United States seemed to be participating with China in creating another vicious circle of fear, hostility and self-fulfilling prophecy such as that in which the United States and the Soviet Union had become involved twenty years earlier, and from which they had only recently begun to extricate themselves.

Like the earlier Soviet-American imbroglio, a Chinese-American confrontation seemed likely to arise out of mutual ignorance or misinterpretation of each other's nature and intentions. China felt directly threatened by American encirclement—by American military power based upon Japan, Okinawa, South Korea, Formosa, Guam, the Philippines and South Vietnam. The United States felt threatened by the possibility of Chinese intervention in Vietnam or Korea and by the declared Chinese intention to support "wars of liberation" against "capitalist imperialism" throughout the world. China appeared to judge the United States by its actions, disregarding Washington's assurances of peaceful intent. The United States seemed to judge China by Peking's belligerent pronouncements, disregarding the fact that throughout the postwar period the Peking regime had actually moved with considerable caution. Neither side appeared to understand the reasons for the other's hostility.

It may be useful to recall a few facts of history.

Chinese hostility toward the West is far older than communism; it has its roots in an ancient culture that considered Westerners inferior barbarians; it is perhaps due even more to the long years of humiliation (1840–1912) during which the Western powers forcibly introduced opium into China (to pay for tea) and, together with Japan, exploited and all but dismembered a weak Manchu Empire. During these years, the United States incurred *relatively* little Chinese hostility because, through its "Open Door" policy, the United States claimed little more than a "me-too" commercial position. American participation in suppressing the Boxer Rebellion of 1900 was in part condoned by American renunciation of any share in the reparations imposed by the European powers. Between the overthrow of the Manchu dynasty in 1912 by Sun Yat-sen's revolution and World War I, relations between the United States and China were, on the whole, friendly although somewhat impaired by the discriminatory exclusion of Chinese immigration and the continued existence of the "unequal treaties" granting American (and other foreign) citizens extraterritorial rights in China.

Chinese anti-Western feeling was increased when, at the end of World War I, German-held Shantung was given to Japan instead of being returned to China. In World War II, China was saved from total defeat at the hands of Japan by the intervention of the United States, but only at the eleventh hour and only after Japanese attack had forced the United States to take action.

Broadly speaking, therefore, Chinese anti-Western sentiment may be said to have focused upon the United States only in the second postwar period, during which the United States first tried unsuccessfully to thwart the Chinese Communist

186

Revolution and then refused to recognize the legitimacy of the victorious Mao Tse-tung regime. We should do well to ask ourselves whether this postwar hostility is justified.

From the Chinese point of view, we intervened in a civil war that was none of our business. After Chiang Kai-shek's defeat and flight to Formosa, we still supported his Nationalist regime as the legitimate government of China and as the rightful representative of the Chinese people in the United Nations. By the interposition of our Seventh Fleet and our military aid to and alliance with the exiled Nationalist regime, we have enabled it to prevent the liquidation of the civil war by retaining possession of Formosa and offshore islands which both sides consider a part of China. We have treated, and endeavored to cause other nations to treat, the Chinese People's Republic as a pariah among the world's nations, denying it so far as possible all normal trade and intercourse.

We should ask ourselves what the Chinese people have done to warrant such hostility other than to adopt a form of government which we dislike and fear. In overthrowing a corrupt and incompetent regime and establishing another regime in its place, the Chinese people exercised a right which our own Declaration of Independence accords to all peoples. The government which they overthrew was at least as anti-democratic and oppressive as the regime they established in its place.

It is true that the new regime arrested and imprisoned a number of Americans and cast the United States in the role of the external enemy upon whom to blame the hardships and suffering caused by its own harsh dictatorship.

It is true that Chinese intervention in the Korean conflict greatly increased American casualties and inflicted a painful defeat upon the American and allied forces. But, before China

187

intervened, an American general, not content with repelling the North Korean aggression and restoring the *status quo ante bellum*, had converted a police action into a war of conquest and, in spite of repeated warnings, had driven his forces right up to China's most sensitive frontier.

It is also true that, in 1959, China brutally suppressed a revolt in Tibet over which it claims an historic right of suzerainty; and that, in 1962, China attacked India, asserting claims to frontier territory dating back to the years before Indian independence. And it is a fact that China asserts claims upon some 500,000 square miles of Soviet territory in Asia. But what has this to do with us? The adjudication of territorial disputes is not the function of the United States; it is the function of the United Nations, from which we have excluded the People's Republic of China.

This brings us down to the more recent period during which China has split away from the Soviet Union, denounced Moscow's policy of peaceful coexistence with the West, and has begun to foment and support "wars of liberation" against "capitalist imperialism." But here again, before Peking ever began to stir up trouble in Africa and in areas such as the Caribbean, where the United States has a vital interest, the United States had intervened in Laos and Vietnam, attempting to convert these two little states on China's doorstep into anti-communist pro-Western bastions, and this in spite of having agreed to respect the Geneva Accords providing for their neutralization. Out of this intervention has come the war in Vietnam.

To say all this is not to deny that China, as the most powerful nation in Asia with unsatisfied territorial claims, is a menace to peace. Indeed, it is. However, the writer has long held that the way to contain that menace is not to indulge once more

188

in the fantasy that all right and all justice are on our side. What is suggested here is that the way to tame China is to remove her legitimate grievances, to treat her not as an outcast but as a legitimate though difficult member of the family of nations and to foster a development within China similar to the gradual mellowing that has been taking place within the Soviet Union during recent years. That process has taken place because, while Soviet expansion was firmly resisted, the Soviet Union was not treated as an outcast, and because the Western powers recognized the Soviet Union's right to have friendly governments on its periphery, provided that it would to some extent at least respect their independent sovereignty. In the writer's opinion, China is entitled no less than the Soviet Union not to be encircled by hostile neighbors, provided that she will refrain from seeking to subject her neighbors to Chinese domination.

In a Senate speech during the Vietnam debate, Senator Fulbright suggested the neutralization of the Indochinese states. In addition, the writer has long maintained that it will be necessary to find some way of neutralizing and withdrawing American military power from the Formosa Strait; this might or might not involve the creation of an independent or semi-autonomous Formosan republic.

Finally, if a dangerous confrontation is to be avoided, Peking must be seated in the United Nations as the legitimate representative of one-quarter of the world's population.

As the debate over Vietnam widened into a discussion of relations with China, it seemed evident that there was little justification for the President's complaint that his critics offered no alternative policies. On the contrary, it seemed that his supporters had nothing to offer except more and bigger

189

doses of the medicine that seemed more likely to kill than to cure. Speeches by some of the warhawks demanding that the bombing of North Vietnam be extended to include the populous industrial and transportation centers, and repeated insinuations that dissenters were giving aid and comfort to the enemy brought to mind an earlier period in American history during which a great American had written:

The loud little handful—as usual—will shout for the war. The pulpit will warily and cautiously object—at first; the great, big, dull bulk of the nation will rub its sleepy eyes and try to make out why there should be a war and will say, earnestly and indignantly, "It is unjust and dishonorable and there is no necessity for it."

Then the handful will shout louder. A few fair men on the other side will argue and reason against the war with speech and pen, and at first will have a hearing and be applauded; but it will not last long; those others will outshout them, and presently the anti-war audiences will thin out and lose popularity.

Before long, you will see this curious thing: the speakers stoned from the platform, and free speech strangled by hordes of furious men who in their secret hearts are still at one with those stoned speakers—as earlier—but do not dare to say so. And now the whole nation—pulpit and all—will take up the war-cry and shout itself hoarse, and mob any honest man who ventures to open his mouth; and presently such mouths will cease to open.

Next, the statesmen will invent cheap lies, putting the blame upon the nation that is attacked, and every man will be glad of those conscience-soothing falsities and will

190

diligently study them, and refuse to examine any refuta-
tions of them, and thus he will by and by convince himself that the war is just and will thank God for the better
sleep he enjoys after this process of grotesque self-decep-
tion.

—Mark Twain, at the time of the Spanish-American
War (*The Mysterious Stranger*, 1898)

Fortunately, just as the clamor of the warhawks reached a
crescendo in March and early April 1966, events took place
within South Vietnam which abruptly altered the situation
and, for the time being, stilled the demand for further escalation.

Falsely feeling himself secure because of the strong endorse-
ment given him at Honolulu by President Johnson, Premier
Ky undertook to rid himself of the one member of his military
junta in whom he saw a threat to his own supremacy. This was
General Nguyen Chanh Thi, who commanded the vital north-
central First Corps area. The move set off a Buddhist revolt in
Hué and Danang which soon spread to Saigon and threatened
to result in a civil war within a civil war. The Buddhist leadership demanded the establishment of a civilian government and
the ouster of Ky whom it considered now more than ever a
puppet of the United States. It appeared that, instead of
strengthening Ky's position, President Johnson's accolade had
given him what many newspapers called "the kiss of death."

Since the revolt clearly showed strong overtones of feeling
against the United States and raised new doubts as to whether
any Vietnamese government would be able to carry on a successful struggle against the Vietcong, some of the leading
warhawks in Washington abruptly changed their tune. In-

191

fluential members of Congress, among them the redoubtable Senator Richard Russell, Chairman of the Senate Armed Services Committee, began to question whether perhaps the United States should withdraw both military and economic aid from South Vietnam. President Johnson went into seclusion at his Texas ranch to ponder anew. No one could foresee what sort of government at Saigon would emerge from the "elections" which Premier Ky reluctantly promised to hold within "three to five months," or whether these elections would ever be held.

Throughout his incumbency, President Johnson's interest in world affairs had been almost exclusively confined to Vietnam, except for a brief but disastrous intervention in the Dominican Republic. However, in early March 1966, President de Gaulle's peremptory demand for the removal from French soil of all troops and installations not under French command finally forced Washington to turn its attention to the long-brewing and now acute European crisis.

Once again, the writer was asked to testify before a hastily convened subcommittee of the Senate Committee on Foreign Relations. The following statement was submitted on March 22:

In order to make my position with regard to our European policy clear at the outset, let me state quite plainly that I think the NATO alliance is obsolete, irrelevant to conditions as they exist today and, in fact, an obstacle to the achievement of what I conceive to be the vital interests of the United States.

I have all my life believed that the United States has a vital interest in the security of Western Europe. I still believe this to be true today.

192

In March 1939, when West European security was threat-ened by Hitler, I publicly advocated a declaration by the United States that it would consider an attack upon any of the nations of Western Europe as an attack upon itself. (This pro-posal was denounced by none other than Mr. John Foster Dul-les on the grounds that "only hysteria would suggest that any of the dynamic nations—Germany, Italy and Japan—would ever dream of attacking the United States.")

Ten years later, in April 1949, I appeared before this com-mittee to testify in favor of the same sort of declaration of soli-darity in the proposed North Atlantic Treaty, in order to warn the Soviet Union that any encroachment upon Western Europe would mean war with the United States. In endorsing the pro-posed treaty, however, I warned against stretching the Amer-ican commitment into a promise to defend Western Europe at the line of the Iron Curtain which ran through the heart of Germany. Previously, in 1947, I had opposed the idea of creat-ing a separate West German state because I thought that it would lead inevitably to the creation of an East German Soviet satellite and to a Russian attempt to oust the Western powers from Berlin. I warned that an undertaking to defend West Germany's frontier would lead to a demand for the remilitari-zation and rearmament of West Germany and its inclusion as a partner in the proposed defense alliance. This would, I said, freeze the partition of Germany and create a serious obstacle to the achievement of a European peace settlement. . . .

The specific problem we face has stared us in the face since January 1963, when General de Gaulle killed President Ken-nedy's design of an Atlantic Partnership. Let us define it.

Lacking economic and military power to make France great in the world of superpowers, de Gaulle has tried to tie West Germany to France and to the fulfillment of his ambitions. In

193

this effort, he has presented the West Germans with the choice between French hegemony or Atlantic cooperation. So far, the Germans have refused to choose French hegemony.

From the American point of view, de Gaulle's desire to have Europe conduct an independent policy under French leadership means that the United States would remain committed to defend Western Europe at the almost certain expense of enormous casualties, without having any control over what actions Europe might take that might provoke war. Obviously such a state of affairs would be wholly unacceptable. What alternatives are open to us?

My own view of what we should do to meet the situation was expressed to President Kennedy before his tragic assassination, repeated to President Johnson in November 1964, and summarized in the following letter to the New York Times:

Among President Johnson's many urgent tasks, none seem to the writer more pressing than the rethinking of our European policy. Nowhere else in the world can there be so hopeful a start toward halting the proliferation of nuclear weapons and toward settling the political issues which spawned and still sustain the arms race.

NATO, the cornerstone of our present policy in Europe, is disintegrating, and not only because of General de Gaulle's disruptive policies but because NATO is irrelevant to circumstances radically changed since 1949 when NATO came into being.

Then, a militarily impotent and economically prostrate Western Europe trembled in fear of Communist penetration or outright Soviet invasion. The United States was the world's paramount power and could afford to aid Europe's recovery and to allay its fear by a military guarantee which did not expose the United States itself to attack.

Today, in the age of mutual deterrence by threat of mutual extinction, doubt has arisen whether any American government would, for the sake of Europe, actually expose its own cities to incineration. The Soviet threat has receded; and a resurgent Western Europe, while still desiring American protection, resents being the political ward of the United States. Paradoxically and dangerously in a new era of universal interdependence, the possession of independent nuclear power threatens to become the symbol of illusory national sovereignty.

The North Atlantic Treaty was conceived as creating more than a military alliance; it envisioned a grouping of like-minded free nations joined together in the cause of freedom. But the NATO nations have not shown themselves to be like minded; they have developed few common political aims or economic goals; they have found no common approach to the liquidation of colonialism or to the pressing problem of harnessing their great resources to meet the needs of the world's underprivileged peoples.

NATO stands today as little more than a half-hearted military alliance against an outdated military danger; as such, it is not only obsolete but seems to this observer an actual obstacle to progress toward peace.

An East-West *détente* in Europe is now the key to world peace. There can be no such *détente* so long as NATO remains the pillar of our European policy, because NATO's very life depends upon continued East-West tension. Nor can the troublesome problem of Ger-

195

many be settled so long as our policy demands keeping part of a partitioned Germany in NATO.

For these reasons the writer ventures to suggest that the United States should aim to eliminate the confrontation in Europe of two hostile and eventually obsolete alliances; that, instead of patching up NATO and trying to solve a political problem by some military device, we should seek the achievement of an all-European security agreement in which, within the framework of the United Nations, the nuclear powers and all the nations of Europe would undertake to prevent the spread of nuclear weapons and to suppress all military aggression, whether emanating from East or West.

Such an agreement would be directed against no "enemy" bloc or nation. Unlike the confrontation of hostile alliances, it would promote rather than obstruct the abatement of tensions, the settlement of divisive issues and the beginning of disengagement and disarmament.

All of Europe, including the Soviet Union, shares a recognized common interest in preventing war. This is more important than the ideological differences between East and West. Instead of a partnership with one-half of a Europe divided against itself, it is suggested that we seek partnership with all of Europe in our quest for peace, not only in Europe but in Asia and throughout the world.

This brief statement raises a number of questions as to the nature of the General European Security Agreement which I propose as a substitute for the NATO and Warsaw Pact Alliances, as well as the nature of the approach to a Germn settle-

ment which I advocate. I have endeavored to answer these questions in a book entitled Time for Statesmanship, *published last year. I ask that the relevant pages be included as an appendix to my testimony.*[10]

The situation, as it developed in April 1966, was not promising. It became apparent that the Johnson administration was determined to patch up the NATO alliance as best it might. A polite but frosty note questioned the right of the French government to abrogate the agreements under which American troops were stationed in France, expressed Washington's determination to maintain NATO as an integrated military alliance with or without France, and was clearly aimed at wooing the Germans and isolating de Gaulle. (What the writer had feared and repeatedly warned against was now in the process of happening—Anglo-American failure to come to terms with Moscow over the future of Germany was about to leave it in the hands of de Gaulle to negotiate with the Kremlin.)

Acheson, recalled to assist Rusk in dealing with the European crisis, appeared on television in an interview remarkable for its lack of diplomatic restraint. Describing the French leader as a stupid, vain and arrogant relic of the past, Acheson suggested that France would come to its senses once de Gaulle disappeared from the scene. Under the heading "Speaking of Relics," the *St. Louis Post-Dispatch* commented editorially:

Mr. Acheson shows all the symptoms of a diplomat who is quite unable to free himself from the stereotypes and clichés of his own past. . . . Like many veterans of public life, especially those who are retired or semi-

[10] See Appendix B for these pages.

retired, he tends to apply to the new facts and the new situations of today the same formulas he applied to quite different problems 20 years ago. . . . It is understandable that Mr. Acheson should want to turn back the clock to his own heyday, but a new generation must face forward.

Unhappily, there was little to indicate that the Johnson administration was inclined to face forward at this time, either in Europe or in Asia. With Acheson, McCloy and all the old hands feverishly engaged in trying to patch up NATO, Secretary Rusk addressed himself to the problem of China. His lengthy statement, delivered in closed session to the House Foreign Affairs Committee on March 16 and released to the press on April 16, was the first such pronouncement of policy made by an American Secretary of State since the days of John Foster Dulles. In fact, with due allowance for China's changed relationships and power-political position, it might have been Dulles speaking, except for a superficially more conciliatory tone and the fact that Rusk finally brought himself to refer to "Peking," rather than "Beiping," as the capital of China.

Reasserting the contention that China had been the aggressor in Korea, Rusk reaffirmed Washington's opposition to seating the Peking regime in the United Nations, as well as the American commitment to defend Formosa. Just as Acheson looked forward to the day when France would no longer be ruled by de Gaulle, so also Rusk expressed the hope that better relations might be established with China once a new regime had succeeded that of Mao Tse-tung. Until then, one gathered, there could be little if any change in United States policy.

It seemed to the writer unlikely that de Gaulle's passing

from the scene would restore the NATO alliance, and even more unlikely that Mao Tse-tung's eventual successors would follow an essentially different policy unless American policy were drastically altered.

PART TWO

WHAT WE HAVE LEFT UNDONE

11

Marx Versus Malthus—
The Threat of Hunger

The preceding chapters have dealt with power politics—with
the behavior of the United States as the most powerful nation
in the postwar world. We have seen how the United States
became obsessed with the fear of communism and devoted its
vast energies and resources to the attempted military containment of what it assumed to be a threat of world conquest by
a Sino-Soviet communist monolith. We have traced the mistakes caused by this obsession: the failure to bring newly discovered atomic energy under control and to deal with the
political problems which, if not solved, would bring about a
nuclear arms race; the failure to arrive at a European peace
settlement; the over-commitment of American power in Asia;
the bungling intervention in the Middle East; the neglect of
Latin America; and, above all, the debasement of such international law as existed by unilateral and illegal action.

We have not yet discussed the errors of omission which
flowed from the same myopic and unbalanced view of the
nature of the postwar world.

* * *

Nuclear war was not the sole threat to the survival of civilization. Less obvious when the war ended, but equally menacing was the specter of hunger and the growing discrepancy between the conditions of life existing in the industrialized and relatively affluent nations, inhabited by approximately one-third of the world's population, and the conditions faced by the remaining two-thirds of humanity inhabiting the less developed parts of the earth.

Half a billion people suffer today from inadequate quantities of food. Another billion subsist on improperly balanced diets, notably a shortage of protein. Three million children die each year from diseases caused by malnutrition. Millions of people go through life permanently crippled, physically and mentally, by inadequate nourishment. Malnutrition breeds human beings who are powerless to break out of ignorance, poverty and degradation and yet are able to breed children born to equal misery. And not only do they breed children, but modern medicine has prolonged the life-span by wiping out many of the plagues and diseases which used to decimate the populations of the food-deficit areas. *It is estimated that the world's population will double, from 3 billion to 6 billion, before the end of the century. And the greatest part of this fantastic population growth will take place in precisely those parts of the world where food supplies are already inadequate and where the prospects for increased food production are least favorable.*

Assuming that mankind does not exterminate itself through nuclear war, the world is headed for a crisis of mass starvation within the next thirty-five years—a crisis the political effects of which are unpredictable.

The problem is not insoluble. We have been witnessing an

explosion of knowledge as well as a population explosion. Progress in science and technology has made possible the production of sufficient food to meet human needs, especially if increased production is accompanied by education in family planning. As the challenge was expressed in the U.S. Department of Agriculture's *World Food Budget, 1970*, "the race is between what could be done and what will be done."

To date, very little has been done. Ten years ago, the writer urged not only that surplus food raised in the United States and other surplus-producing countries be used as "development capital" to assist the developing nations, but also that crop restrictions in the United States be abolished and that farmers be encouraged to grow food specifically for the needs of the food-deficit areas.[1] Since then, the Food for Peace Program has been developed and, under it, American surpluses have been used not only for famine relief but, more constructively, to promote economic development. Since 1954, the United States has distributed $15.4 billion worth of commodities to 114 countries, with the largest share going to India.

But crop restrictions are still in force. American taxpayers still lay out some $2 billion a year to pay farmers to withdraw acreage from production and to reduce crops. Farmers are leaving the land, and much of our finest cropland lies idle while hunger stalks through large parts of Asia and Latin America.

This is not to say that world food needs could be met if the United States and other food-surplus-producing countries produced the maximum of which they are capable. The prob-

[1] See Warburg, *Turning Point Toward Peace*, pages 13–16, reprinted in the *Congressional Record*, April 26, 1956.

lem is not as simple as that. We have been shipping about three million tons of wheat to India each year, but India consumes annually some eighty million tons of grain and will probably need twice that amount in thirty-five years. Even if we doubled our annual shipments, India's food problem would not be solved. It can be solved only by increased Indian food production. And this is where the United States could render invaluable assistance.

American farmers have enjoyed the benefits of modern technology, a healthy and reasonably well-educated rural population, and a government concerned for their welfare. They have been able to use modern machinery, fertilizers, pesticides, hybrid seeds and a plentiful supply of water to increase the productivity of their land. They have adequate credit and storage facilities, transportation and processing plants through which to bring their crops to market. Almost all these benefits are lacking for the food producers in the food-deficit areas, where most agricultural production remains as primitive as it was centuries ago. In part this is due to feudal land-ownership and the absence of credit facilities which combine to make peasants into serfs.

We have only very recently begun to think seriously of helping the food-deficit countries to modernize their agriculture. In 1965, Senator George McGovern of South Dakota introduced a bill entitled "The International Food and Nutrition Act." This measure would have authorized the United States government to spend $500 million in the first year: *first*, to purchase food in the American market for use overseas; *second*, to increase the capacity of the developing countries to receive and efficiently distribute such food; and, *third*, to strengthen the food-producing capacity of farmers in the

206

developing world. The bill would have authorized an increase of $500 million for these purposes each year over a seven-year period to a maximum of $3.5 billion. It would also have authorized a much-needed increased participation by the United States in the excellent work, done with minimal financial resources, of the United Nations Food and Agricultural Organization.

On February 10, 1966, President Johnson urged the Congress to authorize a five-year "Food for Peace" Program, with $3.3 billion a year devoted to financing "a worldwide war on hunger." His legislative proposals followed the general philosophy of the McGovern Bill but, in addition, authorized the vitamin-protein enrichment of farm production for use overseas, the return to cultivation of sixty million idle acres, a 10 percent increase in the 1966 acreage allotment for rice, and a shifting of part of American feed-grain production to soy beans. The proposed legislation would make it mandatory upon the President to take into account efforts by the beneficiary countries to increase their own food production and gradually to achieve self-sufficiency.

It remained to be seen whether Congress would follow this long-overdue constructive recommendation.

The United States has not been alone in almost ignoring this problem for the better part of the postwar period. In fact, the United States has done more than the governments and peoples of the other food-surplus-producing countries. American citizens have invented hybrid corn, new kinds of fertilizers, new seeds and new pesticides. Canada, Australia and New Zealand have supplied the world markets with substantial amounts of foodstuffs, but they have not been much concerned with helping the food-deficit countries. Nor have the surplus-producing countries of Western Europe shown much interest except in cases where it served their own political or economic interests.

Yet the problem is one which concerns the whole Western world and can be solved only by concerted and coordinated effort. A widespread sense of injustice is incompatible with stable peace; and hunger in two-thirds of the world while one-third of the world's population worries about getting too fat on high-calorie diets is perhaps the most explosive of all causes of revolutionary discontent.

Viewed from the standpoint of competitive coexistence between the communist and non-communist countries and their endeavors to secure the allegiance of the emerging peoples, there is no other field in which the non-communist countries could so easily demonstrate their superiority as in the growing and supplying of food. Communism, conceived as a revolution of the oppressed and exploited industrial workers of the world, has become a revolution of oppressed and exploited peasants in China and, to a lesser extent, in the Soviet Union. Yet the outstanding failure of communist governments has been in agricultural production, while the outstanding successes in food production have been achieved in the non-communist countries. While 70 to 80 percent of the population in communist countries is engaged in wresting a living from the soil, less than 10 percent of the American population produces more food than the people of the United States can eat. Nor is this superior agricultural productivity confined to the Western democracies; in Japan, an acre of wheat yields 2,450 pounds, as against about 760 pounds in less developed India. The superiority of non-communist countries in food production is perhaps the most convincing and the least used argument in the Cold War dialogue.

In its preoccupation with the doctrine of Karl Marx, the United States has until recently all but overlooked the more relevant Malthusian specter. In the face of mounting hunger, the United States has permitted the war against communism to bring it into alliance with feudal, land-owning oligarchies, where it should have been insisting upon land reform as a condition for American aid. If the war against hunger is lost, it will not be for lack of knowledge as to how it could be won; it will be because of lack of cooperative effort on the part of the developed nations which, in turn, has been largely though not wholly due to American preoccupation with a crusade waged with the wrong means and in the wrong places.

12

Aid to Economic Development

The Foreign Aid programs of the United States began with UNRRA, the loan to Britain in 1946 and an unprecedentedly generous grant of Marshall Plan aid to the recovery of Western Europe in 1947. The cost of the latter represented about 11 percent of the United States budget. The Marshall Plan was "sold" to Congress and to the American people partly as a moral debt which we owed to our Allies in World War II but chiefly as a means of arresting communist encroachment. And, indeed, the European Recovery Program proved a most effective instrument in saving Western Europe from an economic collapse which might well have resulted in a communist take-over. However, the Marshall Plan dealt with an area which had already been highly developed and required rehabilitation rather than development—an area in which there was keen awareness of the communist threat to long-established democracy and individual freedom. No such awareness could be taken for granted in the less developed areas of the world where people were struggling to emancipate themselves from age-old poverty and colonial exploitation, where there was no experience in democratic self-government and where individual freedom had never existed.

Once Western Europe was on the road to recovery, the foreign aid programs of the United States became explicit functions of the anti-communist crusade, designed primarily to build a dam against communist encroachment rather than to promote economic development. During the decade of the 1950's, American aid was given chiefly to countries on the periphery of the Sino-Soviet orbit which seemed exposed to communist penetration. Much of this aid was given to strengthen military defenses, either by outright provision of arms or by supplying funds to enable the countries concerned to support military establishments which they themselves could not afford to maintain. Military aid was in most cases accompanied by small amounts of economic assistance insufficient materially to forward development or to raise the living standards of the people concerned. Much of it flowed into the pockets of corrupt and reactionary ruling cliques. The net result in most cases was to give an emerging nation arms with which to fight but no cause for which to fight other than one which seemed remote and irrelevant.

In the Eisenhower-Dulles era, almost any government, no matter how tyrannical, corrupt and oppressive, could obtain a hearing in Washington for United States aid so long as it could show evidence of a communist menace and a determination to resist it. On the other hand, a staunchly non-communist and crucially important democracy like India was considered ineligible for American assistance because its government refused to join in the anti-communist crusade. Inevitably, in a program so conceived, there was wastage and lack of progress toward economic development. What was more, vitally important parts of the world were neglected either because, like India and Burma, they refused to align themselves with American policy or because, like Latin America, they did not seem immediately exposed to any communist menace.

During the 1950's, foreign aid was two-thirds military and only one-third economic. The total, amounting to less than half of one percent of the gross national product of the United States, was annually pushed through a somewhat reluctant Congress with bipartisan support on the grounds that it was an effective weapon in the Cold War. That small proportion of the aid program—usually less than one-third—which was not directly related to the Cold War was held to promote "free enterprise" and "democracy." "Buy American" strings were attached to economic assistance to promote American exports. Before this practice was generally adopted by the Kennedy administration in 1961 as a means of combatting the balance-of-payments deficit, the countries receiving economic aid from the United States were spending about forty cents of every American aid dollar in Western Europe, where many of the goods they needed were cheaper. Since "Buy American" strings have been attached to economic aid, the recipient countries are spending at least eighty cents of every American aid dollar in the United States.

By tying drastic "buy American" strings to foreign economic aid, the Kennedy administration thwarted its own efforts to liberalize trade and to induce an increasingly prosperous Western Europe to assume a greater share of the burden of aiding the development of the underdeveloped areas. Having fathered the creation of the Organization for

212

Economic Development (OECD) in order to coordinate assistance from the industrialized nations to the underdeveloped parts of the world, and having sponsored the liberalization of international trade by the Trade Expansion Act of 1962, the Kennedy administration set a bad example by tying its own aid to purchases in the American market. Since 1961, European contributions to development aid have increased, but they have mostly taken the form of individual bilateral efforts on the part of the West European nations to increase their own exports in competition with the United States. Since the primary aim of these programs has been to sell goods, some of them have tended to benefit the donor nation more than the recipient, with the donor often encouraging the recipient to put industrialization ahead of food production, to buy manufacturing plants and equipment not coordinated to any carefully worked out development program, and even to build airports desired solely for reasons of prestige.

So long as the industrialized nations each pursue their own programs of development aid, they are almost certain to compete, rather than to cooperate. In the United States, no less than in Europe, there is strong resistance to multilateral action. Each nation holds tenaciously to the belief that, if it pays the piper, it has the right to call the tune, while, in a multilateral program, its control over the use of its funds is diluted. The American Congress has until recently been unwilling to substitute multilateral development aid for bilateral action, but, thanks largely to Chairman Fulbright of the Senate Foreign Relations Committee, the mood of Congress has been changing. In presenting his foreign-aid program for 1965, President Johnson was able to state that 80 percent of United States development aid would be channeled through multilateral agencies, such as the World Bank and its subsidiary; regional institutions, such as the Inter-American Development Bank, or international consortiums such as that formed for aid to India. Nevertheless, progress in cooperation among the industrialized nations has been slow, and development aid has fallen far behind the need. An interesting report to the Joint Economic Committee of the United States Congress by Representatives Henry S. Reuss of Wisconsin and Robert F. Ellsworth of Kansas, presented on December 20, 1965, pointed out the need for strengthening the OECD and for giving it wider scope in coordinating not only development aid but also fiscal, monetary and trade policies among the Western nations.[1]

The growing need for such coordination had long been evident. In a book published in 1959, entitled *The West in Crisis*, the writer expressed the view that the disorganization of the Western world presented a greater obstacle to progress toward peace than communist aggression. Some progress had been made during the first two years of the Kennedy administration, only to have de Gaulle's nationalist obstructionism wreck the design of an effective Atlantic partnership. Once this had happened, in early 1963, a period of stagnation had set in during which Europe remained at Sixes (EEC) and Sevens (EFTA), while American initiative was almost wholly lacking. The Reuss-Ellsworth report pointed out the vital need of resuming forward motion toward tariff reduction, reform of the balance-of-payments system and coordination of development assistance, urging that the United States develop alternative strategies to meet whatever might be the outcome

---

[1] *Off Dead Center: Some Proposals to Strengthen Free World Economic Cooperation* (Washington, D.C., U. S. Government Printing Office, 1965).

of the battle between French nationalism and the "European-ism" of the five other members of the European Economic Community. It seemed unlikely that this struggle would wholly disrupt the Common Market; too much was at stake in its preservation for all concerned. But it was quite possible that de Gaulle's intransigence might transform the European Economic Community into an inward-looking protectionist customs union, instead of its becoming an outward-looking European community as planned by the Rome treaties. The Reuss-Ellsworth report performed a much-needed service in urging the United States government to make long-overdue preparations for either eventuality.

Apart from lack of coordination among the nations capable of rendering substantial development aid, there was a dangerously growing gap between the *amount* of such aid and the urgent needs of the developing nations. This was due to a number of causes: the niggardliness of the aid appropriations by the donor countries; the increasing burden of interest and amortization payments incurred on loans from the donor countries; the unstable world markets for raw materials produced by the developing countries; the displacement of some of these raw materials by synthetic products; and the unfavorable terms of trade which made it impossible for the developing nations to obtain enough for their exports of raw materials to pay for their imports of food and manufactured products.

In addition, much of the aid that was extended was squandered or found its way into the pockets of corrupt government officials and black marketeers. Fiscal reform was inhibited by ruling oligarchies and land reform was obstructed by absentee landlords, some of them left over from the colonial period. Some of these defects had been remedied by 1965, but, in

215

presenting his foreign aid program for 1966, President Johnson seemed unaware of the magnitude of the job that remained to be done. Reporting on January 17, 1966, on the previous year's program of $3.5 billion, he pointed with pride to the revamping and streamlining of foreign aid, saying that the program had shifted from "simply helping other countries to stay afloat to helping them become more self-supporting," which seemed to imply that he thought the developing countries had reached the point at which they could "take off." This was perhaps true of a very small number of countries, notably Israel, Spain and Formosa, but for most of the developing countries the take-off point was far off—in many cases further off than ever.

The President voiced his "deep concern" over "political unrest" and "an uncertain race between food supplies and population" in the developing countries, but failed to translate this "concern" into remedial action. Asking Congress for another appropriation of only $3.5 billion for the next twelve months, he pointed with satisfaction to the fact that eighty cents out of every aid dollar would be spent in the United States and that foreign aid had become "a smaller burden on our resources," representing only 3.5 percent of the Federal budget as compared with 11 percent when the Marshall Plan was in operation. He did not suggest that our vastly greater resources warranted a contribution on the order of the earlier effort. Out of the $3.5 billion, only $2.1 billion would be spent on development aid, since $1.4 billion was earmarked for military assistance. The $2.1 billion represented less than half of one percent of the nation's gross national product.

Only very recently, George D. Woods, president of the World Bank, had painted a very different picture of the state

216

of the underdeveloped countries, pointing out that they were steadily falling further behind the rich nations and that, as their hopes were frustrated, new and dangerous tensions were being generated. Earlier, on August 3, 1965, Woods had warned the delegates at an OECD meeting that the developing countries could "productively use" from $3 to $4 billion a year more than the $6 billion currently being provided by the donor governments. "Unless a major part of this existing gap is bridged, and on very easy terms," Woods said, "I believe that what lies ahead is an inevitable and a heart-breaking slowdown in economic development and even in international trade." Observing that the donor countries had long since adopted the goal of devoting one percent of gross national product to development aid, Woods noted that their contributions had remained at about $6 billion since 1961, in spite of growth in gross national products amounting to about $40 billion a year. If withdrawals of profits, dividends and interest were taken into account, Woods estimated that the contributions of the donor countries amounted to about six-tenths of one percent of their gross national products.

From the point of view of the developing countries, Woods said, aid had represented a declining amount per capita, due to an increase of 2 to 3 percent a year in their populations. Moreover, he pointed out that the developing countries as a group now had a total external debt of about $33 billion, on which amortization and interest payments came to about $3.5 billion a year. "These levels of debt service," Woods said, "are dangerously high. They mean that a good deal of the proceeds of new loans must be devoted to servicing previously contracted obligations, rather than being invested in new productive development. Indeed, when all service and dividend payments on both public and private investment are taken into account, the backflow from the developing countries off-sets about half the entire gross capital inflow which these countries receive from all sources."

Commenting editorially upon the President's January 17, 1966, statement to the Congress, the *New York Times* remarked with polite restraint:

> If the President means to cope with political unrest, potential famine and other problems that cause him "deep concern," then he faces the necessity of mounting a more effective and expansive program, something considerably bigger than the present minimal effort.

One could scarcely blame the peoples of the world for failing to understand how the world's wealthiest nation could set so miserable an example in its attitude toward the world's underprivileged peoples, while, at the same time, it was appropriating vastly greater sums to the prosecution of a brutal war against a small, underdeveloped country armed with little more than infantry weapons and an indomitable desire for independence and self-determination.

Nor could one blame the peoples of the world for wondering why it should seem more important to the American people to land a man on the moon than to help remedy the injustice and suffering on this planet.

For the past ten years, the writer has advocated the creation of a United Nations Development Authority with a governing body upon which both the donor and recipient nation would be represented. The plan, originally suggested in 1957, provided for regional subsidiaries by which projects would be screened and eventually recommended to the parent body. This proposal was endorsed by the Commission to Study the Organization of Peace in its Tenth Annual Report.

The proposal was put forward with three primary objectives in mind: *first*, to provide a channel for multilateral (as opposed to bilateral) aid to development; *second*, to create an instrument in which the recipients as well as the donors would have a voice as well as a proprietory interest; and, *third*, to strengthen the United Nations by making it the vehicle through which the nations of the world would cooperate in solving one of the world's most pressing problems.

With some modifications suggested by experience during the following decade, the proposal was again advanced in detail in 1965.[2]

Although no such plan has as yet been adopted, there has recently been somewhat more centralization of development aid in the United Nations as well as considerable progress toward converting bilateral aid programs into American participation in multilateral efforts to promote economic development. Thanks largely to Chairman Fulbright of the Senate Foreign Relations Committee, more and more of American development assistance is being channeled through international agencies such as the World Bank and its subsidiaries, or recently established regional banks, or international consortia.

On April 6, 1966, Senator Fulbright proposed certain amendments to the President's 1966 Foreign Aid Bill, designed, he said, "to isolate us from the political and possible military implications that attach to our present bilateral system of aiding developing countries." Bilateral programs, he said, often had "unfortunate side-effects," such as identifying

2 Warburg, *Time for Statesmanship*, pages 59–62.

the United States with certain political regimes in "situations that could grow into Vietnam-like involvements." Therefore, he proposed that the authorization make it mandatory that a larger part of American development aid be channeled through multilateral agencies.

Of equal if not greater importance is the fight which Senator Fulbright has waged to separate military aid completely from development assistance. While most of his Senate colleagues support Chairman Fulbright's view in this respect, the effort has met obstruction in the House of Representatives. Chairman Thomas Morgan of the House Committee on Foreign Affairs has insisted that he would be unable to obtain the necessary authorization and appropriations unless military and economic aid continued to be presented in a single package. (This illustrates the consequences of our government's having for years "sold" foreign aid as an essential weapon in the anti-communist crusade.)

Even if Senator Fulbright's commendable efforts succeed, they will not accomplish all that might be accomplished if all or most development assistance were channeled through a United Nations Development Authority. Multilateralization outside of the United Nations will not create an instrumentality in which all nations, whether providers or recipients of aid, will feel that they have a proprietary interest; nor will it create a forum in which the diverse nations of the world can learn to understand one another's variegated cultural and commercial idiosyncrasies which often frustrate a sincere desire to cooperate. (What seems "fair" and "realistic" to an industrialized nation may seem to a developing country incompatible with its national dignity or aspirations.) Finally, multilateralization of development assistance outside of the United

Nations will not strengthen the world organization as much as would the creation of a center for development programs within the United Nations itself.

Note

Since this chapter was written, there has been a most unfortunate development. Those members of the Senate Foreign Relations Committee who have most consistently favored increased and improved foreign aid have suddenly reversed their position, attacking the Johnson administration's proposals for 1966, not because they are inadequate but from a point of view which seems to be inspired by disagreement with the administration's foreign policy as a whole. A particularly regrettable amendment has been offered which would raise the interest rates on so-called "soft loans" for development. Other amendments would limit technical assistance and reduce the number of countries to which aid may be extended. Much as the writer sympathizes with most of the criticism leveled at the Johnson administration's foreign policy by the Senate Foreign Relations Committee, the emasculation of foreign aid seems a strange method of working toward a better foreign policy.

13

The United States and the United Nations

The United States took the lead in organizing the United Nations, the International Court of Justice, the World Bank and the International Monetary Fund. Its citizens have made meaningful contributions to the United Nations Specialized Agencies, and the American government has provided more financial support to the whole world organization than has any other member state.

Nevertheless, the United States has not consistently supported the principles upon which the United Nations was founded, nor has it carried out some of the obligations imposed by the United Nations Charter.

The Charter, which the United States helped to write, is international law so far as the member nations are concerned. We are not concerned here with whether it could be improved or modified.[1] We are concerned solely with attempting to

1 Though not an expert on international law, the writer has for many years been interested in studies of how the United Nations might be strength-

assess to what extent the United States has, since 1945, promoted or obstructed the purposes for which the United Nations was brought into being. Broadly speaking, these purposes were:

1. To prevent the outbreak of war between nations and to suppress violence when and if it should occur. This is usually called the "Peace-Keeping" function.

2. To promote peaceable settlement of disputes among nations which, if not settled, might lead to war. This is called the "Peace-Making" function.

3. To ameliorate and, if possible, to eliminate the social, political and economic causes of a widespread sense of injustice which will move men to violence. This is chiefly the function of the specialized agencies dealing with food, health, education and general social and economic development.

4. To provide a forum in which the nations of the world may be in continuing close contact, learn to understand one another's points of view and gradually evolve a universally accepted body of law that may eventually provide the basis for world government.

All four of these functions have been impeded by the Cold War.

So far as Peace-Keeping is concerned, the Cold War prevented the functioning of the military staff committee which, under the Charter, was intended to provide the United Nations with a force with which to suppress aggression; and

---

ened. He has greatly admired the pioneer work done by Grenville Clark and Louis B. Sohn, has attended many conferences at which the creation of a stronger world organization was discussed, and has served as a member of the Commission to Study the Organization of Peace for the past ten years. Much more work needs to be done in this area, but the subject lies beyond the scope of this study.

Cold War disputes over the respective authority of the Security Council and the General Assembly and over the financing of peace-keeping operations have imposed a severe handicap upon the Secretary-General. Nevertheless, the strong personalities of the three individuals who have held this office, plus the willingness of some of the countries not directly involved in the Cold War to supply troop contingents, made possible a number of successful peace-keeping operations, notably in Kashmir, Cyprus, West Irian and the Middle East. These were all cases where the U.N. was able to establish itself as a disinterested third party, which it was not able to do in the successful but controversial Congo operation. In Korea, aggression was repelled by the U.N. chiefly by the use of United States forces. In none of these successful operations was *peace-keeping* followed by successful *peace-making;* and the political problems which had caused the outbreak of hostilities remained unsolved. In fact, experience to date seems to show that peace-keeping alone—i.e., the establishment of a cease-fire and the withdrawal of forces to their pre-war positions—seems to have a tendency to freeze over the basic political problems and to make their solution appear less urgent.

The citizens' committees on Peace-Keeping and Peace-Making at the White House Conference in late 1965 made a number of interesting recommendations with regard to both of these functions of the United Nations, involving especially deeper and more continuous expert studies of international disputes, the training of mediators and the use of third-party mediation and advice.

These committees of private American citizens sharply criticized the United States for reserving the right not to accept as final the decisions of the International Court of Justice (the so-called Connally Amendment); and for similarly reserving "the option to make exceptions in supporting United Nations peace-keeping operations," if, in its view, "compelling reasons exist for doing so." The committee expressed the view that both reservations "shook the faith of the faithful and encouraged those seeking easy ways to avoid their responsibilities."

The committee on Peace-Keeping also noted with regret that the United States had as yet made no voluntary contribution toward defraying the U.N. debt of $100 million incurred through peace-keeping operations, although sixteen other member nations had contributed over $20 million, with the amounts ranging from Britain's $10 million to Uganda's $5,000. The committee urged the United States government to contribute $25 million. In the panel discussion, it was suggested that it was absurd for the United Nations to be hampered in its work by constant financial stringency and that Americans should realize that the entire expenses of the world organization came to less than one percent of the gross national product of the United States. (In reply, it was brought out that the U.S. government is prohibited by law from supplying more than 30 percent of U.N. expenses and that it would not be wise to let any one nation assume any greater responsibility. In the writer's opinion, the U.N. should be financed by a percentage tax on the gross national products of all the members, with the calculation of gross national products established by a universally agreed formula.)

The actions of the United States toward fulfilling the third major purpose of the United Nations—i.e., the amelioration of hunger, poverty, disease and ignorance—have been discussed in Chapters 11 and 12.

There remains the general attitude of the American government and of the American people toward the establishment of a world of law through the strengthening of the world organization. In this respect, the American government's attitude has been shockingly negative. A succession of postwar Presidents has paid lip service to the world organization but none, except perhaps Kennedy, has shown any inclination to make the United Nations the cornerstone of United States foreign policy. The same thing is true of a succession of Secretaries of State.

Under Truman, Byrnes paid practically no attention to the United Nations; Marshall respected but scarcely used the world organization; and Acheson expressed in more than one "private" conversation an open contempt for what he considered "a futile debating society." Truman's interventions in China and in Greece and Turkey were undertaken outside of the United Nations framework; and the whole Truman Doctrine amounted to a substitution of unilateral American action for collective action by the world organization. Granted that this was in part due to the paralysis of the Security Council caused by the Cold War split and the use of the Soviet veto, it was also clearly due to a disinclination on the part of the Truman administration to be bothered by the tedious process of consulting world opinion.

When Dulles became Secretary of State under President Eisenhower, he made no secret of his preference for regional organizations over world organization. He proudly boasted of his role in writing Article 51 of the U.N. Charter which authorized regional defense organizations; and his attempt to build a worldwide system of anti-communist alliances bore little relation to the creation of a world of law. The Dulles brothers' clandestine interventions in Guatemala and Iran

226

were violations of the U.N. Charter; and their attempt to convert Laos and South Vietnam into anti-communist allies contravened the Geneva Agreements which the United States had solemnly agreed to respect. There were only two major occasions when Dulles invoked the authority of the United Nations —occasions when other nations violated the Charter.

In the Suez crisis of 1956, which Dulles had to a very large extent precipitated, he invoked United Nations action against Great Britain, France and Israel. But no sooner had United Nations action overcome the crisis in the Middle East, than Dulles proceeded once more to take unilateral action in that area through the promulgation of the Eisenhower Doctrine and the landing of American troops in Lebanon.

In the same month of 1956, Dulles also invoked United Nations action against the brutal Soviet suppression of the Hungarian revolt, but in this case the United Nations was inhibited by the Soviet veto. (It was a debatable point whether the suppression of the revolt had actually been a violation of the U.N. Charter, since the government of Hungary had asked for intervention. The ruthless brutality of the intervention was another matter.)

The Kennedy administration committed a grave violation of the U.N. Charter in carrying out the Eisenhower plan for the clandestine invasion of Cuba. It undid the Dulles policy in Laos, but increased American involvement in Vietnam. Nevertheless, Kennedy, by his own personal attitude and his achievement of a partial test-ban treaty, strengthened rather than weakened the United Nations, especially in the manner in which he handled the Cuban missile crisis in 1962.

Unhappily, the same could not be said of the Johnson administration. The Cuban missile crisis of 1962 had involved a direct threat to the security of the United States and, under the provisions of the U.N. Charter, the United States was legally entitled to act unilaterally in its own defense. There was no such justification for the Johnson administration's intervention in the Dominican Republic; the Johnson administration not only violated the U.N. Charter but also the Charter of the Organization of American States (OAS), which forbids intervention for any cause whatsoever. In defense of this illegal action, the argument has been put forward that existing international law makes no provision for dealing with external assistance to subversive movements against established governments. This is true. It is also true that there has never yet been devised a satisfactory definition of external aggression. But the absence of law surely does not entitle the United States unilaterally to enact law to suit whatever it may consider its own national interests. Even if one could make a case for the unilateral assumption of global police power, the fact remains that a policeman *enforces* law —*he does not create it.*

The Dominican affair raised another question. The United States tried to cover its violation of the OAS Charter by obtaining the *ex post facto* sanction of its intervention by the other members of the OAS—an effort which achieved only limited success, as did the effort to internationalize the peace-keeping force through the addition of contingents from other Latin American nations. Subsequently, the United States tried unsuccessfully to induce the OAS to create a stand-by military force to deal with any further revolutionary movements suspected of being communist-directed. In thus endeavoring to create a semblance of legality for its illegal intervention (and for others that might be deemed "necessary" in the future), the Johnson administration embarked upon an extremely dangerous course.

Regional defense organizations authorized by Article 51 of the U.N. Charter are authorized to deal, if they can, with any threat to the peace arising in their respective areas. If they are unable to do so without enforcement action, they are compelled by the U.N. Charter to bring the matter before the Security Council which alone has the power to order peace-keeping intervention; or, if the Security Council fails to act, they can bring the matter up before the U.N. General Assembly under the "Uniting-for-Peace" Resolution of 1950. In seeking to make the OAS the vehicle for peace-keeping intervention in the hemisphere, in place of the United Nations, the United States, had it been successful, would have established a precedent which might logically have been followed by other regional organizations. Not counting the NATO and Warsaw Pact alliances or the moribund SEATO and CENTO alliances, there were two other regional organizations in existence: the Organization of African Unity (OAU) and the Arab League. Whereas it might be said that OAS intervention could reasonably be considered as third-party intervention, no such claim could be made on behalf of either OAU or the Arab League, the first being committed to the cause of black African versus white settler governments, and the second being committed to the destruction of Israel.

Thus, from every point of view, the United States intervention in the Dominican Republic ran counter to the avowed intention of the United States to help establish a world of law.

Finally, the United States, more than any other nation, has prevented the United Nations from becoming a universal organization. Ever since the Nationalist regime of China was overthrown in 1949, the United States has waged a stubborn and slowly losing battle to prevent the occupation of China's seat in the United Nations by the Peking regime. In so doing, it has prevented one-quarter of the world's population from being represented in what purports to be a world organization.

This is not the place in which to argue the case for seating the Peking government. The points to be made here are, quite simply, three:

1. No other major nation shares the determination of the United States to keep Peking from taking China's seat. The dwindling number of smaller countries that have voted with the United States in the past have done so less out of conviction than out of a desire not to offend Washington.

2. There can be no enduring peace without disarmament, especially nuclear disarmament. There can be no universal effectively enforced disarmament, or even any effective control of nuclear weapons, without the participation of China.

3. The China policy of the United States is without foundation in law or common sense. It increases Chinese hostility toward the West and blocks the road to peaceful coexistence, to the relaxation of political tensions and to peace.

The negative attitude of the government of the United States toward the creation of a world of law cannot be explained as a reflection of American public opinion, except perhaps with relation to China.

Opinion polls have shown a steadily growing majority support of the United Nations. It is true that there is a minority segment of American opinion that is hostile to the world organization, resents its presence on American soil, and suspects it of harboring communist spies and subversive elements. The Americans who feel this way, like the members of the "Know-Nothing Party" in earlier days, are basically xenophobic, and their dislike and suspicion of "furriners" has been magnified by the anti-communist hysteria of the McCarthy era. They constitute a disproportionately vocal minority,

230

often spurred on by irresponsible "public relations" characters who make a living out of organizing and raising funds for *ad hoc* committees and superpatriotic lobbies, some of them financed by Texas oil magnates and other wealthy businessmen. Some of these lobbies do influence a few Congressmen, but their impact is not strong enough to account for the ambivalence toward the United Nations of the Executive Branch. And it must be remembered that it was the Executive Branch —the White House and the Department of State—that embarked the nation upon an anti-communist crusade and indoctrinated its people with the virus of suspicion and fear.

The same thing is true to a very large extent with respect to China policy, except that in this case paid propaganda by the Nationalist regime on Formosa has actually succeeded in creating a substantial body of American opinion. Few of those who are the victims of this propaganda realize that it has been paid for by their own taxes—out of the money given or loaned by their government to the Chiang Kai-shek regime for military defense or economic development. The unfortunately little-publicized investigation of foreign lobbies conducted by Senator Fulbright in 1964 showed that a single American public relations agency (Hamilton Wright) received $300,-000 a year from 1957 through 1962 to "research, create and manufacture" news favorable to the Nationalist regime and to distribute such "news" without disclosing that it was paid propaganda.[2]

This brings us to an interesting question. If United States foreign policy does not reflect American public opinion, whose interests and whose ideas does it reflect?

---

[2] See Fred Cook, "Their Men in Washington," *The Nation*, March 30, 1964, pages 311–330.

PART THREE

WHAT WE CAN AND MUST DO

14

Who Makes Our Foreign Policy?

The Constitution of the United States empowers the President to conduct the nation's foreign relations except for two restrictions. The right to declare war is reserved to the Congress, and the President may sign treaties with other governments only with the advice of the Senate and the concurrence of two-thirds of the Senators present when a treaty comes up for a vote.

The first restriction has been diluted during the postwar period by Congressional acquiescence in the use of the President's power as Commander-in-Chief of the armed forces to involve the nation in the risk of war and, in two instances, in war itself. Truman did this in Korea. Johnson has done it in Vietnam. Eisenhower obtained Congressional resolutions authorizing him to do whatever he thought necessary for the defense of Formosa at the time of the Quemoy crisis, and again with respect to the carrying out of the Eisenhower Doctrine in the Middle East. In neither case, however, did he take the nation into war. Johnson, in taking the United States into an undeclared war in Vietnam, has relied upon a controversial interpretation of the SEATO Treaty and upon a resolution passed by Congress on August 10, 1964, authorizing him to take such reprisal action as he might deem wise against North Vietnam's attacks upon American warships in the Gulf of Tonkin. It is doubtful whether such resolutions actually give the President powers that he does not already possess as Commander-in-Chief, but they diminish the Constitutional role of Congress, especially when they are passed by near-unanimous votes and without serious debate.

The second restriction has frequently been circumvented by a device known as the Executive Agreement, by the use of which, instead of treaties, Presidents have avoided the necessity of obtaining Senate confirmation. Many of the worldwide arrangements for the containment of communism made by Dulles were contracted in this manner.

On the other hand, the President's foreign-policy-making prerogative has been diminished by the fact that the carrying out of most major foreign policies now requires the appropriation of large sums of public funds, and the Constitution made the House of Representatives the keeper of the public purse.

The result of these developments has been that Congress has had both a lesser and a greater influence upon foreign policy than the Founding Fathers intended. It has had a lesser influence than intended upon the broad direction of foreign policy, which has rarely been debated, and a greater influence upon the execution of policy through its control of the purse-strings.

Where major foreign policy decisions have been concerned,

Congress has acted throughout most of the postwar period in a wartime spirit of "closing ranks behind the Commander-in-Chief." Dissent has been muted, almost as if it were treason, and as if its expression meant "giving aid and comfort to the enemy." This has been particularly true since the McCarthy era, in which any form of dissent was equated with pro-communism.

Contrast this behavior with that of the British House of Commons, where, even in wartime, dissent is not equated with disloyalty. Thus, when Britain invaded Egypt in 1956, there was an uproar in Parliament and Prime Minister Eden was forced to resign. Again, in 1958, when British troops were landed in Jordan, there was a stormy full-dress debate in which the government of Prime Minister Macmillan narrowly escaped a vote of censure. Yet, when Congress was informed of the parallel landing of American troops in Lebanon, a single Congressman—Reuss of Wisconsin—arose in the House of Representatives to state that, in his opinion, this action was both unwise and dangerous, only to be gaveled down by the Speaker on the grounds that such comment was "inappropriate at the time." And, in the Upper Chamber, only a handful of Senators voiced their misgivings, while Democratic Majority Leader Lyndon B. Johnson assured the Republican President: "Whatever the future may hold in store for us, the American people will be united behind the President."

The difference between the behavior of the British and American legislatures is only in part the difference between Parliamentary and Presidential democracy. The absence in the United States of a counterpart to "His Majesty's Loyal Opposition" is due to a number of other factors. One of these is the dubious notion of "bipartisanship" in foreign policy. The idea that politics should "stop at the waterfront" in times of peace is an absurdity because foreign and domestic policies are inextricably intertwined. The domestic beliefs and behavior of a nation very largely determine its attitude toward the world beyond its borders; and conversely, the state of world affairs profoundly influences domestic developments. Bipartisanship stultifies the whole process of foreign policy development, depriving the party in power of responsible criticism and depriving the people of a choice between alternatives.

Another factor that tends to inhibit foreign-policy debate is the lack, in American politics, of a recognized leader of the opposition. A President defeated for re-election, or a defeated candidate for election, is called the "titular head" of his party, but he has no recognized right or power to lead his party, no means of exercising leadership, no nationwide organization to lead, and no funds except what private means he may possess with which to operate. (The writer suggested some years ago that the titular leader of a defeated party should be provided at public expense with a salary and equipped with the organization necessary to make his leadership of the opposition effective.

In the absence of national party organization, except for a few months in election years, and in the absence of a recognized leader of the opposition, leadership of the party out of power devolves upon its representatives in Congress; and, so long as the notion of bipartisanship in foreign policy prevails in Congress, little constructive action can be expected from that source.

In part, the lack of Congressional influence upon foreign policy derives from the manner in which both Houses are fragmented into a multiplicity of committees, each jealous of

238

its prerogatives and each dealing with only a limited aspect of national strategy and policy. Expenditures for the armed services are authorized by one Senate committee, while expenditures for foreign aid are authorized by another; the same thing is true in the House of Representatives. Moreover, in both Houses, the major committees tend to subdivide into subcommittees, with each subcommittee chairman jealously guarding his fiefdom. Then, after the authorization bills have been passed, the authorized expenditures go before the appropriations committees in both House and Senate, and only then does each chamber act. If the two Houses pass differing bills, the matter goes to conference, and both Houses must then approve the conference report.

It will be readily seen that this procedure tends to fragment discussion and debate, with various committees offering changes or amendments in their respective limited areas, while neither House normally deliberates upon national policy as a whole. As a result, the major lines of foreign policy are taken for granted unless a major crisis occurs, and, even then, it is likely that the crisis will be discussed without anyone questioning the policy which permitted it to arise.

One way to improve this legislative process might be for an annual joint session of both Houses to review foreign policy as a whole in connection with the President's messages on the State of the Union and the Budget.

Finally, a recently developed tendency to form coalition cabinets has given the President a high degree of immunity from criticism by his political opponents. By placing members of the opposing party in positions of great power and responsibility, a President can ward off much partisan criticism of his policy. In the Johnson administration, for example, a Repub-

239

lican Secretary of Defense and a Republican Ambassador to Saigon provide considerable protection for a Democratic policy in Southeast Asia which otherwise might become a partisan issue, as was the case with "Truman's war" in Korea.

All this does not answer the question: Who makes our foreign policy? It merely goes to show that informed debate in the Congress has had very little to do with shaping it. It may be hoped that this will change.

But if, until now, the postwar Presidents have been little influenced by Congressional debate of their foreign policies, who or what has influenced them?

Several Secretaries of State—notably Acheson and Dulles —have exerted a strong individual influence. But the Department of State as such has been woefully lacking in imagination and courage. Its tendency has been to stick to policies long after they have become obsolete, to oppose any change anywhere in the *status quo*, unless it be a change to a restoration of the *status quo ante*, and to be expert in showing why things *could not* be done, rather than ingenious in finding ways to do them.

This is not to say that the Department has not and does not contain many devoted, able and even brilliant public servants. But in Roosevelt's day, all but a few of these men were submerged by the President's tendency to be his own Secretary of State and to rely upon the advice of others outside of the Foreign Service. Then, in the Truman-Byrnes era, Byrnes rarely consulted his subordinates. Under Marshall and Acheson the Department began to come into its own, with many excellent younger men coming to the fore; but Dulles sacrificed many of the best of them on the altar of McCarthyism. Apart from this lamentable, morale-destroying action,

Dulles ran the Department as if it were a large law firm in which he was the senior partner and his associates merely junior partners, law clerks or office boys. It was small wonder that, when Kennedy became President, he found the Department slow, dull and lacking in initiative or imagination.[1]

Who, then, has influenced the foreign-policy decisions of the first three postwar Presidents?

Truman was originally influenced by Stimson, Byrnes, Harriman, McCloy, Forrestal and Lovett, later by Acheson and Marshall, and, throughout, by his respect for high-ranking generals and admirals.

Eisenhower was chiefly guided by Dulles, to some extent by McCloy, Lovett and General Clay. In addition, he was influenced by a number of big businessmen whom he admired much as Truman had admired the "Big Brass." Indirectly, Eisenhower's foreign policy was strongly affected by Treasury Secretary George Humphrey's McKinleyesque conservatism in fiscal affairs and by Defense Secretary Charles Wilson's philosophy, which held that "What's good for General Motors is good for the United States." (This could be extrapolated to mean "What's good for American business is good for the world.")

Kennedy, like Roosevelt, tended to be his own Secretary of State and collected a White House staff of extremely able foreign-policy advisers drawn largely from academic circles. Among these, McGeorge Bundy was the most important. The foreign-policy veterans Harriman, McCloy and, for a short time, Acheson were often consulted and occasionally assigned

[1] See Arthur Schlesinger, Jr., *A Thousand Days* (Boston, Houghton Mifflin Company, 1965), pages 406–448.

to special missions. Defense Secretary Robert McNamara, a Republican and a former president of the Ford Motor Company, probably had more influence upon Kennedy's foreign policy than Dean Rusk whom he chose as Secretary of State. Adlai Stevenson, who might have been Secretary of State had he not at the last moment sought the Presidential nomination for himself, occupied a curious half-in-and-half-out role in his capacity as chief delegate to the United Nations.

During his first years in office, Johnson was more concerned with domestic than with foreign affairs and showed a desire to leave foreign policy to the Department of State. Gradually, most of the Kennedy staff of foreign-policy advisers departed. Certain changes were made in the top personnel of the State Department, notably among the men responsible for Latin American relations. McNamara remained as Defense Secretary, with his influence upon foreign policy enhanced by the growing involvement of the United States in Vietnam. Harriman became Johnson's roving ambassador at large. McCloy remained a trusted consultant.

For the first time in many years, Congress became seriously concerned in 1965 over the direction of foreign policy. Chairman Fulbright and a number of other members of the Senate Foreign Relations Committee, as well as some other Senators and a substantial number of Representatives—most of them Democrats—criticized the Dominican intervention and expressed mounting concern over the course of the undeclared war in Vietnam, urging the President to seek a negotiated settlement. Other members of Congress, most of them Republicans or Southern Democrats, supported the warhawks in the Pentagon, demanding a further escalation of the conflict.

And, for the first time since the Korean War, the people

242

of the United States became concerned, showing their anxiety in "teach-ins," demonstrations, marches and letters to the editor. As might be expected, peace demonstrations evoked counter-demonstrations and, inevitably, charges of communist sympathy.

One may hope that the belated awakening of Congress and of certain sections of the public will influence the future actions of the Johnson administration, but this has nothing to do with the past. It leaves unanswered the question of what influences caused the United States to embark upon and to continue its ill-conceived postwar policy.

It so happens that the writer has been more or less well acquainted with most of the men who have advised the postwar Presidents on foreign policy. Some of these acquaintanceships date back to common service in the first administration of President Roosevelt. A few date back even further to the writer's days as an international banker in Wall Street. The list includes two former Secretaries of State: Acheson and Dulles. It includes Averell Harriman, Robert A. Lovett, John McCloy, James V. Forrestal, Adlai Stevenson and, on a less intimate basis, Secretary of State Marshall, General Lucius D. Clay and McGeorge Bundy. It includes also a considerable number of State Department officials, Senators and Congressmen.

From the search for a common denominator among the men whom the writer has known well, the following picture emerges:

All of these men were or still are devoted public servants. All of them belonged or belong to the nearest thing there is to an American aristocracy. Before they became public servants, some were lawyers with international reputations; some were bankers or directors of railroads and large corporations. Most of them had connections with their counterparts in European countries. Without exception, they were graduates of Ivy League universities, Europe-oriented and not particularly well informed about other parts of the world. Most of them were or are men who can talk easily to the ruling groups in other countries but are less at ease and less well acquainted with the hewers of wood and the drawers of water in their own country or in other parts of the world. Generally speaking, they are urbane, progressive-minded conservatives, neither radical nor reactionary. Taken as a whole, the group could easily be equated with a comparable group of British Oxonians or Cantabrigians, except that a similar British group would have grown up with a wider knowledge of the world and with less experience in business.

Only three of these men had ever run for elective office. Stevenson had been an extremely successful Governor of Illinois and had twice been the Democratic nominee for the Presidency. Harriman, after serving in various high offices under Roosevelt, had been elected Governor of New York and had been unsuccessfully promoted by Truman for the Democratic nomination for President in 1956. Dulles had been an unsuccessful candidate for the Senate from New York.

Dulles was the only one in this group who had throughout his life aimed at high public office, assiduously preparing himself some day to become Secretary of State, an office which had been held by his grandfather, John Foster, and by his uncle, Robert Lansing. The fact that Stevenson's grandfather had been Vice President of the United States may have inclined him to enter politics, but he eventually did so with ambivalent feelings—with a desire to serve rather than to attain prom-

244

inence. All the others left well-established career
business or the practice of law to serve their co
ever way they might. Acheson, had he not bee
politics by Roosevelt as Under Secretary of the
office for which he was not well equipped, might easily ...
become a distinguished Justice of the Supreme Court. Harriman, had he not been similarly drafted into the New Deal,
could have excelled in any number of fields of activity in which
he was interested. Born to great wealth, Harriman was never
satisfied with being the son of a well-known father. Out of
sheer determination to excel at whatever a restless spirit moved
him to tackle, he had become in turn a Yale oarsman, an
international polo player, a shipping magnate, a prominent
banker, chief executive of the country's most successful rail-
road system, the originator of high-speed diesel-powered
trains, and the founder of the Sun Valley ski resort.

In the best sense of the word, all these men were amateur
public servants. Dulles was the only careerist among them.

What about the influence brought to bear upon foreign
policy by these presidential advisers?

First, as to the Cold War:

Among the men who advised Truman at the beginning of
his administration, only Harriman had any intimate knowledge
of Russia. (There were, of course, others among the professional diplomats, such as George Kennan, "Chip" Bohlen and
Llewellyn Thompson who were or later became "Kremlinolo-
gists," but these were not in the group under discussion.)

As a businessman and financier, Harriman had been one of
the earliest American investors in the Soviet Union. As Roosevelt's ambassador to Moscow during the latter part of World

War II, he had dealt with Stalin and the top Soviet leaders. As an unabashed capitalist, he had earned Stalin's confidence and respect through his firmness, patience and intelligence. When Truman took office, it was natural that Harriman's advice should be sought.

The writer is convinced that it is *not* true that Harriman instigated the Cold War or the anti-communist crusade. He did strongly advise Truman to be firm with Stalin over Poland, but his object was to establish a basis of cooperation with Russia in the postwar world—not to undo what Roosevelt had done at the Yalta Conference (which Harriman had attended) but to see that the Yalta Agreements were carried out.

In the writer's opinion, the men who were chiefly responsible for starting the Cold War and the anti-communist crusade were Truman, Byrnes and Forrestal. Those mainly responsible for carrying on this policy were Acheson and Dulles, the latter with assists from Admiral Radford, Richard Nixon and Joseph McCarthy. However, an important distinction should be drawn between Acheson and the Republican Cold War warriors who followed after him.

Acheson sought primarily to contain the Soviet Union in Europe, not to extirpate communism. He considered it futile to negotiate with Stalin and was convinced that the Soviet leader would eventually be forced to yield to superior Western strength. The weakness of his policy consisted in unwillingness to negotiate when a position of strength had been achieved. Acheson was in no way responsible for Truman's intervention in China; this was undertaken before Acheson became Secretary of State. Acheson may have been partly responsible for the Korean War, but before that outbreak, he

246

favored the liquidation of American involvement in Chinese affairs.

Dulles and his cohorts, on the other hand, aimed at wiping communism from the face of the earth. Dulles believed and repeatedly stated that both the Russian and Chinese communist regimes would perish as the result of their inherent weakness and iniquity—a sort of Marxist philosophy in reverse. (The Marxists believed that capitalism would destroy itself because of its inherent "contradictions.") Pending what he saw as the inevitable triumph of "freedom," Dulles extended the Cold War and the anti-communist crusade to Asia and the Middle East, endeavoring to encircle the entire Sino-Soviet orbit with containing military power.

Dulles was an ideological and moral dogmatist; as such, he catered to the communist witch-hunt in the United States, sacrificing such able China experts as John Paton Davies, John Service, John Carter Vincent and O. Edmund Clubb. Acheson, on the other hand, openly deprecated Truman's Loyalty Order of 1947, rejected the doctrine of guilt by association and courageously refused to "turn his back on Alger Hiss."

Second, as to Germany:

Among the presidential advisers mentioned, McCloy and Lovett supported Secretary Stimson and Secretary Hull in their vigorous opposition to the Morgenthau Plan for the "de-industrialization" of Germany after its unconditional surrender. Nevertheless, parts of this plan crept into the directive given to General Eisenhower and subsequently found their way into the ill-fated Potsdam Agreement.[2]

2 See Warburg, *Germany—Bridge or Battleground*, pages 15–26.

In 1948–1952, McCloy strongly supported Acheson's plan for the creation of a separate West German state in which he eventually became United States High Commissioner. Harriman, too, supported this program. Both McCloy and Harriman backed the rearmament of West Germany. During these years, McCloy was an ardent supporter of Chancellor Adenauer.

From 1953 to 1959, Dulles continued Acheson's policy. He, too, was a great admirer of the German Chancellor and, together with him, blocked all efforts to negotiate a German settlement.

If, as the writer happens to think, the postwar policy of the United States with respect to Germany consisted of a series of blunders, the chief responsibility for these blunders rests upon the pre-surrender planners under Roosevelt and Churchill, upon Acheson and Dulles and, to a lesser extent, upon McCloy and General Clay. (Clay was largely responsible for Eisenhower's support of Dulles-Adenauer intransigence.)

In contrast to the public interest in the question of China, there was little such interest in German policy either among the American people or in Congress. The press featured the recurring crises over Berlin and the failures of the successive four-power conferences, but it was impossible for critics of the German policy, such as the writer, to obtain more than a polite hearing. Where it would have been politically difficult for Truman or even Eisenhower to change an American China policy with which few people outside of the United States agreed, there was no such domestic obstacle to changing a German policy.

Perhaps one reason for the general American acquiescence in the Acheson-Dulles-Adenauer German policy was that the American banking and business community had strong ties to and interests in German industry. Dulles himself had in the past represented a number of German concerns in the United States. To call attention to this fact implies no self-interest in what Dulles did as Secretary of State. It merely illustrates the predilection of American Big Business for cooperation with its German counterparts.

Third, as to foreign aid and especially aid to the under-developed areas:

The Europe-oriented, capitalist-minded nature of the group of presidential advisers under discussion made its impact on aid to Western Europe highly constructive and important. Acheson, more than any one individual, was responsible for developing the concept of the Marshall Plan. Harriman chaired the main study committee. Marshall, Acheson and Harriman were chiefly responsible for getting Truman to act more expeditiously in aiding Europe and for driving the European Recovery Program through Congress.

When it came to aiding the non-industrialized countries of Asia, the Middle East, Africa and Latin America, this particular group of presidential advisers was, as might be expected, less effective and less of a factor. Acheson favored the idea of the Point Four Program but was not very deeply concerned for its effective implementation. Dulles distorted the entire foreign-aid effort into an instrument of the Cold War. Neither Truman nor Eisenhower possessed any great understanding of the anti-colonial revolution of rising expectations; nor were these two Presidents capable of translating their undoubtedly strong humanitarian instincts into constructive action with respect to societies whose nature, needs and aspirations they did not understand. Hence, neither of them attracted to their administrations advisers who knew these countries and recognized the importance of aiding their development.

It remained for the Kennedy administration to begin to emancipate American foreign policy from its anti-communist obsession, to reverse the priorities of military and economic assistance, and to attract to Washington and the Foreign Service men, such as Chester Bowles, J. K. Galbraith, Walt Rostow, David Bell and Richard Goodwin, whose hearts were in the job of aiding and guiding the revolution of rising expectations.

Fourth, as to disarmament:

Three members of the group of advisers we have been discussing performed notable services in this area. Acheson devised with David Lilienthal, then Chairman of the Atomic Energy Commission, the so-called Baruch Plan for the international control of atomic energy. It was not Acheson's fault that the proposal came too late and that it was presented in precisely the manner against which Stimson had warned.

McCloy was instrumental, under Kennedy, in getting organized the Agency for Arms Control and Disarmament. In addition, he negotiated with the Soviet Union the first meaningful agreement as to the principles of disarmament. (The McCloy-Zorin agreement of September 1961.)

Harriman successfully undertook for Kennedy the difficult task of negotiating a partial test-ban treaty with the Soviet Union.

The individuals described from first-hand knowledge in this chapter are fairly representative of a larger group of bankers, industrialists, businessmen, lawyers and educators who are now and then consulted informally by the White House. Some two hundred of these prominent citizens, in various parts of the country, most of whom are on first-name terms with each other and communicate with each other by telephone, might appropriately be called "The Establishment." They are closely connected to the nation's major corporate interests and, perhaps more important, to its major universities; they are on the boards of the major foundations. Yet their collective influence is, in a curious way, more social than economic.

The Establishment contains few mavericks. For the most part, its members "go along with" the administration's foreign policy, irrespective of whether a Republican or a Democrat inhabits the White House. Members of the Establishment occasionally offer suggestions, but rarely express outright dissent or criticism.

The Establishment is basically hostile to government intervention in what its members like to think of as a free market economy, except when such intervention serves their particular interests. The Establishment frowns in principle upon government-planned or government-directed economies in other countries; but most of its members have realized over the postwar years that some degree of government planning and direction is inescapable, especially in countries where there is little or no accumulation of private capital and no experience in "free enterprise."

One might say that Eisenhower was a typical Establishment President, perhaps a little but not much to the Right of the Establishment's views. His stag dinners at the White House were, for the most part, typical Establishment affairs. (Truman had very little to do with the Establishment. Kennedy

251

was in a way part of the Establishment but not much influenced by it.)

The Establishment's views can perhaps be crudely summarized in the dictum: "The business of the United States is business."

Overlapping the Establishment, but with a separate identity of its own, is the "Industrial-Military Complex" whose growing influence President Eisenhower warned against in his valedictory. This complex is an agglomeration of private and public (i.e., government) enterprise. It consists of business executives in the defense industries, many of whom are retired generals and admirals, research institutions maintained by the defense industries, and other research groups subsidized or wholly supported by the government. It is perhaps unfair to say that this complex has a vested interest in *not* making peace; indeed, some members of the complex have contributed notable studies to the problem of cushioning the economic effects of disarmament; but the net impact of the complex has been to increase the reliance of the postwar administrations upon military power in the shaping of foreign policy, thus tending to obscure and prevent the much-needed study of political solutions. The writer would go so far as to say that the government's hiring of research groups in the country's leading universities has tended to dry up an important source of critical analysis of foreign policy and to make some of our institutions of learning into factories of rationalization for policies that would benefit from sharp academic dissent.

The recent outburst of academic criticism of the war in Vietnam is a hopeful sign, but it is a notable fact that most of the leaders of this movement of dissent have been linguists, historians and social scientists rather than political scientists—

that is to say, faculty members not involved directly or indirectly as advisers to the government.

Another hopeful sign has been the recent active participation of the religious leaders of various denominations in the movement of dissent. Until the escalation of the war in Vietnam, such participation had been the exception rather than the rule, with the majority of churchmen standing aloof from political controversy, leaving unto Caesar the things that are Caesar's. There have been notable exceptions throughout the postwar period but, on the whole, it has taken a combination of the civil-rights revolution and the war in Vietnam to mobilize religious leadership as an important influence upon United States policy.

Conclusions

1. The postwar foreign policy of the United States has been motivated less by constructive purpose than by reaction to the actions and assumed intentions of communist leadership.

2. The largely defensive postwar policy has been shaped, not by any true democratic process but by the interplay of Executive power (Truman, Acheson, Dulles); of economic, ethnic and sectional special-interest groups; of foreign-government propaganda (China, Germany); and of an Establishment closely related to the Military-Industrial Complex. The latter includes the Central Intelligence Agency. (It is impossible for an outsider to judge to what extent the clandestine operations of the CIA have merely carried out policy or actually influenced its direction.)

3. From 1945 through 1962, the Cold War acquired a momentum of its own, almost wholly uninfluenced by critical

analysis based upon evaluation of changing circumstance. This momentum seemed to have been halted by the Kennedy administration in 1963, but appears to have been resumed under President Johnson.

15

Whose View of Us Is Correct? One Man's Verdict

Ignorance is only rarely an excuse for wrong or stupid action, or for failure to act in the face of urgent need or great opportunity. But, while ignorance is no excuse, there is sometimes an excuse for ignorance.

In part, the ignorance of the American people concerning their fellow inhabitants of the earth is their own fault, as indicated in the preceding chapter. But, in another sense, it has been the fault of a government which, during most of the post-war period, has not only withheld vitally important information from its people but has passed out misleading "information," and, instead of explaining foreign policies, has "sold" them to the people and to their representatives in the Congress by appeals to suspicion, hatred and fear, rather than by an appeal to reason.

The policy of secrecy, of non-disclosure and of dishing out unwarranted reassurance, instead of providing factual information, destroys the very foundation of democracy, which is an alert and informed citizenry. It creates waves of apathetic complacency alternating with waves of hysterical fear, instead of a public opinion based upon comprehension and reason.

During the Truman-Eisenhower period, it was often impossible for an informed observer to recognize the world as portrayed by the highest officials of his government, especially when Secretary Dulles boasted of the "successes" of his diplomacy which had patently been failures, and when he confidently predicted the impending overthrow of communist governments.

Writing more than a century and a quarter ago, Alexis de Tocqueville, that amazingly shrewd observer of the American scene, warned against the coming of that time in America when "each individual man becomes more like all the rest, more weak and more insignificant," and when government acquires the habit of "ceasing to notice the citizens, to consider only the people, and of overlooking individuals to think only of their kind."

When the government of the United States ceases to respect the individual citizen and treats the American people as a faceless mass to be collectively manipulated rather than individually informed, then American democracy is in danger. Once the pluralism of a democratic society is forgotten, the people break up into a series of mobs, and a mob can be easily taught to fear, to hate and to kill; but only individual man is capable of reason, love and compassion.

Surely there are enough factors in a centralized, mechanized, corporation-dominated modern society that unavoidably tend to depreciate the individual citizen, without adding the fatal denigration of his dignity and worth by denying him the right to know the facts concerning the complicated and danger-fraught world in which he lives.

This is a matter which deserves President Johnson's earnest consideration, if he wishes to gain the full support of the American people in his admirable efforts to create the Great Society at home and to bring peace to the world.

There is another lesson to be learned. It is bad enough when a government deceives its own people by misinforming them as to the facts of its overt action. It is infinitely worse when the government of a democracy countenances and supports a secret organization which, with vast unnumbered sums of the tax-payers' money at its disposal, is permitted to engage in clandestine operations all over the world under the guise of existing solely to procure intelligence. The Central Intelligence Agency was the child of the Office of Strategic Services, an organization created for the purposes of espionage, subversion and counter-intelligence in wartime, as well as for the procurement of information relevant to the conduct of the war. It has been permitted to continue its existence in time of peace with vastly increased manpower and resources, not fully supervised, as are the armed services, by Congress. It has engaged in activities contrary to international law and to the treaty commitments of the United States in overthrowing or attempting to overthrow governments considered unfriendly to the United States. No one knows to what extent its secret operations have been sanctioned by the President. (President Eisenhower did not appear to know that a spyplane was traversing the Soviet Union and taking pictures of its secret installations at the time of the Paris Conference of May 1960. President Kennedy was told only a part of the plan for the invasion of Cuba's Bay of Pigs.) American citizens have no means of knowing where the CIA is operating and for what purposes.

No one would deny that it is necessary for governments to base their policies upon carefully evaluated intelligence concerning all the areas of the world in which they are interested. Nor would anyone deny that, when the world is in a state which is neither one of war nor one of peace, all governments find it necessary to preserve a certain amount of secrecy; and that this, in turn, invites espionage. Until peace under law is established throughout the world, espionage and counter-espionage are ugly but unavoidable facts of international life.

But it is one thing to employ secret agents to ferret out intelligence, and quite another thing to maintain a secret organization to engage in clandestine subversive activities in other countries. The one is an accepted practice, in which most governments indulge and expect others to indulge. The second is a form of warfare which, even in the present twilight zone between war and peace, is both illegal and highly dangerous. The fact that other governments, notably communist governments, engage in this type of covert activity is, in the writer's judgment, no excuse for the United States to indulge in similar illegal practices that are wholly inconsistent with its avowed aim of establishing peace under law.

From a purely pragmatic point of view, it is unwise to entrust the same secret organization with the procurement of intelligence and the carrying out of clandestine operations based upon that intelligence. As wartime experience should have taught us, and as the Bay of Pigs fiasco should have proved, combining intelligence procurement with secret subversive operations in the same organization and under the same command produces both bad intelligence and bad planning.

Finally, the U-2 incident in 1960 and the Bay of Pigs disaster in 1961 illustrate how such operations, when discovered, tend to discredit the highest and most trusted officials of our government. In one case, the Department of State was caught in a series of flat lies; in the other, our greatly respected Ambassador to the United Nations was placed in the invidious position of innocently supporting a CIA "cover story" which, within a few hours, was exposed as utter falsehood.

To say that the American people have been uninformed or misinformed, that American foreign policy has not been shaped by any democratic process, that, indeed, so far as foreign policy is concerned, the democratic process has been suspended—to say all this is not to exonerate the American people. The majority of American citizens have been too concerned with their own private affairs to notice, much less to protest against, being manipulated rather than consulted. And yet, the writer has enough confidence in the inherent common sense and decency of the American people to believe that, if they had been given or had demanded a voice in shaping their government's postwar foreign policy instead of suffering themselves to be indoctrinated and led like sheep, the resulting postwar policy might not have been much wiser at the beginning, but its unwisdom would probably not have become frozen into inflexibility for so long a period.

Foreign critics might well take into consideration the enthusiasm with which Americans reacted to the constructive reversal of their government's policy by President Kennedy, and their overwhelming vote, in 1964, against the belligerent, undiscriminating anti-communism of Barry Goldwater. And foreign critics should note that, when a President whom they had elected as a man of peace took them into war, the American people and some of their leading representatives in the Congress began—belatedly to be sure—to call their President to account. These considerations do not excuse the past, but they provide some reason for keeping an open mind as to the future.

So far as criticism emanating from other Western democracies is concerned, the writer does not believe that any other Western democracy, except possibly Sweden with its tradition of progressivism and neutrality, would have done any better or even as well as the United States during the postwar period, had that other nation possessed the unrivaled military and economic power possessed by the United States at the conclusion of the war. Not just the United States, but the whole of Western civilization has been progressively perverted by greed and lack of consideration, by nationalistic competition instead of international cooperation, and by the brutalization of the human spirit spawned by modern war.

Within the memory of men now living, wars between Western nations were still fought with a certain amount of chivalry toward the enemy and with consideration for civilian life. But, within the last fifty years, Western man has invented air power, napalm and weapons of mass murder and destruction, using them more and more indiscriminately against whole populations and against peoples unable to retaliate in kind. The American people share in this shame, but they are not alone. The two great wars of the century were generated in Europe. In World War II, one supposedly civilized Western European nation set out to conquer the world, began the bombing of sleeping cities and the murder of hostages, and resorted to genocide in seeking to establish its people as the "master race."

In the writer's judgment, the peoples of the Western world, and especially the peoples of Western Europe, are not entitled to find much fault with the American people. The United States has made mistakes in its European policy, chiefly with respect to Germany, but the United States twice saved Western Europe from German conquest and twice helped it to repair the ravages of wars generated in the Old World.

Latin Americans, on the other hand, may justly complain of neglect and lack of sympathetic understanding during the postwar period. They may justly resent the economic imperialism of North American business interests. And, above all, they have every right to condemn United States intervention in Guatemala, Cuba and the Dominican Republic.

For the native African peoples, Liberia is a constant reminder of the fact that the United States once imported Africans as slaves, practiced slavery for more than a century and still has not given its Negro citizens full equal rights and opportunity. And black Africa resents, not without some justice, American business investments in racialist South Africa and, until recently, American support (for Cold War reasons) of the remnants of European colonialism. Development assistance and the work of the Peace Corps have mitigated these resentments, and much of the recent improvement in American relations with the newly independent African states can be ascribed to the tact and sympathy displayed by Adlai Stevenson as United States Ambassador to the United Nations.

Asians have every right to criticize American postwar policy, beginning with the atom-bombing of Japan, American intervention in China and continuing through various phases to the current war in Vietnam, with its brutal use of air power

261

and napalm by white men against Asians.

Most of American postwar policy must, in fact, seem quite incomprehensible to the majority of Asian peoples. They know that China was our ally and Japan our enemy in World War II; that Japan attacked both China and the United States, while China later intervened against the United States in Korea only after American armed forces marched up to China's most sensitive frontier. Yet they see how the United States has made peace with Japan and wisely aided its recovery, while pursuing a policy of implacable hostility toward China simply because a corrupt and incompetent Kuomintang government was overthrown by a communist revolution.

To most Asians, the American anti-communist obsession is incomprehensible. They see no threat to the security of the United States arising from the Chinese revolution, nor any threat to their own security. They fear Mao's China, not because it is communist, but as they would have feared the China of Chiang Kai-shek as the most powerful nation in Asia and as the inheritor of the expansionist tradition of the Middle Kingdom.

Indians do not understand why, if the United States was so determined to contain communism, it showed so little interest during the Truman-Eisenhower years in helping their democratic country with its more than 400 million people to grow strong; nor why their refusal to align themselves with an anti-communist crusade that made no sense to them should have created hostility on the part of the United States. They resented American arming of Pakistan as a supposed ally in that crusade, fearing that Pakistan wanted arms primarily to strengthen itself against India. In recent years, some of these resentments have been diminished by American military aid

262

when China invaded Indian territory in 1962, by generous American food shipments and by belated large-scale assistance to India's economic development. But the memory lingers.

Thailand is probably the only Asian country which sympathizes with the United States in its war against the communists in Vietnam. Its government is a military dictatorship. South Korea's American-supported government has sent the only Asian troop contingents to fight alongside of the American forces. Most of the Asian peoples, and particularly the people of Japan, are alienated by the escalation of the war and fearful of its consequences.

There is not a single Asian nation whose people support the United States in its determination to ostracize the People's Republic of China and to prevent Peking from taking China's seat in the United Nations. Those few governments of Asian countries which have voted with the United States in the United Nations probably do not reflect the majority sentiment of their people. This is true even of the native Formosans under the rule of the Chinese Nationalist regime who are not pro-communist, and do not wish to be handed over to the Peking regime.

If the United States wishes to retain any influence at all in Asia, there are two things it must do:

1. End a war in Vietnam which is increasingly becoming a white man's war against Asians; and

2. Adopt a less implacably hostile policy toward the People's Republic of China.

There is still a great opportunity for the United States to help Asia in the fight against hunger and to assist its economic development. This opportunity will be lost, unless the United States ceases, in its fear of communism, to act as a counter-revolutionary force, imagining itself to be the protector of Asian freedoms which have never existed.

Finally, what we do or fail to do here at home in granting equal rights and equal opportunity to our own Negro citizens will eventually affect our influence in Asia, Africa and in every corner of the world. The notion of white supremacy is the last hated symbol of the dying age when Western man ruled supreme.

Are we, then, what we think we are—a true democracy—a country with an economy based upon free enterprise in a free market—a nation dedicated to the cause of freedom throughout the world?

Or are we what others seem to think we are—a democracy in name only—a country in which monopoly capitalism has made a mockery of free enterprise—a nation more concerned with property rights than with human rights and more interested in preserving the *status quo* than in aiding peaceable change?

The answer, in this writer's opinion, is that neither picture is wholly correct.

1. *We are not a democracy in name only, but our democracy is imperfect, especially so in the formation of foreign policy.*

At home, except for the exclusion of Negro citizens from the democratic process, now at long last being remedied, we have what might be called a good infrastructure of democracy. That is to say, we have a system of established law and custom which assures different political parties, interest groups and individuals the right to state their views and to have them weighed against the views of others. (Admittedly, some interest groups and a few individuals have a disproportionate power to make their voices heard but, broadly speaking, we have government by discussion and debate.)

In foreign-policy formation, this has not been the case. Since the ordinary citizen has not been educated to have a sense of belonging to the human race analagous to his very definite sense of belonging to the nation, and since there is as yet no solid framework of international law and no true international community, the ordinary American citizen has only a nationalistic frame of reference within which to consider questions of international relations. Thus, when the United States finds itself in a conflict of interest or opinion with another nation, the ordinary citizen thinks chiefly in terms of patriotic loyalty, holding his own government to be "right" and the foreign adversary to be "wrong."

This leads to an authoritarian formation of foreign policy, with the people more or less blindly supporting a foreign policy determined by a small group of individuals in the Executive Branch of their government. And this, in turn, leads—since all governments make mistakes and are reluctant to admit them—to false rationalization supported by distortion of fact on the part of the policy-makers. In the end, the authoritarian policy-makers tend to become the victims of their own propaganda, believing their distortions of fact as if they were the truth. This happens in other democracies and not only in the United States.

People in foreign countries should be aware that there has always been an outspoken minority of American citizens who have not hesitated to express a lively dissent from foreign policies which appeared to them unwise or unjust. At times, this dissent has been muffled but never entirely stilled. Just recently, widespread citizen participation in the Negro revolution has led by a sort of osmosis to widespread demonstrations against the war in Vietnam which, hopefully, may cause the Johnson administration to reconsider its course. However, it must be admitted that, throughout most of the postwar period, the democratic process has had little impact on the international behavior of the United States.

2. *It is true that our economy is not free from monopolistic restriction nor from government intervention; and that "free enterprise" exists to only a limited extent for the individual.* But it does exist for the corporate agglomerations of individuals only a few of which are regulated in the public interest. We have not made a mockery of free-enterprise capitalism, but we have only just begun to learn how to harness its energies to serve the greatest good of the greatest number. Indeed, we have progressed further in this direction than all but a few other nations. The fact that our huge productive capacity is self-centered and directed chiefly toward providing affluence for our own people may not be admirable, but the same criticism may be leveled at all national economies in a world still anachronistically divided into national compartments. Granted that we could produce more for others without producing less for ourselves, especially if we reduced the huge sums we spend for "defense," what other nation has done more to share its prosperity than the United States?

3. *It is true that, in our dealings with other nations and peoples, we are often more concerned with property rights than with human rights.* Remember our business-dominated attitude toward the Cuban revolution, the aborted Dominican revolution, and toward such mineral-rich countries as the Congo and South Africa, where there is heavy private Amer-

266

ican investment. Nor can it be denied that our businessmen's desire to make profits in foreign countries has combined with our anti-communist phobia to make us into defenders of the *status quo* in many countries where our own revolutionary heritage as well as our professed principles should cause us to support progressive change.

But, as a nation and as a people, we are not neo-colonialists in the sense of wanting to stake out an empire over which to exercise political control. (This could more correctly be said of the Soviet Union and China.)

The fact is that, throughout the postwar period, we have been a powerful yet absurdly frightened nation, a nation that has committed itself to the foolish notion that a repugnant ideology can be contained by military means—which is like attempting to contain water in a sieve.

The worst that can justly be said of us is that we have wasted our powers in an ill-advised and stubborn pursuit of an essentially negative purpose, instead of using them for the affirmative purpose of bringing justice and peace to mankind. Yet, in spite of this, we have done more for other nations and peoples in the last twenty years than any other country has done in the long history of man.

16

The Interrupted Transition

This study has dealt with an appraisal of the recent past. But what of the future? Did a new era in American foreign policy begin in June 1963 with President Kennedy's proclamation of a "strategy of peace"? Or has the United States since receded from what merely appeared to be a new beginning?

When John F. Kennedy entered the White House in 1961, he was young enough to be the son of his predecessor— young enough to be the son of such world figures as Harold Macmillan, Charles de Gaulle, Konrad Adenauer, Chiang Kai-shek, Mao Tse-tung and Nikita Khrushchev. His advent symbolized throughout the world the coming to power of a new generation. The old leaders suddenly seemed and probably felt more aged, while the younger aspirants to power began to feel that their day had dawned.

The dream was shattered by an assassin's bullet. Here, in the United States, the tragedy at Dallas, Texas, interrupted the transfer of power to a new generation of Americans and, for the time being, handed back the management of the nation's affairs to the older men who had shaped the postwar policy that we have been discussing.

Nevertheless, during his brief tenure, Kennedy had aroused a new generation of Americans to a sense of political awareness and responsibility, instilling in many of its members a determination to complete the unfinished task of revitalizing the nation and reshaping its relation to the world. People in other countries probably do not realize the growing antithesis between the awakened aspirations of many young Americans and the frozen clichés of the generation into whose hands power was unexpectedly returned by Kennedy's untimely death.

The politically conscious part of the new American generation is bored with the rhetoric of the Cold War and with the older generation's smug satisfaction with "the American Way of Life." The Cold War seems to them an outdated and irrelevant abstraction; they are interested in the solution of specific problems of foreign policy, not in ideological confrontations. As for "the American Way of Life," they see it as far from perfect and badly in need of overhaul.

In the opinion of this perhaps over-optimistic observer, the rising generation, while perplexed with the complexities of a rapidly changing world, sees more clearly than those in power the close connection between domestic life in the United States and the important challenges of foreign policy. It understands that the civil rights movement in the United States is intimately related to the process of decolonization taking place in Asia and Africa. It realizes that the rising demand for equality constitutes a major force within as well as among nations. It identifies itself more than the older generation with the vic-

269

tims of injustice, discrimination and oppression, wherever they may happen to be. What is more, this identification with the underprivileged, or what they would probably call the "voiceless," leads to action.

Kennedy gave these young Americans not only a sense of participation but a new impetus toward public service, opening for them new vistas as to how that service might be performed by ordinary citizens. The Peace Corps provided them with an opportunity to share what knowledge and skills they possessed with peoples in unfamiliar lands by living among them and learning as well as teaching. This new concept of citizen service has found expression both at home and abroad. Whether in distant lands or in Mississippi, many young Americans have recently acquired an understanding of and a sympathy for the underprivileged to an extent not often found among older citizens or in the official bureaucracy.

While it is true that only a relatively small percentage of the rising generation has served in the Peace Corps or taken an active part in the civil-rights revolution, their newly acquired attitudes have shown a marked tendency to rub off upon many of their contemporaries. This augurs well for the future of America's relation to the world.[1]

A closely related development arising from the civil-rights revolution within the United States may also have a hopeful bearing upon international relations. In the period of 1960 through 1965, the Negro revolution developed new and highly successful tactics of non-violent conflict resolution. In the past, resort to violence by underprivileged or unjustly treated minor-

[1] An interesting proposal for expanding the idea of the Peace Corps by creating an International Development Corps, composed of scientists and engineers, was put forward in March 1966 by Congressman William F. Ryan (D) of New York.

ities has led to counter-violence. The race riots of 1919 were, for example, met by lynch mobs and brutal police action. Similarly, the early strikes of industrial workers were attended by violence on both sides. In these earlier conflicts, those who sought to change what seemed to them an unjust state of affairs did so by methods which brought them into open conflict with existing law and thus invited repression in the name of law enforcement. Modern Negro leadership has, however, adopted new methods of bringing about change which, though illegal, are non-violent and, therefore, tend not to evoke counter-violence. Negro leaders in the civil-rights revolution have adopted Mahatma Gandhi's doctrine of non-violence but not his preachment of *passive* resistance; they have taught their followers *active* resistance in non-violent defiance of the law. Sit-ins, defiance of police orders banning demonstrations or protest marches, and other technically illegal actions have not only mobilized moral support on the part of the general public but have actually changed the attitude of the law-enforcement agencies. Increasingly in recent years, the police have used non-violent methods of conflict control and have themselves adopted more of an unbiased, third-party attitude as between those who seek to preserve the *status quo* and those who seek to change it. What has been evolving in the United States is a tacit sanction by government of illegal methods of obtaining a change of law and custom, provided only that the illegal methods used remain non-violent. (Similar tactics have been adopted by white university students in an effort to bring about changes in the educational system, by activist elements in the peace movement and—interestingly enough—by parents resisting school integration in the North.)

We are, in other words, perhaps witnessing within the

271

United States a new form of conflict resolution without violence which may well become relevant to the control of violence in international affairs.

These are hopeful signs but they are not, of course, sure indicators of a more constructive American foreign policy. We do not know when the interrupted transfer of power to a new generation of Americans will be consummated; nor can we predict how that generation will behave when it becomes exposed to the corruption of power. Moreover, there was a certain ambiguity in the rising generation's inheritance from the President who symbolized and gave expression to most of its ideas and aspirations.

In the realm of foreign affairs, Kennedy's actions began to conform to his liberalizing rhetoric only a little over a year before his career was cut short. One might say that the turning point came with the Cuban missile crisis of October 1962. Prior to that time, Kennedy had spoken in a new language of peace, while feeling compelled to act as if he still believed in the clichés of the Cold War. Paradoxically, Kennedy, more sincerely interested in disarmament than his predecessors, proceeded, during 1961–1962, to build up American military power to the point at which he could confidently declare that the United States was "ahead" in the arms race. On the one hand, this liberated young Americans from the paralyzing fear of nuclear attack while, on the other hand, it failed to fortify their revulsion against a possible use of nuclear weapons by their own country. This may account for the fact that most young Americans are apparently less concerned than their elders over the possibility of a nuclear holocaust and less interested in the creation of a warless world than in putting an end to current conflicts in which they themselves seem likely to be involved. The new generation of Americans would be

272

as willing as any previous generation to fight for their country if it were attacked, but they resent being drafted into a war in Vietnam which seems to many of them remote, senseless and barbaric and in the making of which they have had no voice. Broadly speaking, they are neither pacifists nor super-patriots, more interested in universal justice than in universal peace, and not yet fully aware that justice and peace are indivisible.

The more activist elements of the rising generation sometimes describe their movement as "the New Left." Actually, it seems to have taken over from the traditional American Right its non-interventionist, not necessarily isolationist stance in international affairs, as well as its hostility to centralized power here at home. Forgetting the isolationism of La Follette's Progressive Movement, "the New Left" sees the traditional Liberal Left in American politics as interventionist abroad and as the advocate of an ever more powerful paternalistic welfare state at home. Essentially, the movement, if such it may be called, is neither Left nor Right. It is humanistic rather than nationalistic. It is against what Wright Mills called "the Power Elite," less for reasons of neo-Marxist opposition to the concentration of economic power than because the Power Elite is paternalistic, denying participation in the democratic process to large segments of the American population.

As this observer sees it, the rising generation may, if it fulfills its promise, turn the United States away from the idea that "the business of America is business," and toward an as yet dimly seen vision of a nation and a people whose business it is to foster the dignity of the human individual throughout the world.

Long ago, the French philosopher Montesquieu wrote:

"The sentiment of justice was created in man before his power to reason." If this is true, and if a sense of injustice is the primary cause of man's inhumanity to man, then a generation of Americans devoted to a simple sense of justice at home and abroad is precisely what the world needs today. And, if the writer's appraisal of the rising American generation comes somewhere near the truth, then the day when the interrupted transfer of power is consummated cannot come too soon.

What of the immediate future? A new generation of Americans cannot be expected to come to power before 1972. What changes in United States foreign policy, if any, is it reasonable to expect of the generation now in power before that date?

Let us make two hopeful assumptions: *first*, that the war in Vietnam will not be permitted to escalate into a major conflict; and, *second*, that an inconclusive dragging on of the war in Vietnam will not cause the coming to power in 1968 of an ultra-conservative administration which will either dangerously declare that "there is no substitute for victory" or else seek to withdraw the United States into isolationism.

On these two assumptions, what changes in direction and emphasis should we hope and work for? Here are one citizen's thoughts on the subject.

1. We should ask and expect our government to move simultaneously on two broad fronts: (A) *toward ending the arms race and the creation of a world of law;* and (B) *toward accelerated world economic development.*

These two aims go hand in hand. Establishing them as our major objectives will shift the emphasis of our involvement in world affairs from military to political and economic considerations.

(A) Ending the arms race and moving toward the creation of a world of law means:

a) Halting the proliferation of nuclear weapons, reducing existing stockpiles of such weapons, and eventually confining the use of fissionable materials to peaceful purposes;

b) Ultimately empowering the United Nations to enforce universal national disarmament down to the level of lightly armed internal police forces (this will involve modification of the voting procedures in the United Nations and, probably, some degree of Charter revision);

c) Strengthening the peace-keeping and peace-making capability of the United Nations;[2]

d) Strict compliance by the United States with its obligations under the United Nations Charter (as noted, such compliance has been far from complete in the past);

e) Making the United Nations the cornerstone of United States foreign policy, in place of reliance upon unilateral or multilateral action in pursuit of national objectives.

(B) Accelerated World Economic Development involves:

a) Diverting resources now pre-empted by the arms race to raising the agricultural production, aiding the industrialization and promoting the political and economic development of the presently disadvantaged peoples. It means a substantial

---

2 In connection with b and c, see Grenville Clark and Louis B. Sohn, *World Peace Through World Law;* Richard A. Falk and Saul H. Mendlovitz, *The Strategy of World Order* (4 vols., New York, World Law Fund, 1966); and Commission to Study the Organization of Peace, *Seventeenth Annual Report* (New York, 1966).

increase of contributions to development on the part of the industrialized nations *even before disarmament releases resources;*

b) Multilateralization of development aid, preferably through a United Nations Development authority, with cooperation replacing competition among the industrialized donor nations;

c) Much greater international cooperation toward freeing world trade, toward improving the terms of trade for the developing nations, and toward stabilizing the world prices of the raw materials which they produce.

These two major aims should supplant the containment of communism as the primary motivation of United States foreign policy. They are affirmative aims, not merely reactions to the policies of Moscow or Peking. Together, these two aims are directed at the elimination of war and of the just grievances that might lead to war. They reflect not only the vital national interest of the United States but the vital interests of all humanity.

2. Progress toward the achievement of these two aims depends very largely upon liquidating the Cold War between the United States and the Soviet Union; and upon our government's having the wisdom not to embark upon a second Cold War with China in which many of the mistakes of the past would very likely be repeated.

3. Two major obstacles stand in the way of finally liquidating the Cold War between the United States and Russia— namely, the escalation of the war in Vietnam and our failure to solve the problem of Germany. The writer's views on both of these subjects have been indicated in preceding chapters;

briefly, they are: that we should at the very least stop our attacks upon North Vietnam and de-escalate the conflict; and that we should prepare the way for a German settlement by substituting a general European security agreement for the present tension-creating confrontation of two obsolete military alliances. This would prepare the way for the reunification of Europe, for a German settlement and for the gradual withdrawal from the Continent west of the Soviet frontier of Russian, British and American forces.[3]

De Gaulle's withdrawal from NATO has left the United States face to face with a choice which should have been made long ago—the choice between letting NATO become to all intents and purposes an Anglo-American military alliance with an increasingly dissatisfied West Germany as the anchor, or taking the lead toward the reunification of Germany and of Europe by ending the confrontation of two outdated military alliances. The first alternative will make West Germany, with its unsatisfied territorial claims, into the dominant power in Western Europe and increase the tensions between Russia and the West. The second alternative will solidify the East-West *détente* and make it possible for the Soviet Union to do what its own vital interests demand—namely, to cooperate with the United States in the containment of China.

We have a right to ask that our government face this decision, recognizing that changed circumstances have made urgently necessary the abandonment of a no longer relevant NATO policy.

4. As for the avoidance of a second Cold War with China, the writer has for years advocated the sort of policy which now seems to be slowly emerging; that is to say, a policy of

[3] See Appendix B.

firm resistance to Chinese expansionism combined with a willingness to see the Chinese point of view, to seek a *modus vivendi* and to establish normal diplomatic, cultural and trade relations.

The containment of Chinese expansionism should not, however, be effected by a ring of encircling American military power but by the consensus and cooperation of China's neighbors, backed by the United Nations, which, in turn, would rely upon both the Soviet Union and the United States as well as upon India and Japan. These major powers would, in effect, back the United Nations in guaranteeing the independence and territorial integrity of all of China's smaller neighbors, with any boundary disputes to be settled by impartial adjudication.

Even the Formosa (or Taiwan) problem is not insoluble. At present, some 11 million native Formosans are ruled, with only nominal representation, by a refugee Nationalist clique as the thirty-fifth province of the China which it has lost. By reason of their history, the Formosans are entitled, no less than any other people, to self-determination and self-government. If the Peking regime, which rightfully claims that Formosa is a part of China, refuses to permit the establishment of an independent Taiwanese or Formosan Republic, the problem might be solved by making Formosa an autonomous republic under Chinese suzerainty, with the United Nations (*not the United States*) guaranteeing the Formosans against the imposition of any government not freely elected by themselves. As an autonomous republic under Chinese overlordship, Formosa might be entitled to separate membership in the United Nations, just as the Ukraine and Byelo-Russia hold separate memberships although they are parts of the Soviet Union.

We have a right to ask that our government take the initiative in trying to find a *modus vivendi* with the government that rules one-quarter of the world's population. We have a right to insist that our government stop rationalizing a dangerously unwise and now wholly obsolete China policy by repeating over and over again (as it does also with respect to Vietnam) that "it is all the fault of the other side." Secretary Rusk, who, in 1952, still thought that the Peking regime was "not Chinese," is fond of saying that nothing can be done to improve our relations with that regime because "it insists that we surrender Formosa." We should ask our Secretary of State by what right Formosa is ours to hold or surrender—by what right we support the continued rule over a part of China by an exiled remnant of a defeated faction in a Chinese civil war. If we are concerned for the "freedom" and self-determination of the 11 million natives of Formosa, how do we justify our support of a carpetbagger government which denies Formosans the right to govern themselves?

5. These, as the writer sees it, are the major changes in United States foreign policy that American citizens have a right to expect of the generation now in power before a younger generation takes over the reins of government.

But there is something more that Americans have a right to expect. They have a right to expect that their government will in the future keep them fully and honestly informed; that it will in the future explain rather than "sell" its policies; that it will foster free discussion of alternatives instead of seeking a consensus of uninformed or misinformed acquiescence in its decisions—in short, that it will permit the democratic process to operate freely in determining the nation's course of action.

This great and beloved country of ours can play the constructive role in the world of which it is capable only if there is full mutual trust between government and people. Such mutual trust can exist only when facts are freely disclosed, mistakes freely admitted and alternative courses of action freely discussed.

The establishment of such a relationship is not a one-way street. Government cannot do it alone. If we, the citizens of the United States, desire to have a democratic process determine our nation's foreign policy, we must consider it our duty to participate in it. If we want full and honest information, we must study such information conscientiously and not content ourselves with a mere scanning of newspaper headlines or a casual listening to news summaries. If we want alternative courses of action laid before us, we must be prepared to form reasoned opinions based upon knowledge of background and fact. Until we stop thinking of our government as something apart from ourselves, it will be a thing apart from ourselves, and we shall continue to be a nation of sheep, responding to the manipulation of our desires, hopes and fears rather than to an appeal to our reasoned judgments.

No other people in the world has as much background material available or as much leisure time in which to study it as we. To say that one is too busy to fulfill the elementary duty of citizenship is nothing less than a betrayal of democracy. And if we, the people of the United States, betray democracy, how can we expect other less fortunate people to foster its growth throughout the world?

APPENDIX A

Excerpt from
REPORT OF THE AD HOC CONGRESSIONAL CONFERENCE ON VIETNAM

Held January 21 and 22, 1966, Washington, D.C.

CONGRESSIONAL SPONSORS
Benjamin S. Rosenthal (D-L), New York, Chairman
Charles C. Diggs, Jr. (D), Michigan
Don Edwards (D), California
Leonard Farbstein (D), New York
Donald M. Fraser (D), Minnesota
Robert W. Kastenmeier (D), Wisconsin
Henry S. Reuss (D), Wisconsin
William F. Ryan (D), New York

CONFERENCE PARTICIPANTS

CHAIRMAN: *Dr. Arthur Larson*, director, Rule of Law Research Center, Duke University; former director of the United States Information Agency; and Special Assistant to President Eisenhower.

Mr. Richard Barnet, co-director, Institute for Policy Studies; former deputy director, Office of Political Research, U.S. Arms Control and Disarmament Agency.

Professor Robert Browne, professor of economics, Fairleigh Dickinson University; former A.I.D. official in Vietnam.

Mr. Benjamin V. Cohen, former counsellor to the Department of State.

Professor Richard Falk, associate professor of international law, Princeton University; editor, *American Journal of International Law*.

281

Professor Bernard Fall, professor of international relations, Howard University; author of *The Two Vietnams*.

Mr. Arnold Fraleigh, lecturer in political science, George Washington University; former Foreign Service officer.

Dean Edmund Gullion,[1] dean, Fletcher School of Law and Diplomacy; former Counsellor of American Legation in Saigon; former Ambassador to the Congo.

Professor George McT. Kahin, director, Southeast Asia Program, Cornell University.

Professor John Lewis, professor of government, Cornell University.

Mr. Robert Nathan,[2] economic consultant.

Mr. Marcus Raskin, co-director, Institute for Policy Studies; former member of the special staff of the National Security Council.

Professor Louis Sohn, Bemis Professor of International Law, Harvard Law School.

Mr. James P. Warburg, writer on foreign policy.

Dr. Betty Goetz Lall, rapporteur; research associate, School of Industrial and Labor Relations, Cornell University.

Paul T. Gorman, Executive Assistant.

FOREWORD

On January 21 and 22, 1966, a group of experts and scholars met in Washington at the invitation of eight Members of the House of Representatives to analyze the current situation in Vietnam and prepare realistic proposals to help end the war and facilitate a negotiated settlement.

The sponsoring Congressmen have felt unsatisfied with the

---

[1] Dean Gullion participated in the conference but was not a signatory to the report. He is not in agreement with a majority of the findings and recommendations.

[2] Mr. Nathan attended that part of the conference dealing with economic aid but did not participate in the preparation of the report.

recent role of Congress in foreign affairs. They believe their office requires a more fundamental examination of foreign policy than that allowed by even the most careful consideration of specific legislation. The sponsors are convinced that the level of congressional analysis can be raised through greater intimacy between the legislative branch and the intellectual and university community. It was with this in mind that they invited to Washington a group of experts particularly qualified to discuss with them Vietnam and its implications for American diplomacy.

Some of the participants have spent considerable time in Vietnam, and have obtained intimate association with conditions there. Others offered the important perspectives of experience in negotiation, study of economics, diplomacy, or international law, or expert knowledge of relevant geographical areas.

Participants were requested not to dwell on episodes or errors of the past. Instead, they were asked to discuss present policies and possible alternatives to them; to analyze the problems involved in reaching and enforcing a settlement in Vietnam; and to project the outlines of a creative American policy toward Asia.

Certain conclusions and recommendations by the participants emerged in the discussions and these are stated explicitly at the beginning of the report. The subsequent summary of the discussions also includes some individual points which contributed to the analysis, although they were not unanimously endorsed.

The sponsors regard the proposals made by the conference as important contributions to their own thinking about Vietnam and the formulation of American foreign policy. They feel the report deserves the attention of their congressional colleagues, members of the executive branch, and the American people. Finally, they view the conference as having set an important precedent for future congressional initiatives in foreign affairs.

Conference Recommendations

The Conference reached the recommendations and conclusions set out below. A summary of the discussions from which they were developed follows:

Present Strategies

1. There are diplomatic alternatives, not yet fully explored, to continued military escalation of the war in Vietnam.

2. Continued bombing of North Vietnam is not in the American interest either in shortening the war or in improving prospects for a negotiated settlement.

3. There should be no further escalation of American troop commitment. There are serious risks of inviting greater North Vietnamese and Chinese activity.

4. Unilateral withdrawal of all American troops prior to a cease-fire or peace conference is not in our national interest.

New Policy Initiatives

5. The most productive course for the future is a de-escalation of military activity and commitment.

6. The National Liberation Front must be recognized as a principal belligerent in the war, and as a necessary party to any peace conference and settlement.

7. To improve the likelihood of negotiations, the Saigon government should be broadened to include representatives less hostile to negotiations.

8. The United States must help promote greater contact between all South Vietnamese factions—representatives of the National Liberation Front, the Saigon government, and influential private citizens.

Negotiations and the Convening of a Conference

9. The differences between the several negotiating positions are not insurmountable. The United States might agree to Hanoi's Four Points, treating them as one interpretation of the 1954 agreement and thus an appropriate basis for nego-

tiations. The controversial Point Three of the Hanoi program would then be a subject for subsequent discussion rather than prior approval.

10. The 1954 Geneva Conference should be reconvened with all parties to the hostilities represented.

11. A procedure for reconvening the Geneva Conference would be to have the three nations on the International Control Commission (Canada, India, Poland) request a conference to receive new instructions on enforcement of the 1954 agreements.

12. The inability of the United Nations thus far to use its good offices to help end the Vietnam war dramatizes the urgency of including China as a full member of that institution. Despite the difficulties of involving the United Nations in a settlement of the war all parties should seek opportunities to utilize the United Nations in appropriate ways.

Terms of a Settlement

13. A cease-fire must be secured. Given the dispersed nature of the conflict, such a cease-fire might be more easily reached at a conference, though the possibility of a prior cessation of hostilities should be explored carefully.

14. Agreements must be reached on a provisional government in South Vietnam and procedures for the holding of elections to form a constituent assembly. A provisional government might be established on the basis of geographical areas controlled, with contested areas to be administered temporarily by the International Control Commission. Alternatively, decisions regarding such a government could be reached by prior negotiations between all parties in the south.

15. All parties must firmly adhere to the results of free elections.

16. Amnesty must be granted for all parties in the conflict.

17. Guarantees of the cease-fire, the provisional government, free elections, troop withdrawals, amnesty, and neutralization must be enforced by an effective International Control Commission. The International Control Commission must therefore be significantly strengthened. United Nations par-

ticipation in this process might reduce administrative difficulties and set precedent for future United Nations participation in the solution of other civil conflicts threatening world peace.

18. A settlement should assure the neutralization of the two zones of Vietnam, Laos, and Cambodia. Arms control agreements must be reached applying to other nations of the area, prescribing their non-participation in military alliances, the freedom of their territory for foreign military bases, and their protection from outside arms, material, and armed personnel infiltration.

CONFERENCE SUMMARY

THE CURRENT SITUATION IN VIETNAM

In discussing the present situation in Vietnam, the conference concentrated on two major issues: the status and relations of the several Vietnamese parties in conflict and the political effect of various military tactics and strategies.

The Vietnamese Antagonists

There is little information about the National Liberation Front and its military arm, the Vietcong. Their top leaders are not easily contacted, and below the top leadership few of their personnel have been adequately identified by Americans. Many of the participants felt this lack of knowledge itself obstructed needed initiatives in the diplomatic sphere. Several participants acquainted with politics in South Vietnam reminded the conference that the Vietcong had grown out of the resistance movement when all of Vietnam was struggling against the French. The National Liberation Front is clearly dominated by the Communists, although several experts pointed out that the Front does consist of various factions, some of them more nationalist than Communist. It was felt that attempts must be made to learn more about the structure of the Front, constituting, as it does, such a significant force in the south.

There were varying viewpoints regarding the strength of

the South Vietnamese government, and the conference was aware of the extreme mutability of circumstances in Saigon. Some participants believed there was no organic non-Communist political structure left in South Vietnam, and that the military government was simply an extension of the American presence. Others argued that there was a viable structure intact. The conference agreed that the stability and prestige of the government was largely a function of the degree of American support.

Many participants were deeply disturbed by the Ky government's insistence that talk of negotiations jeopardizes its life and threatens to dissolve its army's will to fight. All agreed that this position should not be allowed to prevail. In fact, it was felt that a broadening of the South Vietnamese government would be a prerequisite for moves toward a negotiated settlement.

Relations Between Saigon and the National Liberation Front

Given the above evaluation, the participants were deeply convinced that steps must be taken to promote greater contact between the National Liberation Front, members of the Saigon government, and influential South Vietnamese citizens. American policy, in its insistence that the war is a simple case of external aggression, may be undercutting this goal. While many noted the intransigence of Saigon on stimulating contacts, several of the participants pointed out that some South Vietnamese officials, Buddhists, independent political figures, and non-Communist intellectuals are undoubtedly acquainted with the National Liberation Front agents and officials. The United States, through local aid and intelligence officials, should actively seek to promote these relations. The participants thought that the United States must persuade the Ky government not to obstruct this process and inflict punishment on citizens engaged in promoting contact between presently hostile groups. If, as all parties to the conflict agree, a future South Vietnam must be autonomous and free from foreign interference, then attempts at reconciliation within the country must be made.

*Relations Between the National Liberation
Front and Hanoi*

Many in the group believed there are differences between the National Liberation Front and the North Vietnamese government regarding the conduct of the war. Some argued that those fighting in the south are likely to feel less inclined to compromise for a settlement. An example of this difference was the variation in interpretation given by the National Liberation Front and North Vietnam to the statement first issued by the Front on March 17, 1965. The North Vietnamese version, broadcast three days after the National Liberation Front account, was much toned down.

The difference in outlook between the Front and North Vietnam was cited as another reason why the United States should encourage the government in South Vietnam to make contact with the National Liberation Front. We could be committing serious errors if we assumed that Hanoi had such complete authority over the National Liberation Front that it could speak for it on all issues of stopping the war and negotiating a settlement. We do not know definitely that the National Liberation Front would accept Hanoi's terms for a settlement. In fact, it was felt that one of the reasons why reunification of North and South Vietnam is no longer an issue of priority was the recognition by Hanoi that even with a Vietcong victory, reunification would involve a complicated process of bargaining between Hanoi and whoever formed a South Vietnamese government.

*The Political Effects of Military Tactics:
Bombings in the North*

The conference participants were in agreement that the bombings in the north were of little military value, while the diplomatic disadvantages were very serious. It was agreed that the bombings had helped bolster South Vietnamese morale; but it was believed this factor did not outweigh harmful diplomatic effects. Further escalation of the bombings, it was felt, could not be expected to improve the situation.

The Political Effects of Military Tactics:
Operations in the South

The conference expressed extreme anxiety over the prospect of increased American troop commitments in the south. Echoing the conclusion of the recent Mansfield Report, the participants argued that an escalation of troop commitment would likely result in stalemates on yet higher levels of engagement. There was profound awareness of the risks of provoking greater North Vietnamese and possible Chinese ground participation. No member of the group believed the United States should withdraw all its forces from Vietnam prior to a settlement. But the group agreed that the most desirable future course would be a de-escalation of military activity and involvement. Many held that American initiatives on staged withdrawals would be more in the United States interest than a continued enlargement of our involvement.

The conference also noted that bombings in the south and ground clear-and-hold operations were creating a serious refugee problem. The number of refugees, estimated at one million in 1965, was growing beyond the capacity of pacification programs to absorb them. The problem was thought to be of increasing importance to the stability of the South Vietnamese government.

Throughout the discussion there was concern expressed that the more the United States makes the war our war, the less chance we have of building attitudes congenial to a settlement. With respect to United States economic efforts, for example, it was argued that without the willingness of the South Vietnamese government to commit itself to improving conditions in the countryside, large increases of United States economic aid and personnel are not likely to achieve intended political results.

NEGOTIATIONS AND A PEACE CONFERENCE

The conference discussed in some detail the present bargaining positions of the parties in conflict. From here, it turned to an examination of the problems involved in initiating negotiations and convening a peace conference.

Current Negotiating Positions

On the surface it appears that both sides in the war are agreed on what should constitute the basis for negotiations and a peace conference. The United States and North Vietnam have said that the 1954 Geneva Agreement should form the foundation of a settlement; the United States has presented Fourteen Points as representing its own position. The North Vietnamese position is represented by the Four Points announced on April 8, 1965. Of these, Point Three has been the principal obstacle to agreement. This point reads: "The internal affairs of South Vietnam must be settled by the South Vietnamese people themselves, in accordance with the program of the NFLSV (the South Vietnam National Liberation Front) without any foreign interference." The United States has indicated that all Points, Four or Fourteen, could be dealt with in negotiation. Yet there is still considerable controversy regarding the true nature of Hanoi's Point Three. One view was that Point Three meant that Hanoi would settle for nothing less than a settlement based entirely on the program of the Front. Many, however, disputed this interpretation, arguing that the Four Points are but an elaboration of Hanoi's understanding of the 1954 agreement. Cited as documenting this contention were the preamble and postscript to the Four Points. The preamble states that it is the intention of the North Vietnamese government "to strictly respect the 1954 Geneva agreements on Vietnam and to correctly implement their basic provisions as embodied in the following four points":

A significant number of participants felt that the negotiating positions of the parties were not so irreconcilable. It was then proposed that the United States should accept the Four Points of Hanoi, treating them as one interpretation of the Geneva Accords, and thus an appropriate basis for negotiations. The controversial Point Three would then become a subject for discussion at a conference rather than prior to it. This American diplomatic initiative would give Hanoi less reason to oppose negotiations.

There was some belief that Hanoi was not disposed to negotiate now since it felt that the United States could be worn down psychologically.

If, however, the above view is not entirely the case, and if the positions of the several parties are not so opposed, what then is holding up the convening of negotiations and a conference? There appears to be the lack of conviction on each side that the other side does in fact accept the conditions proclaimed for a settlement. There may also be conviction that military success is still possible. And clearly there is ambiguity regarding the role of the National Liberation Front, in addition to other procedural difficulties regarding the convening of a conference.

Dealing With the National Liberation Front

A main stumbling block to negotiations has been the refusal of the United States to accept the presence of the National Liberation Front as one of the necessary parties to the negotiations and settlement. The United States position has been, in the words of the President, "The Vietcong would not have difficulty being represented and having their views represented if for a moment Hanoi decided she wanted to cease aggression. I don't think that would be an insurmountable problem." This has appeared to be insufficient recognition to satisfy the Front and North Vietnam. And Hanoi has sometimes seemed to take the extreme view that the Front is the only group from South Vietnam that should be dealt with.

The group felt strongly that the United States should be clearer about its willingness to deal with the Front at the negotiating table. While the United States should consult fully with the South Vietnamese government on its view, the Ky government should not be permitted to exercise a veto power over United States policy in this respect. One approach to dealing with the Front might be an American decision to grant the Front belligerent status.

Reconvening of the 1954 Geneva Conference

The reconvening of the 1954 Geneva Conference is almost a certain prerequisite to negotiating an end to the war. There is, however, a procedural problem as to which government or body should request the reconvening of this conference.

While there are considerable uncertainties regarding future developments, the participants thought it important to discuss likely alternative procedures for convening a conference.

The co-chairmen of the 1954 Conference—the United Kingdom and the Soviet Union—are unlikely to issue a conference call because the Soviet Union might not wish to expose itself to further denunciations by China or complicate its good relations with North Vietnam. So this avenue was therefore considered unpromising.

Another possibility is that the United Nations might request the reconvening of the conference. The principal problem here is that neither North nor South Vietnam nor China are members of the United Nations; and North Vietnam and China may continue to regard any United Nations action as likely to be partisan and therefore unacceptable.

A third possibility, now unlikely, is to act on a former (1964) Cambodian request to reconvene the conference to guarantee its neutrality and borders which Cambodia charged were threatened by the Vietnam war. This conference might then be used by the parties to discuss a settlement of the war in South Vietnam.

There is a fourth possibility, as yet untried, which might be most acceptable to all parties. The three countries of the International Control Commission, India, Canada, and Poland, could request that the Geneva Conference be reconvened in order that they receive further instructions on the implementation of the 1954 Agreement. At this Conference, the terms of a settlement to the present war could be considered.

In requesting such a Conference, the International Control Commission members might propose that representation be determined along the lines of the 1961–62 Laos Conference, which allowed each of the warring factions to participate in discussion. One of the major functions of that Conference was to provide a channel through which leaders of the three groups met and eventually agreed on the formation of a government. The Laos accord was then intended to be a guarantor of the settlement.

292

RELATED ASPECTS OF A VIETNAMESE SETTLEMENT

China

At a number of points in the conference China was discussed. These discussions covered China's view of the Vietnamese conflict, and the relation of its domestic affairs to foreign policy. Thought to be particularly important were the problems of providing sufficient food for its expanding population, the succession question, and the adaptation of the army to political rather than professional military purposes. Chinese food needs cannot be met by extending control over small states in the area. Only in the Loess region of north China can total food production be substantially raised, something in the order of 40 percent. As to the question of succession, the older leadership has attempted—with only moderate success—to instill revolutionary and anti-American attitudes in those younger men likely to replace them. American policies, however, can affect the degree of success the older leadership has with this indoctrination process.

It was also noted that the Maoist leadership fears that the United States may attack the mainland soon and that China must be prepared to meet this attack by various forms of defense encompassing guerrilla-type operations. There are signs, however, that army leaders may be seriously resisting the role assigned them by the party in the defense of China.

On Chinese foreign policy, the specialists in the group noted the gross misinterpretation given by many to the September 1965 statement of the Chinese Defense Minister, Lin Piao. This statement, contrary to popular and some official beliefs, advocated scaling-down of overt Chinese action and those militant policies which increased the risk to China itself. The Chinese espoused the view that revolutions and wars of liberation could not be imported, and that conditions within a country had to be ripe in order for such revolutions to succeed. This did not mean that China would not send out agents and propaganda to foment revolution. Yet such tactics should be differentiated from the likelihood of repeated large-scale Chinese

293

aggression and the sending of Chinese troops and arms to local Communist groups in the developing areas of the world. Notable too in the Lin statement was the absence of threats to the United States in Vietnam, even though China had issued many such threats in the earlier months of 1965.

Thus in Vietnam, China has exercised caution. Yet in assessing future Chinese intentions it was stressed that there undoubtedly was a threshold for China's active participation in the war. At some point in a continued United States escalation the Chinese would doubtless feel compelled to enter.

Many believed that since 1963 Chinese foreign policy had suffered a series of significant setbacks in the developing areas primarily because of the hostile reactions of indigenous populations and leaders.

Wars of Liberation

The group considered the above evaluation as having particular relevance to Communist policy on wars of liberation. Given Chinese inability or reluctance to commit military force to support wars of liberation, and what some felt was a growing uneasiness on the part of the Soviet Union unilaterally to promote these conflicts, the participants felt it important that the United States revise its conception of Communist aggression.

American response to Communist agitation for conflict in developing areas must not be to react unilaterally with military forces. United States aid to certain governments with antidemocratic features appears to have pressed the Soviet Union into increasing its agitation for disorder. Yet Soviet and Chinese exhortations to developing countries have met with little success. Those nations which are in their post-colonial stage are anxious for periods of sustained economic growth which increased revolution and violence would only disturb. There are still some nations, nevertheless, in which revolution is, or may soon be ripe. This must be anticipated by the United States. It was felt that our own particular revolutionary tradition was not appropriate to guiding these revolutions. But our interests are most likely to be served by a sympathetic rather than a hostile response when these events finally occur.

In discussion of possible responses to revolutions in the developing nations, the conference emphasized the need for discovering new roles for international organizations. Likewise, the participants thought the United States should seek to explore new avenues of cooperation with the Soviet Union within the United Nations.

In discussing the role of major powers in local conflicts of the future, many favored stress on developing procedure within international law rather than emphasis on securing agreement on general principles.

There was some discussion of whether Communist-inspired violence was likely to break out in Thailand. The topic was considered to be highly speculative, though several experts expressed the view that a major outbreak of hostility was unlikely. Local tension and increased terror, on the other hand, were thought to be a distinct possibility. Some thought was given, therefore, to the possibility of multilateral action to anticipate strife and prevent a crisis analogous to that in Vietnam.

The group also noted the need for arms control agreements in Thailand and possibly other areas. Such agreements might prohibit the import of arms or armed personnel, the establishment of foreign military bases, and the joining of military alliances. These steps could be incorporated into a general conference on Vietnam, or be an adjunct to a Vietnamese settlement. Our greatest interest, finally, should lie in insulating these conflicts from outside interference.

On the relationship of Vietnam to other countries in southeast Asia, including Thailand, it was pointed out that Vietnam was the only case in southeast Asia where the Communists effectively identified themselves with the country's nationalists. Elsewhere in southeast Asia, nationalism has not been forced into fusion with Communism. Indeed, the failure of Communist insurrections in Burma, Indonesia, Malaya, and the Philippines testifies to the positive contribution of Asian nationalism. In each of these cases, the inability of Communist insurgents to secure nationalist backing defeated their ultimate goals.

295

APPENDIX B

Excerpt from Time for Statesmanship (*1965*) *included in the writer's statement of March 22, 1966, before the Senate Subcommittee on Foreign Relations*

I

1. The United States should not let itself be irritated into some sort of neo-isolationism. In spite of all difficulties, it should adhere to the belief that the security of Western Europe is vital to American security.

2. The Brezhnev-Kosygin regime in the Soviet Union appears determined to pursue a policy of *détente* with the West. The Soviet Union urgently needs this *détente* for domestic reasons and in order to secure its European rear in dealing with the rising menace of China.

3. The United States needs a *détente* with the Soviet Union in order to make progress toward arms control and disarmament without which there can be no real security for Europe, for the Americans or for any other part of the world.

4. No real *détente* in Central Europe can be achieved so long as two hostile alliances confront each other at the Iron Curtain in Central Germany. The very life of these alliances depends upon the maintenance of tension. Both the NATO and the Warsaw Pact alliances are obsolete and irrelevant to present-day circumstances.

5. No dismantling of the two alliances is possible without (a) a German settlement acceptable to both West and East Germans, the Soviet Union and the Western powers; and (b) a general European security agreement in which, within the framework of the United Nations, the nuclear powers and *all* the nations of Europe, including the Soviet Union, undertake

297

to prevent the spread of nuclear weapons and to suppress military aggression by any European nation against another.

6. *Instead of trying to patch up an obsolete alliance or seeking a partnership with one half of a Europe divided against itself, the United States should seek partnership with all of Europe in its quest for peace—peace not only in Europe itself but peace throughout the world.*

II

How is this to be accomplished? What obstacles will have to be overcome?

The first step is to lay before the British and West German governments and eventually before de Gaulle a proposal to be presented to the Soviet government for an all-European security agreement and an all-German settlement. This should be done through quiet diplomacy without any publicity whatever.

The drafting of an all-European security agreement will present fewer problems once the basis for a German settlement has been agreed upon. (It should be recalled that at the 1954 Foreign Ministers' Conference in Berlin, the Soviet Union agreed with the Western powers that an all-German settlement should be sought in the context of a general European security agreement but that the conferees were unable to agree upon which came first. The West insisted that a German settlement must precede, while the Soviet Union insisted that it come after a security agreement. It is suggested that the two agreements should be presented to Moscow simultaneously in order to avoid a similar experience.)

As for coming to grips with the problem of an all-German settlement:

Until now, efforts to break the deadlock have foundered on Soviet insistence that a reunified Germany must be a "socialist" state friendly to the Soviet Union, while the West has insisted that reunification come about through free, all-German elections and that a reunified Germany must be free to join the NATO alliance if it so desires. Thus each side has, in essence, demanded the unconditional surrender of the other as a precondition for German reunification. Recently, Western leadership has begun to realize—though this has not been openly admitted by any Western statesman—that German reunification and German membership in the anti-Soviet NATO alliance are two mutually exclusive aims and that, if Germany is to be reunified, it will have to be militarily neutralized. As yet, however, neither Washington nor London seems to have decided which is more important: reunification at the price of military neutralization, or a West German military contribution to NATO at the price of Germany's permanent partition.

The British government has consistently pushed for negotiations, though without suggesting any plan which faced the inescapable choice. With the Labour Party in power, it seems likely that Britain will put forward some updated version of the late Hugh Gaitskell's plans for disengagement as set forth in his Godkin Lectures at Harvard University in January 1957.

De Gaulle opposes disengagement now and appears to think that German reunification can come about only when universal disarmament is achieved and all of Europe west of the Urals is reunited. He does not seem concerned over German partition. He, alone among responsible Western leaders, has sensibly recognized the permanence of the Oder-Neisse frontier between Germany and Poland.

In the United States, Senator Claiborne Pell (D) of Rhode Island, has advocated recognition of the Oder-Neisse frontier and the *de facto* recognition of the East German state in exchange for Soviet-East German guarantees of the freedom of West Berlin and open access to Berlin for the Western powers. Senator Mansfield of Montana, Democratic majority leader, and several other Senators have put forward similar suggestions. These proposals imply a willingness to accept German partition as permanent, provided that the freedom of and Western access to Berlin are assured.

On the other hand, Mr. Walter Lippmann and a few others, among them the writer, have pointed out the danger to peace which would result from leaving Germany partitioned with

Moscow in possession of the powerful instrument of seduction resulting from its being the sole arbiter of whether reunification shall ever come about. Khrushchev once explicitly stated his belief that the Germans would sooner or later seek another Rapallo and, unlikely as another Russo-German deal may seem at present, the long history of German-Russian relations since the time of Frederick the Great is full of sudden swings from hostility to cooperation and from cooperation back to hostility. As time goes on, partition will more and more appear to the Germans as a grievance that must be remedied. The only way to prevent their turning east to seek redress is to make sure that, if Germany is to remain partitioned, it will be through the free choice of the German people, and not because the Western powers connived with the Soviet Union to make partition permanent.

De Gaulle's disruption of the NATO alliance serves only to accentuate, not to create, the choice which the Americans, British and Germans have long failed to face. If it is decided to seek German reunification at the price of Germany's military neutralization, the Germans must be willing to accept debarment from military alliances with either East or West. If the decision is to keep West Germany in NATO, the Germans must of their own free will concur in this decision and accept the permanence of partition.

II

In September 1962, before the NATO alliance fell into its present state of disarray, the writer submitted to the Kennedy administration a plan which would provide a cooling-off period of ten years during which the West and East Germans would be left free to decide, without outside interference or pressure of any sort, whether they wished their country eventually to be reunited and militarily neutralized, or whether they preferred it to remain partitioned, with West Germany allied to NATO and East Germany remaining a member of the Warsaw Pact.

The plan provided that, during the ten-year period, the

status quo in Berlin would be maintained under United Nations supervision, with each side agreeing not to use its sector as a base for espionage, subversion or hostile propaganda. The Soviet and East German governments would guarantee the Western powers unhampered access to West Berlin and the freedom of its inhabitants during the ten-year period. Meanwhile, pending an all-German decision, both of the two German states would be admitted to membership in the United Nations without prejudice to their eventual coming together as a single nation.

During the ten-year period, all of Berlin would be considered the potential capital of a reunited Germany and, as such, would be placed under the protection of the United Nations; the present garrisons would remain as agents of the United Nations; and any disputes as to the misuse of any sector for espionage, subversion or hostile propaganda would be submitted to a United Nations Berlin Commission.

If, within the ten-year period, the two German states should decide to unite, the Federal Republic of Germany would be released from NATO and the German Democratic Republic would be released from the Warsaw Pact. All foreign troops would be withdrawn from German soil, provided that a new all-German government would voluntarily accept debarment from joining any military alliance whatsoever, it being understood that such debarment would not apply to non-military political or economic affiliations. If and when reunification were to take place, the United Nations Berlin Commission and the four garrisons serving as its agents would be withdrawn, allowing Berlin to become the capital of a united Germany.

If, on the other hand, the two German states should fail to unite within the ten-year period, thus leaving Berlin in the center of a permanently separate East German state, a new arrangement would be made concerning the people, the land and the property of the three Western sectors. The inhabitants of the Western sectors would be given ample time and complete freedom to remove themselves and their movable property. They would be adequately compensated by the German Democratic Republic for privately owned immovable property, such as real estate and buildings thereon, at values to be determined by the United Nations Berlin Commission. And the publicly owned parts of the 185 square miles comprising the Western sectors of Berlin, together with buildings and improvements thereon, would be acquired by the German Democratic Republic either through purchase from the Federal Republic or exchange for some suitable part of East German territory contiguous to the Federal Republic; the value of land and other properties thus purchased by the Federal Republic or acquired through cession of East German territory would be determined by the United Nations Berlin Commission.

Were a proposal of this sort put forward by the West including the Federal Republic, and accepted by the Kremlin, its adoption would for the next ten years take the heat off the most troublesome question at issue between the West and the Soviet Union. A breathing space would be provided during which the German people could work out their own destiny. If they failed to reunite in a single nation, they would not be able to blame others for their continued partition. Meanwhile, there would be no recurring crises over Berlin.

This proposal is cited as an example of one way in which the German nettle might be grasped. There may well be other and perhaps better ways to seek the same ends but, so far as the writer knows, none have been suggested.

III

What are the obstacles to any such proposal?

There is unlikely to be any British obstacle. The Labour Party has long favored some form of disengagement and Britain's balance-of-payments situation will cause not only the Labour government but a considerable number of Conservatives to welcome any plan that relieves Britain of the obligation to keep its 55,000-man Army of the Rhine in Germany.

The West Germans will probably be sharply divided. The nationalistic Adenauer wing of the Christian Democratic Party and the Bavarian Christian Socialists under Franz Josef

Strauss will probably object to military neutralization and the withdrawal of foreign troops, even though the proposal merely provides that this shall be one of two choices presented to the German people.

In East Germany, one must expect the Ulbricht regime and its *apparatchiks* to oppose the withdrawal of Soviet troops but, if given a chance freely to express their views, the majority of East Germany's 17 million inhabitants would probably favor the proposal.

Poland would certainly welcome any scheme which derived to a large extent from the Polish Rapacki Plan.

Under Khrushchev, the Soviet government endorsed the 1957 Rapacki proposal for a denuclearized zone. Whether the Brezhnev-Kosygin regime would favor it will not be known until the plan is put forward. Much will depend upon how sincerely the Kremlin wants a *détente* and upon how the proposal is presented. The possibility of having Poland put forward a new Rapacki Plan, amplified and modified along the lines indicated in the foregoing, should not be overlooked. Not only the Soviet Union but also de Gaulle might react more favorably to a Polish proposal than to one put forward by either the "Anglo-Saxons" or the Bonn Republic.

De Gaulle may well turn out to be a greater obstacle than the rulers of the Kremlin. It would be rash to predict what will be his future attitude. One can say only that he has been known to change his mind as he did with respect to Algeria and the French colonial empire. One can say further that, if the United States, Britain and the West Europeans (including the Germans) and the Soviet Bloc were all to agree upon a plan such as has been outlined, while de Gaulle refused to sanction a European Security Agreement and an approach to an all-German settlement, he would place France in a position so isolated and so invidious that even he might hesitate.

IV

An all-European security agreement obviously cannot go into full effect unless and until the Germans have reached their decision. If the Germans opt for reunification at the price of military neutralization, the pact will take a somewhat different form than it will if the two German states decide to remain separate. Nevertheless, if agreement is reached on a cooling-off period, as suggested, certain elements of the all-European security pact can and should go into effect immediately.

1. All the European nations could agree that, pending the German decision, no nuclear weapons are to be installed in either of the two German states. (This agreement might include Poland and Czechoslovakia.)

2. The Western powers and the Soviet Union might agree to withdraw their conventional military forces from the area between the Oder-Neisse Line and the Rhine.

3. To guard against surprise attack, the Soviet Union might be permitted to install a radar screen on the east bank of the Rhine, while the Western powers would install a similar screen on the west bank of the Oder-Neisse Rivers.

4. A United Nations Commission might be appointed to verify the withdrawal of troops and the removal of all nuclear weapons from the two German states. This commission would also be charged with the responsibility for seeing to it that the Germans would be left to make their decision without pressure from either East or West and that the agreement by both sides not to use their sectors of Berlin for espionage or propaganda purposes would be kept.

The Security Agreement should provide for two contingencies: a) a German decision in favor of unification at the price of military neutralization; and b) a German decision to allow partition to become permanent.

In the case of a decision to unite, the Security Agreement might provide that all Soviet Bloc troops should be withdrawn behind the frontier of the Soviet Union, while all American, British and French troops would be withdrawn from West Germany.

Should the Germans elect to remain partitioned, the question of Berlin would be handled in the manner suggested above. The Security Agreement would have to be renegotiated with respect to the status of East Germany as an ally of the Soviet Bloc and West Germany as an ally of the West. Should this result in something like the reconstitution of the NATO and Warsaw Pact alliances, there would at least be no foreign troops confronting each other on German soil, and no nuclear weapons in German hands.

The mere establishment of a cooling-off period during which the Germans would reach their decision, and the creation of a neutralized belt across Central Europe would enhance the prospects of arms control and disarmament and might lead to a relaxation of tensions in other parts of the world.

SELECTED BIBLIOGRAPHY

Acheson, Dean. *Power and Diplomacy*. Cambridge, Mass., Harvard University Press, 1958.

Alperovitz, Gar. *Atomic Diplomacy*. New York, Simon and Schuster, 1965.

Aron, Raymond. *An Explanation of De Gaulle*. New York, Harper & Row, 1966.

Baade, Fritz. *Race to the Year 2000*. Garden City, N.Y., Doubleday & Company, 1963.

Barnet, Richard J. *Who Wants Disarmament?* Boston, Beacon Press, 1960.

————, and Marcus G. Raskin. *After Twenty Years*. New York, Random House, 1965.

Barnett, A. Doak. *Communist China and Asia: A Challenge to American Policy*. New York, Harper & Row, 1960.

Blackett, Patrick M. S. *Atomic Weapons and East-West Relations*. Cambridge, England, Cambridge University Press, 1956.

Byrnes, James F. *Speaking Frankly*. New York, Harper & Row, 1947.

Carr, Edward H. *Nationalism and After*. New York, St. Martin's Press, 1957.

Chang Hsin-hai. *America and China*. New York, Simon and Schuster, 1966.

Churchill, Winston S. *The Second World War*, Vol. VI, *Triumph and Tragedy*. Boston, Houghton Mifflin Company, 1953.

Clark, Grenville, and Louis B. Sohn. *World Peace Through World Law*. Cambridge, Mass., Harvard University Press, 1958.

Clay, Lucius D. *Decision in Germany*. Garden City, N.Y., Doubleday & Company, 1950.

Clubb, Oliver E., Jr. *The United States and the Sino-Soviet Bloc in Southeast Asia*. Washington, D.C., The Brookings Institution, 1962.

Dean, Vera M. *Foreign Policy Without Fear*. New York, McGraw-Hill, 1953.

Deane, John R. *The Strange Alliance*. New York, The Viking Press, 1947.

De Gaulle, Charles. *War Memoirs of Charles de Gaulle*, Vol. III, *Salvation, 1944–1946*. New York, Simon and Schuster, 1960.

Djilas, Milovan. *Conversations with Stalin*. London, Rupert Hart-Davis, 1962.

Drummond, Roscoe, and Gaston Coblentz. *Duel at the Brink*. Garden City, N.Y., Doubleday & Company, 1960.

Dulles, John Foster. *War or Peace*. New York, The Macmillan Company, 1950.

Eisenhower, Dwight D. *Mandate for Change*. Garden City, N.Y., Doubleday & Company, 1963.

Fairbank, J. K. *The United States and China*. Cambridge, Mass., Harvard University Press, 1958.

Feis, Herbert. *Churchill–Roosevelt–Stalin*. Princeton, Princeton University Press, 1957.

———. *Japan Subdued*. Princeton, Princeton University Press, 1961.

Fitzgerald, Charles P. *The Birth of Communist China*. New York, Frederick A. Praeger, 1966.

Fleming, Denna F. *The Cold War and Its Origins, 1917–1960*. Garden City, N.Y., Doubleday & Company, 1961.

Forrestal, James V. *The Forrestal Diaries*, edited by Walter Millis. New York, The Viking Press, 1951.

Grew, J. C. *The Turbulent Era*, Vol. II. Boston, Houghton Mifflin Company, 1952.

Halberstam, David. *The Making of a Quagmire*. New York, Random House, 1965.

Harriman, W. Averell. *Peace with Russia?* New York, Simon and Schuster, 1959.

Hinton, Harold C. *Communist China in World Politics*. Boston, Houghton Mifflin Company, 1966.

Horowitz, David. *The Free World Colossus*. New York, Hill and Wang, 1965.

Ismay, Hastings Lionel Ismay, Lord. *Memoirs*. London, William Heinemann, 1960.

Jones, Joseph M. *The Fifteen Weeks*. New York, The Viking Press, 1955.

Kennan, George F. *Russia, the Atom and the West*. New York, The Viking Press, 1955.

———. *Russia and the West Under Lenin and Stalin*. Boston, Little, Brown and Company, 1961.

Kohn, Hans. *American Nationalism*. New York, The Macmillan Company, 1957.

Lacouture, Jean. *Vietnam: Between Two Truces*. New York, Random House, 1966.

Leahy, William D. *I Was There*. New York, Whittlesey House, 1950.

Lippmann, Walter. *The Cold War*. New York, Harper & Row, 1947.

———. *Isolation and Alliances*. Boston, Little, Brown and Company, 1952.

———. *Western Unity and the Common Market*. Boston, Little, Brown and Company, 1962.

Lukacs, John A. *A History of the Cold War*. Garden City, N.Y., Doubleday & Company, 1961.

McCloy, John J. *The Challenge to American Foreign Policy*. Cambridge, Mass., Harvard University Press, 1953.

Mecklin, John. *Mission in Torment*. Garden City, N.Y., Doubleday & Company, 1965.

Myrdal, Gunnar. *An International Economy*. New York, Harper & Row, 1956.

Raskin, Marcus G., and Bernard Fall. *The Viet-Nam Reader*. New York, Random House, 1965.

Reischauer, Edwin O. *Japan, Past and Present*. New York, Alfred A. Knopf, 1964.

Shaplen, Robert. *The Lost Revolution*. New York, Harper & Row, 1965.

Sherwood, Robert E. *Roosevelt and Hopkins*. New York, Harper & Row, 1950.

Smith, Howard K. *The State of Europe*. New York, Alfred A. Knopf, 1949.

Snow, Edgar. *Journey to the Beginning*. New York, Harper & Row, 1959.

————. *The Other Side of the River*. New York, Random House, 1962.

Steele, Archibald T. *The American People and China*. New York, Published for The Council on Foreign Relations by McGraw-Hill, 1966.

Stettinius, Edward R. *Roosevelt and the Russians*. Garden City, N.Y., Doubleday & Company, 1949.

Stimson, Henry L., and McGeorge Bundy. *On Active Service in Peace and War*. New York, Harper & Row, 1948.

Truman, Harry S. *Memoirs*, 2 vols. Garden City, N.Y., Doubleday & Company, 1955–1956.

Ward, B. *The Rich Nations and the Poor Nations*, New York, W. W. Norton & Company, 1962.

Waskow, Arthur I. *From Race Riot to Sit-in, 1919 and the 1960's*. Garden City, N.Y., Doubleday & Company, 1966.

Wilson, Harold. *The War on World Poverty*. London, Victor Gollancz, 1953.

The following books by the author are relevant to this study. Those marked with an asterisk contain chronologies, texts of important speeches, official documents and proposals for policy revision.

Our War and Our Peace. New York, Farrar & Rinehart, 1941.

* *Foreign Policy Begins at Home*. New York, Harcourt, Brace, and Company, 1944.

Unwritten Treaty. New York, Harcourt, Brace, and Company, 1946.

* *Germany—Bridge or Battleground*. New York, Harcourt, Brace, and Company, 1947.

* *Put Yourself in Marshall's Place*. New York, Simon and Schuster, 1948.

* *Last Call for Common Sense*. New York, Harcourt, Brace, and Company, 1949.

How to Co-exist Without Playing the Kremlin's Game. Boston, Beacon Press, 1952.

* *Germany, Key to Peace*. Cambridge, Mass., Harvard University Press, 1953.

310

The United States in a Changing World. New York, G. P. Putnam's Sons, 1954.

Turning Point Toward Peace. New York, Current Affairs Press, 1955.

Danger and Opportunity. New York, Current Affairs Press, 1956.

* *Agenda for Action: Toward Peace Through Disengagement.* New York, Academy Books, 1957.

* *The West in Crisis.* Garden City, N.Y., Doubleday & Company, 1959.

* *Disarmament, the Challenge of the Nineteen Sixties.* Garden City, N.Y., Doubleday & Company, 1961.

* *Time for Statesmanship.* New York, Current Affairs Press, 1965.

INDEX

Acheson, Dean: Cleveland, Miss., speech (May 8, 1947), 45; fosters Federal Republic of West Germany, 65; and rearmament of West Germany, 75ff, 113; *references to*, 41, 44, 63, 64, 70, 76, 91, 99, 107, 111, 116, 119, 135, 143, 197–98, 240ff; statement on defense perimeter and Korea, 72

Acheson-Lilienthal proposal (1946), 27, 250

Adams, John, 75

Adenauer, Konrad, 65, 70, 77, 82, 99, 107, 110, 115, 119, 143, 145–46, 149, 150–51, 158, 248, 268

Agency for Arms Control and Disarmament, 250

Agenda for Action: Toward Peace Through Disengagement (Warburg), 110n

Agriculture, U.S. Department of, 205

Agriculture, world, 203ff

Alien and Sedition Acts, 75

Alliance for Progress, 131, 155, 166

Allied Control Council, 17, 61

Alperovitz, Gar, 15n

American Strategic Airforce, 111

American University (Georgetown), 146

Anglo-Iranian Oil Company, 86

ANZUS (Australia, New Zealand and U.S.) mutual-aid treaty, 85

Chinese Communists
(*continued*)
160ff, 229–31, 261–63,
277–78; *see also* Korean
war; Vietnam
Christian Democrats (Italy),
61
Churchill, Winston: Fulton,
Mo., speech (March 5,
1946), 37–38; on anti-
communism, 37–38; *refer-
ences to*, 4–5, 6, 14, 15,
18, 24, 25, 41–42, 49–
50, 57, 59, 88, 95, 144,
168, 248; and Yalta Con-
ference, 8
CIA. *See* Central Intelligence
Agency
Civil rights, 264–65; *see also*
Negro revolution
Civil Rights Bill, 154
Clark, Grenville, 223*n*, 275*n*
Clark, Joseph, 165, 179
Clay, Lucius D., 62*n*, 98,
241, 243, 248
Clifford, Clark, 41
Clubb, O. Edmund, 247
Cold War: beginning of
(Sept. 1945), 24, 36ff;
Kennedy's policy toward,
146–48; *references to*, 11,
52ff, 64ff, 89ff, 209, 212,
223–24, 226, 245–47,
249, 261, 269, 272, 276,
277–78; *see also* Soviet
Union; Stalin, Joseph;
Truman, Harry S
*Cold War and Its Origins,
The* (Fleming), 15*n*, 42*n*

Commission to Study the Organization of Peace: Tenth
Annual Report, 219
Common Market: refusal to
admit Britain, 145; *references to*, 110, 215
Communism: American
Party, 49; gains in prestige
for, 33–34; growth in
Latin America, 126; ideol-
ogy in the Soviet Union,
31–32; and McCarthy
hearings, 91, 230, 237,
240; Polish and Hungarian
revolts against (1956),
106; *references to*, 23, 54–
55, 87; *see also* Chinese
Communists; Soviet Union
Congressional Committee on
Government Operations,
132
Congressional influence on
foreign policy, 236ff
Congressional Record: Apr.
26, 1956, 205*n;* May 11,
1965, 165*n*
Connally, Tom, 67
Connally Amendment, 225
Conversations with Stalin
(Djilas), 41*n*
Cook, Fred, 231*n*
Council of Foreign Ministers,
16, 21, 23–24, 54
Cuban missile crisis, 140ff,
227, 272

Davies, John Paton, 247

317

JAMES P. WARBURG

James P. Warburg is a well-known commentator on world affairs. As one of Wall Street's youngest bank presidents, he was summoned by F.D.R. to Washington as a financial adviser and participated in the First Hundred Days of the New Deal and in the World Economic Conference in London. During World War II Mr. Warburg had charge of American propaganda policy in the European theater. Since 1945 he has been an outspoken critic of our nation's foreign policy. This is his thirtieth book. Mr. Warburg is a trustee of the Institute for Policy Studies, Washington, D.C.